The Java 2 Cram Sheet

This Cram Sheet contains the distilled, key facts about the Sun Certified Programmer for the Java 2 Platform exam. Review this information last thing before entering the test room, paying special attention to those areas where you feel you need the most review. You can transfer any of the facts onto a blank piece of paper before beginning the exam.

JAVA SOURCE CODE

1. If a **package** statement is present, it must be the first noncomment statement in the file.

2. You don't have to import the **java.lang** package. However, every other package you use must be named in an **import** statement, or you must use the fully qualified name of the class every time it is mentioned. An **import** statement can use an asterisk (*) to import all classes in the package or explicitly name the imported class, as in the following example:

```
import java.util.* ; // or
import java.util.Hashtable ;
```

3. Each source code file can have only one class declared **public**. If there is a **public** class in a file, the file name must match the class name exactly. Resolution of Java names *always* considers case.

MODIFIER KEYWORDS

4. The Java keywords that control the accessibility of a class and class members (variables, methods, and inner classes) are as follows:

- **public**—Any part of a program can access this class or class member.

- **protected**—Only methods in the same package or in subclasses can access **protected** class members. This keyword is *not* applied to classes.

- **private**—Only methods in the same class can access a **private** member. This keyword is *not* applied to classes.

- **(none)**—If no access modifier is present, the class or member is visible only from classes in the same package. This is sometimes called "package" or default visibility.

5. The **abstract** modifier. An **abstract** method declares just the return type and signature of a method, not its body. Any class that contains an **abstract** method must be declared **abstract**. Interfaces are always **abstract**, but the keyword is optional in the declaration. Variables can't be declared **abstract**.

6. The **final** modifier. A **final** method can't be overridden, and a **final** variable can't have its value changed after initialization. A local variable or method parameter must be declared **final** if it is to be used by an inner class declared inside a method.

7. The **static** modifier. Methods, variables, and nested classes can be declared **static**, in which case they belong to the class as a whole, not any particular instance. Blocks of

name as the enclosing class. If the class is declared **static**, it is called a nested class and can access only **static** methods and variables. Inner classes can be named or anonymous. Inner classes are most commonly used for event handling. For a local inner class (inside a method) to use local variables or method parameters, it must be declared **final**.

EVENTS, LISTENERS, AND ADAPTERS

40. **AWTEvent** is the parent of all events created by user interface objects. The naming convention for event-related classes and methods is very strict. For an **XXXXEvent**, there will be an **XXXXListener** interface, an **addXXXXListener** method in any **Component** that can generate the event, and, in most cases, an **XXXXAdapter** class.

THE MAIN METHOD AND THE COMMAND LINE

41. An application must have a **main** method declared, as shown here:

```
public static void main(String[]
args )
```

42. The **args** array contains any command-line parameters and is always created, even if there are no command-line parameters.

GARBAGE COLLECTION

43. Calling the **System.gc()** or **Runtime. getRuntime().gc()** methods may start the garbage collection **Thread**, but this is not guaranteed by the language standard.

THE JAVA.UTIL PACKAGE

44. The properties of the various collection classes are defined by interfaces. Some of the most significant are as follows:

- *List*—A collection in which elements are kept in a known order and can be addressed by an index. Examples: **Vector**, **ArrayList**.
- *Map*—A collection in which elements are addressed by keys. Examples: **Hashtable**, **HashMap**.
- *Set*—A collection that contains no duplicate elements. Examples: **AbstractSet**, **HashSet**.

45. The **Collections** and **Arrays** classes contain **static** utility methods for manipulating and sorting collections and arrays.

46. All collections return an **Object** reference, so a specific cast is needed before you can use the reference for a specific type.

THREADS

47. The main **static** methods in the **Thread** class are **sleep**, **yield**, and **currentThread**. You do not call the **run** method directly; instead, call the **start** method and the **Thread** will execute **run**.

CORIOLIS™
Certification Insider Press

BITWISE OPERATIONS

23. The shift operators, **>>**, **>>>**, and **<<**. These operators work with integer primitives only; they shift the left operand by the number of bits specified by the right operand, except that they never shift more than 31 places for **int** and 63 places for **long** values. The **>>** right shift extends the sign so a negative number stays negative, whereas the **>>>** operator shifts in zero bits, creating a positive number. The **<<** left shift always shifts in zero bits at the least significant position.

REFERENCE VARIABLES AND ARRAYS

24. Objects, interfaces, and arrays are "reference" data types. The default value of a reference variable that has not been initialized is the special value **null**.

25. The **null** value has no numeric equivalent, but you can compare a reference to **null** with ==.

26. Because an array is an object, it must be created with the **new** operator. Creating an array of primitives automatically initializes all values to zero for numeric primitive arrays and **false** for **boolean** arrays. Creating an array of reference variables automatically initializes all values to **null**. Array addressing starts at zero.

27. Any reference—even classes, interfaces, and arrays—can be cast to the **Object** type.

28. The **instanceof** operator takes a reference variable on the left side and a reference type on the right side. It cannot be used with primitives.

THE DIFFERENCE BETWEEN == AND EQUALS

29. The == operator can be used with primitives or reference variables. When used with reference variables, it returns **true** only if both references are to the same object. The **equals** method is used to test objects for equality of content.

EXCEPTIONS AND ERRORS

30. The **Exception** and **Error** classes descend from **java.lang.Throwable**. Many methods declare that they may throw an exception; whether or not you must provide for catching the exception depends on the type. Exceptions that descend from **RuntimeException** are called "unchecked" and do not have to be declared or caught.

31. The **try**, **catch**, and **finally** clauses. Any exception thrown in a **try** clause may be caught in a matching **catch** clause. The code in a **finally** clause is guaranteed to execute, no matter what happens in the **try** clause, except in the case where the following is executed:

```
System.exit (0);
```

The order in which **catch** clauses are written is significant; the most specific exception should always come first.

32. You declare that a method may throw an exception with the **throws** keyword. The keyword **throw** is used in a statement that actually throws an exception. Only checked exceptions must be declared.

33. When you override a method that throws an exception, the compiler does not allow the overriding method to declare that it throws a more general exception.

CLASSES AND CONSTRUCTORS

34. Constructors look like methods—they have the name of the class but *don't* specify a return type.

35. A class may have any number of constructors as long as the parameter lists differ.

36. A constructor may call another constructor in the class, but only as the first statement. A constructor may call a parent class constructor using the **super** keyword, but it must be the first statement in the constructor.

37. If your class does not specify a no-arguments constructor, the compiler provides one—if and only if the immediate superclass has a no-arguments constructor.

38. You can call methods in the superclass with the **super** keyword.

NESTED AND INNER CLASSES

39. A normal Java class can have another class declared inside it: a member of the normal class. Member classes cannot have the same

code outside a method can be declared **static** for the purpose of initializing **static** variables.

8. The **synchronized** modifier. Methods and code blocks can be declared **synchronized** to prevent more than one **Thread** from executing the code at the same time. When used with a code block, **synchronized** must be applied to an object.

ENTITY NAMES

9. The only nonalphabetic characters allowed to start a name are $ and _ (underscore). The compiler tries to convert any string of characters that starts with a numeral into a number.

PRIMITIVE VALUES

10. Integer variable types. Java integer primitives are always signed except for the **char** primitive type. Note that the maximum positive magnitude is always one less than the maximum negative magnitude. The default value for an integer primitive is zero. The ranges are as follows:

Name	Size	Min Value	Max Value
byte	8-bit	-128	127
short	16-bit	-32768	32767
char	16-bit	\u0000	\uFFFF
int	32-bit	$-(2^{31})$	$2^{31} - 1$
long	64-bit	$-(2^{63})$	$2^{63} - 1$

11. Integer literals are assumed to be of type **int** unless the letter L or l is appended.

12. Floating-point variable types **float** and **double** use 32 and 64 bits, respectively, and conform to the Institute of Electrical and Electronics Engineers (IEEE) 754 floating-point standard. The default value of a floating-point primitive is zero.

13. Floating-point literals are assumed to be of type **double** unless the letter F or f is appended.

14. The **boolean** primitive type can have only **true** and **false** values. The default value of a boolean is **false**. The **boolean** primitives do not have integer equivalents.

ARITHMETIC OPERATIONS

15. When evaluating an arithmetic expression with two operands, the compiler converts primitives by widening according to these rules:
    a. If either is of type **double**, the other is converted to **double**.
    b. Otherwise, if either is a **float**, the other is converted to **float**.
    c. Otherwise, if either is of type **long**, the other is converted to **long**.
    d. Otherwise, both operands are converted to **int**.

16. Division by zero in integer arithmetic produces a runtime **ArithmeticException**.

17. Division by zero in floating-point-arithmetic: No exception occurs; instead, the result is one of the special values—**NaN** (Not a Number), **NEGATIVE_INFINITY**, or **POSITIVE_INFINITY**— that are defined in the **Float** and **Double** wrapper classes.

18. The only way to see if a floating-point result is **NaN** is to use the **Float.isNaN** or **Double. isNaN** static method.

19. Special floating-point values. In addition to **NaN**, the **Float** and **Double** classes define **MAX_VALUE, MIN_VALUE, POSITIVE_ INFINITY**, and **NEGATIVE_INFINITY**.

LOGIC OPERATIONS

20. The logic AND operators **&** and **&&**. The **&&** operator "short-circuits" an evaluation and does not evaluate the right-hand term if the left-hand result is **false** because the final result is bound to be **false**.

21. The logic OR operators **|** and **||**. The **|** operator always evaluates both operands. The **||** operator "short-circuits" an evaluation and does not evaluate the right-hand term if the left-hand result is **true** because the final result is bound to be **true**.

22. The **if** and **while** statements require a **boolean** input, so C tricks that evaluate zero as **false** do not work in Java.

Java 2

Second Edition

Bill Brogden

Java 2 Exam Cram, Second Edition

Limits of Liability and Disclaimer of Warranty

The author and publisher of this book have used their best efforts in preparing the book and the programs contained in it. These efforts include the development, research, and testing of the theories and programs to determine their effectiveness. The author and publisher make no warranty of any kind, expressed or implied, with regard to these programs or the documentation contained in this book.

The author and publisher shall not be liable in the event of incidental or consequential damages in connection with, or arising out of, the furnishing, performance, or use of the programs, associated instructions, and/or claims of productivity gains.

Trademarks

Trademarked names appear throughout this book. Rather than list the names and entities that own the trademarks or insert a trademark symbol with each mention of the trademarked name, the publisher states that it is using the names for editorial purposes only and to the benefit of the trademark owner, with no intention of infringing upon that trademark.

The Coriolis Group, LLC
14455 N. Hayden Road
Suite 220
Scottsdale, Arizona 85260

(480)483-0192
FAX (480)483-0193
www.coriolis.com

Library of Congress Cataloging-in-Publication Data
Brogden, William B.
    Java 2 exam cram / by Bill Brogden.--2nd ed.
        p.   cm. -- (Exam cram)
    Includes index.
    ISBN 1-58880-139-X
    1. Electronic data processing personnel--Certification.   2. Java (Computer program language)--Examinations--Study guides.
I. Title.   II. Series.
QA76.3.B76   2001
005.13'3--dc21
                                        20010289994
                                        CIP

Publisher
Steve Sayre

Acquisitions Editor
Sharon Linsenbach

Product Marketing Manager
Brett Woolley

Project Editor
Cheryl Gilbert

Technical Reviewer
Sheldon Barry

Production Coordinator
Todd Halvorsen

Cover Designer
Laura Wellander

Layout Designer
April Nielsen

Printed in the United States of America
10 9 8 7 6 5 4 3 2

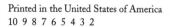

The Coriolis Group, LLC • 14455 North Hayden Road, Suite 220 • Scottsdale, Arizona 85260

A Note from Coriolis

Our goal has always been to provide you with the best study tools on the planet to help you achieve your certification in record time. Time is so valuable these days that none of us can afford to waste a second of it, especially when it comes to exam preparation.

Over the past few years, we've created an extensive line of *Exam Cram* and *Exam Prep* study guides, practice exams, and interactive training. To help you study even better, we have now created an e-learning and certification destination called **ExamCram.com**. (You can access the site at **www.examcram.com**.) Now, with every study product you purchase from us, you'll be connected to a large community of people like yourself who are actively studying for their certifications, developing their careers, seeking advice, and sharing their insights and stories.

We believe that the future is all about collaborative learning. Our **ExamCram.com** destination is our approach to creating a highly interactive, easily accessible collaborative environment, where you can take practice exams and discuss your experiences with others, sign up for features like "Questions of the Day," plan your certifications using our interactive planners, create your own personal study pages, and keep up with all of the latest study tips and techniques.

We hope that whatever study products you purchase from us—*Exam Cram* or *Exam Prep* study guides, *Personal Trainers*, *Personal Test Centers*, or one of our interactive Web courses—will make your studying fun and productive. Our commitment is to build the kind of learning tools that will allow you to study the way you want to, whenever you want to.

Help us continue to provide the very best certification study materials possible. Write us or email us at **learn@examcram.com** and let us know

Visit ExamCram.com now to enhance your study program.

how our study products have helped you study. Tell us about new features that you'd like us to add. Send us a story about how we've helped you. We're listening!

Good luck with your certification exam and your career. Thank you for allowing us to help you achieve your goals.

ExamCram.com Connects You to the Ultimate Study Center!

Look for these other products from The Coriolis Group:

About the Author

Bill Brogden is LANWrights, Inc.'s VP of Technology and Development. A full-time programmer and writer based in Leander, Texas, Bill has over 20 years' experience in the programming field. He's worked for clients as diverse as The Psychological Corporation, Litidex, and Cox Newspapers, and has written programs ranging from text indexing and retrieval software to online courseware. Bill has written significant software in Fortran, Forth, C, C++ and—of course—Java.

Acknowledgments

I would like to thank Ed Tittel for his encouragement and support of the idea of an *Exam Cram* book for Java. Thanks also to Dawn Rader and Bonnie Trenga for straightening out my tangled syntax. Thanks also to Sheldon Barry for his technical review and to Tim Griffin for indexing under a tight schedule. Most of all, I would like to thank my wife, Rebecca, for her continued support.
—*Bill Brogden*

Contents at a Glance

Table of Contents

. . . .

Introduction

Welcome to *Java 2 Exam Cram, Second Edition*. This book is intended to prepare you for taking and passing the Sun Certified Programmer for the Java 2 Platform exam, number 310-025 as administered by the Prometric testing organization. This Introduction explains Sun's certification program in general and talks about how the *Exam Cram* series can help you prepare for certification exams. You can learn more about Prometric by visiting their Web site at **www.prometric.com**.

Exam Cram books help you understand and appreciate the subjects and materials you need to pass certification exams. *Exam Cram* books are aimed strictly at test preparation and review. They do not teach you everything you need to know about a topic. Instead, the series presents and dissects the questions and problems that you're likely to encounter on a test. In preparing this book, I've worked from preparation guides and tests and from a battery of third-party test preparation tools. The aim of the *Exam Cram* series is to bring together as much information as possible about certification exams.

Nevertheless, to completely prepare yourself for any test, I recommend that you begin by taking the Self-Assessment immediately following this Introduction. This tool will help you evaluate your knowledge base against the requirements for the Sun Certified Programmer for the Java 2 Platform exam under both ideal and real circumstances.

Based on what you learn from that exercise, you might decide to begin your studies with some classroom training, or to pick up and read one of the many study guides available from third-party vendors, including The Coriolis Group's *Exam Prep* series. I also strongly recommend that you install, configure, and fool around with the Java 2 Software Development Kit (SDK) 1.3 software and documentation, because nothing beats hands-on experience and familiarity when it comes to understanding the questions you're likely to encounter on a certification test. Book learning is essential, but hands-on experience is the best teacher of all!

Whom Is This Book For?

This book is for you if:

➤ You are a programmer who is already familiar with Java to some extent and are seeking certification. Maybe you have written a couple of applets or applications and worked through one or two of the introductory books.

➤ You have been working with Java on and off for a couple of years. You have even done a fairly large application, but it was with Java 1.1 and you have not done much with more recent versions.

➤ You are an experienced Java programmer but you have heard that even experienced programmers can fail the exam because it covers a lot of basics that you don't use every day.

➤ You see that more and more employment ads, especially for the more interesting Internet-related jobs, mention Java and you think that "Sun Certified Programmer" would help your resume.

This book is *not* for you if:

➤ You are just getting started in programming and have little experience in any language.

➤ You have done a lot of programming but none of it in an object-oriented language.

➤ You have a theoretical understanding of Java but want to work with a lot of code examples so you will feel comfortable.

➤ You are curious about this suddenly popular language called Java and want to find out what the fuss is about.

If you fall into the category that indicates this book is not for you, you should start your Java certification path somewhere else. Please consider my other book, *Java 2 Exam Prep, Second Edition* (The Coriolis Group, Scottsdale, AZ, June, 2001. ISBN 1-58880-140-3), because it is full of programming exercises and has even more sample exam questions.

Sun's Java Certifications

Sun has several forms of certification for Java, as listed at **http://suned.sun.com/USA/certification/java/index.html**. There is now a multicorporation initiative for Java certification. Corporations involved are IBM, Novell, Oracle, and Sun. The Sun Certified Programmer exam is the first step in the proposed certification standard. The main Web page is at **www.jcert.org/**. Here is the list of possible Java certifications offered by Sun:

➤ Sun Certified Programmer for the Java 2 Platform, Standard Edition

➤ Sun Certified Developer for the Java 2 Platform, Standard Edition

➤ Sun Certified Enterprise Architect for the Java 2 Platform, Enterprise Edition

The Certified Developer tests involve a programming project that you can work on on your own time, followed by an exam with questions related to your design decisions. The Architect certification appears to involve more theoretical design considerations.

Signing up to Take the Exam

After you have studied this book, have taken the sample test, and feel ready to tackle the real thing, you first have to deal with Sun's Education branch. Sun will take your money ($150 in the United States), give you a voucher number that you can use to sign up for the test, and then mail you paperwork with the voucher number (but you can sign up with just the voucher number, so you don't need to wait for the mail). You will have to provide a unique ID number, such as your Social Security number. All of this can be done by telephone with a credit card. The number to call for U.S. residents is (800) 422-8020, (303) 464-4097, or fax (303) 464-4490.

Signing up with Prometric

After you have gotten a voucher number, you can contact Prometric to locate a nearby testing center that administers the test and get an appointment. The last time I visited the Prometric Web site, a searching system to find the testing center nearest you was located at: **www.2ittrain.com**.

To schedule an exam, call at least one day in advance, but do not count on getting an early appointment. In some areas of the United States, tests are booked up for weeks in advance. To cancel or reschedule an exam, you must call at least 12 hours before the scheduled test time (or you may be charged). When calling Prometric, please have the following information ready for the telesales staffer who handles your call:

➤ Your name, organization, and mailing address.

➤ A unique test ID. For most U.S. citizens, this will be your Social Security number. Citizens of other nations can use their taxpayer IDs or make other arrangements with the order taker.

➤ The name and number of the exam you wish to take. For this book, the exam number is 310-025, and the exam name is "Sun Certified Programmer for the Java 2 Platform."

➤ The voucher number you obtained from Sun.

Taking the Test

When you show up for your appointment, be sure that you bring two forms of identification that have your signature on them, including one with a photograph. You won't be allowed to take any printed material into the testing environment, but you can study The Cram Sheet from the front of this book while you are waiting. Try to arrive at least 15 minutes before the scheduled time slot.

All exams are completely closed book. In fact, you will not be permitted to take anything with you into the testing area, but you will be furnished with a blank sheet of paper and a pen. I suggest that you immediately write down on that sheet of paper any of the information from The Cram Sheet that you have had a hard time remembering.

You will have some time to compose yourself, to record memorized information, and even to take a sample orientation exam before you must begin the real thing. I suggest you take the orientation test before taking your first exam, but because they're all more or less identical in layout, behavior, and controls, you probably won't need to do this more than once.

About This Book

Each topical *Exam Cram* chapter follows a regular structure, along with graphical cues about important or useful information. Here's the structure of a typical chapter:

➤ *Opening hotlists*—Each chapter begins with a list of the terms, tools, and techniques that you must learn and understand before you can be fully conversant with that chapter's subject matter. I follow the hotlists with one or two introductory paragraphs to set the stage for the rest of the chapter.

➤ *Topical coverage*—After the opening hotlists, each chapter covers a series of at least four topics related to the chapter's subject title. Throughout this section, I highlight topics or concepts likely to appear on a test using a special Exam Alert layout, like this:

This is what an Exam Alert looks like. Normally, an Exam Alert stresses concepts, terms, software, or activities that are likely to relate to one or more certification test questions. For that reason, any information found offset in an Exam Alert format is worthy of unusual attentiveness on your part.

Pay close attention to material flagged as an Exam Alert; although all the information in this book pertains to what you need to know to pass the exam, I flag certain items that are really important. You'll find what appears in the meat of each chapter to be worth knowing, too, when preparing for the test.

Because this book's material is very condensed, I recommend that you use this book along with other resources to achieve the maximum benefit.

➤ *Practice questions*—Although I talk about test questions and topics throughout each chapter, this section presents a series of mock test questions and explanations of both correct and incorrect answers. I also try to point out especially tricky questions by using a special icon, like this:

Ordinarily, this icon flags the presence of a particularly devious inquiry, if not an outright trick question. Trick questions are calculated to be answered incorrectly if not read more than once, and carefully, at that. Although they're not ubiquitous, such questions make regular appearances on the exams. That's why I say exam questions are as much about reading comprehension as they are about knowing your material inside out and backwards.

➤ *Details and resources*—Every chapter ends with a section titled "Need to Know More?" It provides direct pointers to Sun and third-party resources that offer more details on the chapter's subject. If you find a resource you like in this collection, use it, but don't feel compelled to use all the resources. On the other hand, I recommend only those resources I use regularly, so none of my recommendations will be a waste of your time or money.

The bulk of the book follows this chapter structure slavishly, but there are a few other elements that I'd like to point out. Chapter 15 is a sample test that provides a good review of the material presented throughout the book to ensure you're ready for the exam. Chapter 16 is an answer key to the sample test. Additionally, you'll find a glossary that explains terms and an index that you can use to track down terms as they appear in the text.

Finally, the tear-out Cram Sheet attached next to the inside front cover of this *Exam Cram* book represents a condensed and compiled collection of facts, tricks, and tips that I think you should memorize before taking the test. Because you can dump this information out of your head onto a piece of paper before answering any exam questions, you can master this information by brute force—you need to remember it only long enough to write it down when you walk into the test room. You might even want to look at it in the car or in the lobby of the testing center just before you walk in to take the test.

Typographic Conventions

In this book, listings of Java programs and code fragments are in a monospaced font. In some cases, I have used a line number at the start of each line of code to facilitate referring to a particular statement, as in the following example:

```
1.  int n = 42 ;
2.  long j =  4096L ; // appending L or l makes it a long
3.  long k =  0xFFFFFFFL ;
4.  byte b2 =  010 ; // an octal literal
```

If you are typing code into an editor to experiment with one of my examples, do not type the line numbers.

When Java keywords, class names, and other words or phrases that could literally occur in a Java program are mentioned in the text, they are bolded. For example, "classes similar to **java.lang.Integer** are provided to wrap **byte, short,** and **long** integer primitives." Many classes and Java keywords are similar to words used in normal discussions, such as **Integer** in the preceding sentence. The bolding convention is used to alert you to the fact that the word or phrase is being used in the Java programming sense. You should also pay close attention to the occurrence of uppercase letters. The use in Java of **Boolean** and **boolean** is *not* interchangeable. Finally, I occasionally use *italics* to emphasize a term, particularly on the first use.

How to Use This Book

The order of chapters is what I consider to be a logical progression for someone who wants to review all of the topics on the exam. If you feel that you are already up to speed with Java at the Java Development Kit (JDK) 1.1 level, the main thing you will need to review is the Collections application programming interface (API), as discussed in Chapter 10. In any case, you should try all of the questions in the chapters and the sample test in Chapter 15.

If you find errors, sections that could be worded more clearly, or questions that seem deceptive, please feel free to let me know by email at **learn@examcram.com**.

Self-Assessment

Since Sun first released Java freely over the Internet, over three million curious programmers have downloaded the Java Software Development Kits (SDKs) or bought a book with the intent to teach themselves how to program in Java. Although many schools are now teaching beginning programming using Java, most Java programmers have been largely self-taught.

Sun's program for certifying Java programmers is designed to help both programmers and potential employers by providing benchmarks of programmer confidence. In addition to the programmer certification this book is devoted to, Sun offers developer and architect certifications. Offering these certifications is part of Sun's plan to make Java the language of choice for many applications, especially those involving networks.

Java in the Real World

Due to the rapid expansion of applications and toolkits, Java is now being applied in a huge range of scenarios. Java programmers might find themselves working in many different areas, such as the following:

➤ Multi-tier Web service projects using servlets, JavaServer Pages, and Enterprise JavaBeans in a "server farm"

➤ Applications with graphical user interfaces (GUIs) on wireless devices such as Palm Pilots and telephones

➤ Applications that are part of an interconnected web of devices that spontaneously organize themselves with Jini technology

➤ Applications that run on traditional desktop systems

No matter which area you are interested in, the language basics as tested in the Sun Certified Programmer for the Java 2 Platform exam will be important.

The Ideal Programmer Certification Candidate

One thing the ideal candidate does not have to have—although it is highly recommended—is years of experience. The certification test does not cover esoteric items that you pick up only by burning the midnight oil while slaving over a two-year project. Instead, the test requires sound knowledge of the fundamentals. The ideal candidate for the certification exam will be able to do the following:

➤ Know all of the Java keywords and how they are used.

➤ Be able to create legal Java identifiers and reject illegal ones.

➤ Know the distinction between primitives and reference variables.

➤ Know how to create and initialize primitive variables, strings, and arrays.

➤ Know the range of values and limitations of all Java primitive variables.

➤ Understand what is meant by the *scope* of variables.

➤ Know the conventions that govern the way the Java Virtual Machine (JVM) starts and runs applications and applets.

➤ Know what every Java mathematical, logical, and bitwise operator with primitives does.

➤ Be able to apply the functions in the **Math** class.

➤ Know what every Java operator with reference variables does, especially the operators that work with strings.

➤ Be able to decide when to use the **equals** method and when to use the == operator.

➤ Correctly use casts with primitive variables and reference variables.

➤ Use the primitive wrapper classes in the **java.lang** package and predict the consequences of the immutability of wrapper class objects.

➤ Choose the right access modifiers to control the visibility of classes, variables, and methods.

➤ Know the implications of declaring a class or method to be **abstract**.

➤ Know the implications of declaring a class, method, or variable to be **final**.

➤ Know the implications of declaring a method or variable to be **static**.

➤ Understand how to design programs using the concept of interfaces.

➤ Be able to use the interfaces specified in the **java.lang** and **java.util** packages.

➤ Predict when a default constructor will be created for a class.

➤ Distinguish between overloading and overriding methods and be able to write both types of code.

➤ Understand the uses of all forms of inner classes.

➤ Use all of Java's program flow control statements, including **break** and **continue**.

➤ Create, throw, catch, and process exceptions and be able to predict for which exceptions the compiler requires a specific provision.

➤ Understand the benefits of encapsulation and inheritance in object-oriented design and be able to design classes that demonstrate the "is a" and "has a" relationships.

➤ Be able to predict when objects may be garbage collected and know the implications of Java's garbage collection mechanism.

➤ Know how to create **finalize** methods and predict when a **finalize** method will run.

➤ Be able to write code that creates and starts threads using both the **Runnable** interface and extensions of the **Thread** class.

➤ Use the **synchronized** keyword to prevent problems with multiple threads that interact with the same data.

➤ Write code using the **wait, notify,** and **notifyAll** methods to coordinate threads.

➤ Select the correct interface or class from the Collections API to accomplish a particular task.

➤ Write user interfaces with the AWT classes and layout managers that present a required appearance and behavior.

➤ Write code that implements listener interfaces to receive events and extract information from them.

➤ Understand how **File** class objects are used.

➤ Write code using streams to read and write text files using specified language encoding.

➤ Write code using Java's **RandomAccessFile** class to read and write binary data.

Assessing Your Readiness

People come to Java from a variety of backgrounds; however, even years of experience are not a guarantee of good preparation for the test. In fact, even experienced Java programmers may have problems with the test if they have let their fundamental skills slip.

Programming Background

1. Do you have significant experience with C or C++? [Yes or No]

   No C experience: People frequently ask if they should learn C before starting Java. My emphatic answer is *no*, Java is easier to learn than C. The idea that Java users should know C may have gotten started before there were good books for beginners in Java. Many schools have switched to Java for beginner programming courses.

   Yes: The syntax of Java will be familiar; just watch out for some traps that I point out in the book. Don't expect any of your C tricks to work in Java.

2. Do you have significant experience with creating object-oriented programs? [Yes or No]

   Yes: Proceed to Question 3.

   No significant experience with creating object-oriented programs: Java is the right place to start because it is so much simpler than C++. Several good books on Java are available. *Thinking in Java, Second Edition*, by Bruce Eckel, is widely recommended as a good starting book if your object-oriented programming background is weak. You can download it for free from **www.bruceeckel.com** or purchase a paper copy (Prentice Hall Computer Books, 2000, ISBN 0-13-027363-5).

   A very convenient resource is the design of the Java language itself. Study the way the graphical interface components in the **java.awt** package make use of inheritance. The source code for all of these classes comes with the SDK download.

Experience with Java

3. Have you written Java programs as both graphical and nongraphical applications? If not, you must expand your experience in this area because each type of program has its own unique requirements. You should experiment with each of the AWT package layout managers in at least one graphical interface program.

4. Have you written programs that read and write text and binary data using both Java stream classes and the **RandomAccessFile** class?

5. Is your experience entirely with Java 1.1 or 1.02? If it is, you must act to get some experience with Java at the SDK 1.2 to 1.3 levels, especially with the Collections API classes.

6. Do you have a good set of up-to-date Java resources? At a minimum, you should have downloaded the Java SDK and documentation from the Sun Web site (**http://java.sun.com**)—this is still referred to as SDK 1.3, although Sun marketing literature refers to Java 2.

   You should download the current copy of Sun's Java tutorial from **http://java.sun.com/docs/books/tutorial/**. Sun is continually adding to this, so refresh it if your copy is more than two months old. This tutorial comes with many sample programs in a range of complexities. For test preparation, you should concentrate on the simple ones.

   Books that were written for the JDK 1.1 level of Java will still be useful for Java basics. The Collections-related classes will be on the test but are missing from older books.

7. In your current Java projects, does the first pass of the compiler over your new class turn up frequent type-casting errors and other mistakes related to Java basics? If so, use these errors to direct you to the topics you need to review.

8. Can you solve Java problems? For example, if you read the "help me" messages on the **comp.lang.java.programmer** newsgroup, does the correct solution for basic problems usually occur to you? (I'm not talking about problems involving Swing or databases or other advanced topics, just the basic problems.) Helping other programmers with Java problems is a great way to assess your own knowledge.

I Think I'm Ready, so What's Next?

Before you put up some money and schedule the test, try some of the mock Java exams that can be found at various places on the Web. Two sites with high quality mock exams are **www.jchq.net** and **www.javaranch.com**. Unfortunately, not all certification-related web sites have well formulated mock exams, so double check if you find contradictory information.

When you can do well on these tests and can check off every item on the list presented at the start of this chapter, you're ready to sign up. Good luck!

Java and the Sun Certification Test

Terms you'll need to understand:

✓ Radio button

✓ Checkbox

✓ Text entry question

Techniques you'll need to master:

✓ Assessing your exam-readiness

✓ Preparing based on the objectives

✓ Practicing, practicing, practicing

✓ Pacing yourself

✓ Not panicking

✓ Guessing in an informed manner

This book is intended to prepare you for taking and passing the Sun Certified Programmer for the Java 2 Platform exam. In this chapter, I cover the way the test is administered, suggestions for test-taking strategy and tactics, how to prepare for the test, and a short history of the various versions of the Java language.

Subsequent chapters explore various aspects of Java that are likely to appear on the test or are essential to understanding the Java programming language. This book is not intended to cover all aspects of Java; that task takes a whole bookshelf these days.

Assessing Exam-Readiness

I strongly recommend that you read through and take the Self-Assessment included with this book (it appears just before this chapter, in fact). This will help you compare your knowledge base to the requirements for passing the Sun Certified Programmer exam, and it will help you identify parts of your background or experience that may be in need of improvement, enhancement, or further learning. If you get the right set of basics under your belt, obtaining Sun certification will be that much easier.

Once you've worked through the *Exam Cram*, have read the supplementary materials as needed, and have taken the practice test, you'll have a pretty clear idea of when you should be ready to take the real exam. The practice test included in this book is considered slightly harder than the real one. We strongly recommend that you keep practicing until your scores top the 70 percent mark; 75 percent would be a good goal, to give yourself some margin for error in a real exam situation (where stress will play more of a role than when you practice). Once you hit that point, you should be ready to go. But if you get through the practice exam in this book without attaining that score, you should keep taking the practice test and studying the materials until you get there.

Preparing for the Test

I feel that it will be very helpful for you to have available a working copy of Java Development Kit (JDK) 1.2 or 1.3. As of this writing, the only source is the Sun Web site at **http://java.sun.com/products/index.html**.

The total installation file is over 20MB, but you can download it in pieces if necessary. It takes a huge amount of disk space to install—over 65MB after you have the installation file downloaded, so clean out your hard disk. You can also download the JDK documentation, which is very complete but also very bulky.

Naturally, you should practice with the questions at the end of each chapter and the practice test in Chapter 15. There are also a fair number of Web sites devoted to preparation for the Java 2 programmer certification exam. I've listed some in the "Just the FAQs" section later in this chapter, but more will probably appear, so try a Web search engine.

Practicing with Mock Exams

A number of practice tests other than the one in this book are available on the Web. I recommend Marcus Green's Java Programmer Certification Page at www.jchq.net and the JavaRanch site at www.javaranch.com. Both of these sites also have tutorials and discussion groups that can help you prepare for the exam.

Finally, I will be maintaining and adding to the mock exam at www.lanw.com/java/javacert. I used this practice test to evaluate sample questions for this book and to locate topics that most new Java programmers have a hard time with.

Write! Write! Write!

Finally, and I can't emphasize this enough, write lots of code. I keep seeing questions that ask whether a piece of code will compile or run in online discussion groups. You can decide the answers to these questions in a few minutes by writing a simple Java class. If you get compiler or runtime errors, learn from them.

The Test Environment

Tests are administered by the Prometric organization using typical Windows-based computers. You will be in a quiet environment with one or more testing stations in a separate room. Typically, this room will have a large picture window that enables the test coordinator to keep an eye on the test takers to make sure people are not talking to each other or using notes. Naturally, you are not allowed to take any notes into the room.

There will be scratch paper or an erasable plastic sheet with a felt tip marker. You can use this to write down key information; however, you are not allowed to take any notes out of the exam. If there is any topic you have a hard time remembering, you might want to scan the Cram Sheet from the front of this book just before taking the test and then make a few quick notes when you get into the testing room.

The computer will be a pretty typical system with mouse and keyboard. The initial screen gives you the option to run a quick tutorial test. If you have never taken one of these tests before, you should take the tutorial. The real test timer does not start until you have specifically chosen to start the real test.

As of this writing, you are allowed 120 minutes to answer 61 questions, of which 59 are for the certification and 2 are related to Sun's privacy policy. This is plenty of time if you have studied the material. I have to say "as of this writing" because in earlier versions of the test, only 90 minutes were allowed, and Sun may change again.

Question Types

Questions are presented on the screen in a scrollable window. There are three styles of questions:

➤ *Multiple choice with radio buttons*—This type of question presents a number of possible choices labeled with lowercase letters and presented with a round radio-style button. You can answer by either clicking the button with the mouse or typing the letter on the keyboard. Only one item can be chosen.

➤ *Multiple choice with checkboxes*—In this type of question, the number of correct answers may vary from one to all of them. To indicate this, you will be presented with square checkboxes instead of radio buttons. As of the October 2000 version of the test, the question text includes the number of correct answers, so all you have to do is select the correct ones. Because Sun may revert to the earlier style that did not give this hint, I suggest that you not rely on it. All correct answers must be checked for you to get any credit for the question; no partial credit is awarded for partially correct selections.

➤ *Text entry questions*—This type of question presents a one-line text area for you to type the answer. Pay close attention to what the question is asking for so you don't type more than what it wants. For example, do not enclose your text in quotation marks unless the answer specifically requires them. In most cases, a list of possible words is presented as part of the question, so what you have to do is select the correct words and type them in the right order. Remember that Java is case sensitive.

Questions that require presentation of more than about eight lines of code will provide an Exhibit button to pop up a separate scrollable window that shows the code. The purpose of this is to let you see the option text and question text as close together as possible. Don't be too eager to see the code; read the question and the options first so you will know what to look for.

Here is a sample multiple-choice question that requires you to select a single correct answer. Following the question is a brief summary of each potential answer and why it is either right or wrong.

Question 1

Here are some statements about the **java.lang.System** class. Which of the following statements is correct?

- ○ a. You must initialize **System** with a path and file name if you want to use the **System.err** output.
- ○ b. The **System.timer** method allows timing processes to the nearest microsecond.
- ○ c. The **System.arraycopy** method works only with arrays of primitives.
- ○ d. The **System.exit** method takes an **int** primitive parameter.

Answer d is correct. The **System.exit** method takes an **int** primitive value that can be used as an error code returned to the operating system (OS). Answer a is incorrect because the **System.err** print stream is automatically created by the Java Virtual Machine (JVM). Answer b is incorrect because there is no **System.timer** method and the **System** method that does return the time is precise only to the millisecond. Answer c is incorrect because **System.arraycopy** works with both primitive and reference arrays.

Let's examine a question that requires choosing multiple answers. This type of question provides checkboxes rather than radio buttons for marking all appropriate selections.

Question 2

Which of the following statements about the **java.util.Vector** and **java.util.Hashtable** classes are correct? [Check all correct answers]

- ❑ a. A **Vector** can hold object references or primitive values.
- ❑ b. A **Vector** maintains object references in the order they were added.
- ❑ c. A **Hashtable** requires **String** objects as keys.
- ❑ d. A **Hashtable** maintains object references in the order they were added.
- ❑ e. Both **Vector** and **Hashtable** use **synchronized** methods to avoid problems due to more than one **Thread** trying to access the same collection.

Answers b and e are correct. A **Vector** maintains the order in which objects are added but a **Hashtable** does not. Answer e is true—**Vector** and **Hashtable** use **synchronized** methods. Answer a is incorrect because a **Vector** can hold only references, not primitives. If you need to store primitive values in a **Vector**, you must create wrapper objects. Answer c is incorrect because any object may be used as a **Hashtable** key (although **Strings** are frequently used). Answer d is incorrect because a **Vector** maintains the order in which objects are added but a **Hashtable** does not.

Conventions of Code Presentation

For maximum clarity, Sun and the questions in this book observe the following conventions of code presentation:

➤ *Code fragments*—It would make no sense to present the code for an entire Java class for each question; therefore, you will usually be presented with code fragments. When the code represents an entire source file, it should be obvious.

➤ *Numbered lines*—Code fragments are presented with line numbers for reference in the question—you should assume that these are not part of the code and will not cause compiler errors.

➤ *Sources of errors*—When you are confronted with code fragments, it is possible to imagine all sorts of reasons the code might fail to compile or run. Don't let your imagination run away with you; examine the options carefully and concentrate on deciding which is correct.

Navigating the Test

There are clickable buttons near the bottom of the screen that are used to move to the next question or back to the previous one. Pressing the Enter key also moves you to the next question.

There is a checkbox at the top of the screen that lets you mark a question to consider later. Before the test is finished, you will be given a chance to review all of the questions or go directly to those you have marked. You should mark a difficult question and leave it for later rather than spending too much time on it. It is quite possible that a later question will provide a clue and remind you of the correct answer.

Finishing and Scoring

The test is scored in the 11 categories described in the test objectives document at the Sun certification Web site, as discussed in "The Test Objectives" section later in this chapter. After you complete the test, your test results will be printed out with a bar graph showing how you did in each category. Only the aggregate score determines whether you pass or fail. As of the October 2000 version, the lowest passing score is 61 percent, which corresponds to getting 36 questions out of 59 correct.

Test-Taking Techniques

The most important advice I can give you is to read each question carefully. Be sure you answer the question as written and don't jump to conclusions. For example, you may be asked to check all of the correct names for Java variables or the question may ask for all those that would cause a compiler error.

With questions that have code samples, don't start by reading all of the question and code in detail; scan all of the possible answers first. It may turn out that keeping the possible answers in mind will help you understand what the question is really about.

Typos

It is possible (but not likely) that a typo in a question may make all of the possible answers impossible. In that case, make your best guess as to what was intended, answer the question, and move on.

Guessing

Because scoring is based on the number right out of the total number in the test, it is better to guess than to leave a question blank. You can frequently eliminate some of the possible answers to improve the odds of guessing correctly.

The Test Objectives

Sun publishes a rather general statement of the test objectives at **http://www.jcert.org/level1.html**. The major sections of the objectives list are the 11 categories used for grading the test:

➤ Declarations and Access Control

➤ Flow Control and Exception Handling

➤ Garbage Collection

➤ Language Fundamentals

➤ Operators and Assignments

➤ Overloading, Overriding, Runtime Type, and Object Orientation

➤ Threads

➤ The java.awt package-Layout

➤ The java.lang package

➤ The java.util package

➤ The java.io package

Note that none of the specialized libraries and toolkits—such as the Swing graphics components, Java Database Connectivity (JDBC), or JavaBeans—as mentioned. This test covers nothing but the basics, and it covers them thoroughly. Even programmers who have been working with Java for years and have created significant applications may get tripped up by basic language details they have forgotten.

Several certification test takers have remarked that many questions seemed designed to trap C and C++ programmers who don't really get the fundamental differences between C++ and Java. We have made special notes on topics that may cause trouble if you are thinking like a C programmer.

What Happens When You Pass?

After your test is graded, there will be a button on the screen to print the results. Be sure you click on that button a couple of times. The test administrator will stamp one copy (only one) with an "Authorized Testing Center" seal. Keep that one safe and use the other one to brag on. Sun will be notified automatically, which should start the ball rolling on your getting an official certificate from Sun. See **http:// suned.sun.com/USA/certification/certificates.html** for Sun's current policy on official certificates and the use of a special logo for your business stationery.

Will It Help You Get a Job?

There has been a lot of discussion on Java-related newsgroups on the value of certification when applying for a job. Some employers say that they like to see applicants who have passed the exam, and some say they ignore certifications. The headhunters I talked to agreed that most employers are very aware of the Sun certification. Everybody agrees that years of experience with a variety of languages and successful projects carry more weight than any certification.

I feel that the greatest value of the exam is that it gives you confidence that you have mastered the basics, but "Sun Certified Programmer" is a pretty nice thing to have on your resume.

How We Prepared This Book

The idea of an *Exam Cram* book for the Java programmer certification exam got started in late 1997. The Coriolis Group had originally planned a book on the Java 1.1 exam, but then Sun announced that there would be a new test when JDK

1.2 came out, so we thought we would wait for that. As you may know, the 1.2 release was delayed several times, and the final version was not released until December 1998 and is now called the Java 2 Platform. As of this writing, JDK 1.3 has been out for a while, and JDK 1.4 is expected soon. These new versions will not cause a change in the programmer certification exam because the test concentrates on the basics.

This long lead-time gave The Coriolis Group a unique opportunity. Since 1998, we have offered a mock Java certification exam administered by a Java applet on the LANWrights Web site at **www.lanw.com/java/javacert**. Using this Web site, we have been able to test proposed questions to be used in this book. Thanks to user feedback, we have been able to eliminate typos and ambiguous questions and to determine those topics that are most likely to cause trouble for the typical programmer. Thousands of tests have been administered and evaluated. We feel that this unique resource has enabled us to create sample questions to emphasize the points that are most likely to cause you trouble.

Study Resources

To prepare for the exam, you should certainly have downloaded and installed the JDK 1.2 or 1.3 package from the Sun Web site. When in doubt about a detail in Java, by all means, try some sample programs. The compact format of an *Exam Cram* book keeps us from publishing extensive sample programs. If you want lots of examples, look for our *Java 2 Exam Prep* (Brogden, Bill, The Coriolis Group, Scottsdale, AZ, 1999, ISBN: 1-57610-261-0), which includes a large number of projects illustrating various important points.

The Java 2 (JDK 1.2 or 1.3) package includes a large number of demonstration programs, many of them very elegant and spectacular. However, most of these programs are designed to demonstrate advanced Java features that are not a major part of the test, so your time may be better spent writing your own programs and making your own mistakes. There is nothing like tracking down the cause of a compiler error message to reinforce your understanding of basic Java concepts.

Java Books

A truly astonishing number of books have been published on various aspects of Java programming. Those that dealt with version 1 of the language are not of much use anymore. Fortunately, practically all aspects of language basics have remained the same with the move from Java 1.1 to Java 2. Citations for these books appear at the end of each chapter. When contemplating buying a book, you should check one of the online bookstores to see if an updated version is available. In addition, there is a great Java section at **www.fatbrain.com**.

Java Developers Connection

Sun's Web site for developers has tutorials, articles on advanced topics, and the current bug list. This site also has early release versions of various advanced toolkits. You need to register but it doesn't cost anything. This site is located at **http:// developer.java.sun.com/developer/**.

Just the FAQs

There is a tremendous Java support community on the Web, with many pages devoted to Java programming. Some of the most useful are those devoted to frequently asked questions (FAQs). The following list points to the best sites I've found:

➤ *http://www-net.com/java/faq/*—This has pointers to a number of Java FAQ collections.

➤ *www.afu.com/javafaq.html*—One of the oldest and largest FAQs is maintained by Peter van der Linden.

➤ *http://mindprod.com*—This is another extensive collection of FAQs and a Java glossary, maintained by Roedy Green.

➤ *http://javacert.com*—This provides an ongoing discussion of the certification tests.

Notes on Java History

It has been quite a wild ride for those of us who have been following the fortunes of Java. There have been two major changes and any number of minor changes on the route from the first beta release in the spring of 1995 to the present Java 2. Although none of the following will be on the test, I am including the information in Table 1.1 on Java history to help orient you to the vast amount of Java-related material you will find in bookstores and on the Internet. When considering a book to buy, look at the publication date.

That brings us up to the present—now it's time for you to get to work!

Table 1.1	The history of Java.	
Year	**Month**	**Detail**
1995	May	Sun's first announcement of Java (1 alpha).
	August	Netscape licenses Java for the Navigator browser.
1996	January	Sun releases the JDK 1 production version with major changes from beta. Every week brings new announcements of licensing deals, new application programming interfaces (APIs), and scads of publicity. Programmer and Developer certification tests become available.
	December	Sun announces JDK 1.1 with major changes and improvements.
1997	March	The release of draft specifications for Java 2D, the graphics toolkit that eventually ends up in Java 2. JDK 1.1.1 is released.
	December	The first public release of JDK 1.2 beta 2.
1998	March	JDK 1.2 beta 3 is released.
	June	A preliminary list of objectives for the 1.2 programmer certification exam is much more complex than the 1.1 objectives.
	July	The beta 4 release includes major changes in the Collections API.
	September–November	Two "Release Candidate" versions appear in this time period with major changes. Fortunately, these changes were not related to the exam objectives.
	December	The final release of JDK 1.2 appears. Sun is now calling the entire package Java 2, but the Sun technical documentation continues to refer to JDK 1.2.
1999	January	The final version of the test objectives is released.
	February	The Sun Certified Programmer for the Java 2 Platform exam is released.
2000	May	Sun releases Standard Edition Software Development Kit (SDK) 1.3.
	October	A revised exam with all new questions is released.

Language Fundamentals

Terms you'll need to understand:

- ✓ array
- ✓ Package
- ✓ **import**
- ✓ Public
- ✓ Protected
- ✓ Private

- ✓ Instance variable
- ✓ Reference variable
- ✓ **main** method
- ✓ Javadoc
- ✓ Deprecated

Techniques you'll need to master:

- ✓ Distinguishing the correct order and usage of items in Java source code files
- ✓ Identifying Java keywords from a list of keywords and nonkeywords
- ✓ Recognizing legal and illegal Java identifiers
- ✓ Stating the range of values in the primitive types: **byte**, **short**, **char**, **int**, and **long**
- ✓ Knowing the state of member variables that have not been explicitly initialized

- ✓ Determining the value of an element of an array of any base type
- ✓ Giving the correct form of a **main** method and using parameters passed on the command line to a Java application
- ✓ Using the standard Javadoc format documentation to identify and use methods and variables in classes and in superclasses

In this chapter, I review the basics of Java source code files: keywords and identifiers. Because Java borrows much of its syntax from C++, I will point out areas in which C++ programmers may go astray. I also cover the basics of Java variables and the behavior of Java primitive data types. Finally, I discuss the Javadoc format of the Java application programming interface (API) documentation and how to use it.

Although many different commercial Java development environments exist, the Software Development Kit (SDK), previously known as the Java Development Kit (JDK), as released by Sun Microsystems, is the only one the Certified Java Programmer exam covers. Incidentally, we old-timers frequently use the term JDK, although Sun calls it the SDK most of the time.

Structure of Java Programs

Programming in Java consists of writing source code that defines one or more classes. Because Java is completely object-oriented, all Java code is inside a class definition. When a Java program runs, it uses these class definitions to create objects that contain all of the program variables and instructions.

 In Java, there is no such thing as a global variable or any function that is not part of a class, and therefore an object. Java groups the various utility calls you might expect to find in a system library into classes, frequently as "static" methods. The implications of the **static** keyword are discussed in Chapters 3 and 4.

Java programs are defined in source code files, which always have a file type of **java** and which follow strict rules for their naming and contents. You can create source code files with any editor that generates ASCII text. Each Java class is completely defined in a single file. More than one class can be defined in the file as long as there is only one public class.

Source Code Comments

Three styles of comment notation are used in Java. Any text between "//" and the end of the line is a comment. Text starting with "/*" and terminated with "*/" is used to make multiple-line comments. The special form starting with "/**" and terminated with "*/" is used to create comments that can be processed by the Javadoc program to produce HTML-formatted documentation. Creating Javadoc comments is beyond the scope of this book, so consult the resources cited at the end of the chapter if you want more details.

Packages, Class Names, and Imports

Java uses the concept of *packages* to control naming of classes. For instance, many standard library math functions are in the **Math** class, which is in the **java.lang** package along with the classes for other commonly used objects, such as strings. Therefore, **java.lang.Math** is the complete name of this class.

All Java programs are automatically assumed to use the **java.lang** package, but the compiler must be specifically instructed to use classes in other packages. This instruction is in the form of one or more **import** statements. The **import** statements tell the compiler where to look for classes. They don't require classes to be loaded, and they don't add to the final bulk of the compiled class files. You can import an entire group of classes in a package using the familiar wild card "*" to imply any name, as shown in line 1, which imports all classes in the **java.applet** package, or a specific class, as shown in line 2:

```
1.   import java.applet.* ;
2.   import java.applet.AudioClip ;
```

Note that the **import** statements end with a semicolon, like all Java statements.

As an alternative to specifying a package in an **import** statement, you can use the fully qualified name of a class in an expression. For example, instead of the **import** statement in line 2 of the previous code, you could refer to the **java.applet.AudioClip** class.

The result of compiling a Java source code file is the creation of a single class file for each class defined in the source code. The Java compiler turns your class definitions into bytecodes, which are in turn interpreted by a Java interpreter. The name of this file will be the name of the class, and the file type will be class. Case is significant when you're naming Java files and classes, and long file names must be supported by the operating system.

When you're creating your own classes, you can place them in a package by means of the package declaration. There can be only one package declaration in a Java file, and if it appears, it must be the first noncomment statement. If no package declaration appears, the class will belong to the default package. Because any **import** statements must precede any class definitions, the required order for these primary elements is as follows:

1. 0 or 1 package declaration

2. 0, 1, or many **import** statements

3. 1 or many class definitions, but at most one public class definition

Being able to apply these rules is one of the objectives of the Java Programmer Certification Exam.

More about Package Names

All of the standard Java library is in packages whose names start with **java,** and Sun has suggested rules for naming your own packages that are generally observed in the industry. For instance, custom classes provided in the Symantec development environment are in packages with names that start with **symantec.** The package name implies a directory structure in which the class files will be found. Packages also have significance in terms of the "visibility" of classes, as you will see in the following section.

Java Reserved Words and Keywords

Table 2.1 lists all of the words the Java language reserves as keywords. Note that keywords are always all lowercase. You will need to be extremely familiar with the words in this list.

In addition to the keywords shown in Table 2.1, Java reserves the Boolean literal values **true** and **false**, the special literal value **null**.

In earlier releases, the Java language had many more words that were reserved but not used, presumably because the authors thought they might eventually be used. However, all but **const** and **goto** have been quietly dropped from the list of reserved words.

Table 2.1	All the Java keywords.			
abstract	default	if	private	this
boolean	do	implements	protected	throw
break	double	import	public	throws
byte	else	instanceof	return	transient
case	extends	int	short	try
catch	final	interface	static	void
char	finally	long	strictfp	volatile
class	float	native	super	while
const	for	new	switch	
continue	goto	package	synchronized	

Packages and Visibility

Our exploration of Java keywords starts with those (used) that affect the visibility of classes, variables, and methods. *Visibility* of a class controls the ability of other classes to create objects or gain access to the variables and methods in the class. This subject is covered in greater detail in Chapter 4. There are various types of visibility:

➤ *Public visibility*—A class, variable, or method declared public can be used by any class in the program.

➤ *Protected visibility*—A variable or method declared protected can be used only by classes in the same package or in a derived class in the same or a different package.

➤ *Default, or package, visibility*—If none of the visibility keywords are used, the item is said to have package visibility, meaning that only classes in the same package can use it.

➤ *Private visibility*—The **private** keyword is not used with classes, only with variables and methods. A private variable or method can be used within a class only.

Familiar but Wrong Words

You may run into words that sound as if they should be Java keywords because of your familiarity with C or C++, or because they are used in casual discussion of programming in Java. For example, the word "friend" is sometimes used in the discussion of class relationships, but it is not a keyword. Other familiar words that are not used in Java include delete, inline, using, and virtual. Also, Java does not use any of the C preprocessor directives, such as **#include**, **#ifdef**, or **#typedef**. Furthermore, because pointer arithmetic is impossible in Java, **sizeof** is not used.

Identifiers

Words used in programs to name variables, classes, methods, or labels are *identifiers* and are subject to strict rules. None of the Java reserved words may be used as identifiers. An identifier can begin with a letter, a dollar sign, or an underscore character. Letters can be drawn from the Unicode character set, but the ASCII character set will probably be used on the test. The compiler generates an error if you try to use a digit or any punctuation other than the dollar sign and underscore to start an identifier. Identifiers are case sensitive.

Common errors that you may be asked to spot in test questions include inconsistent use of case in identifiers of classes or variables, and incorrect starting characters in identifiers.

The Java Interpreter and the JVM

In the Java SDK environment, a Java program consists of class files that are interpreted by the Java Virtual Machine (JVM), which creates the objects defined in the class files and interacts with the host operating system to handle user input, file reading, and other hardware interactions. The JVM can detect many types of errors in class files, security violations, and runtime errors.

Web browsers that support Java contain a JVM that is independent of any SDK components you have installed in your system. A JVM in a Web browser has many security restrictions imposed on it and deals with the operating system indirectly through the browser.

Java programs can also be compiled to binary code, which does not need an interpreter, but the Java Programmer Certification Exam covers the SDK environment only.

Variables and Data Types in Java

Java has two categories of variables and four kinds of named data types. Variables can either contain primitive values or refer to objects. *Reference variables* refer to objects—you can think of the variable as containing a handle to the object. Naturally, the internal workings of the JVM deal with real pointers to memory, but these details are all concealed from you as a programmer. The four kinds of data types are primitives, classes, interfaces, and arrays, all of which are discussed throughout this chapter.

Instance Variables and Static Variables

When a class is used to create an object, we say that the object is an *instance* of the class. Variables associated with the object are *instance* variables. It is also possible to have variables that belong to a class as a whole. These are referred to as *class* or *static* variables. Essentially, when the JVM reads a class file, it creates a class type object to represent the class and the static variables that belong to that object.

Reference Variables

Reference variables are declared in Java with a statement that gives the type of object to which the variable is expected to refer. For example, consider the following statements that declare two variables:

```
1.   Object anyRef ;
2.   String myString ;
```

The types of references these variables can hold depend on the object hierarchy. Because every class in Java descends from **Object, anyRef** could refer to any object. However, because **String** cannot be subclassed, **myString** can refer to a **String** object only. The rules about the relation of the declared type of a variable and the types of object references it can hold are discussed in detail in Chapter 6.

The contents of a newly declared reference variable depend on where it is declared. For instance, in variables and class variables, the content is the special value **null**. Variables that are declared inside code blocks are uninitialized. The Java compiler is able to detect the possibility of an uninitialized variable being used and issues an error.

References to a given object may be stored in any number of reference variables. The declared type of a variable may not match the type of the object it is referring to, but the object never forgets the class of which it is an instance.

Primitives

Java provides for certain common data types as primitives instead of objects to achieve acceptable performance. Java has four basic types of primitives: integers, character types, floating-point types, and boolean logic types. The integer types are all treated as signed, and range in size from 8 through 64 bits. The character types represent 16-bit Unicode characters and can be considered as unsigned integers for many purposes. The floating-point types are in the standard Institute of Electrical and Electronics Engineers (IEEE) 754 format in 32- and 64-bit size. These formats are the same regardless of the hardware. The boolean logic types are simply true and false with no number of bits implied. Conversion among primitive types is discussed in Chapter 6.

Integer Primitives

Table 2.2 characterizes the integer primitives. You should become very familiar with these characteristics. Note that the only integer primitive that is not treated as a signed number is **char**, which represents a Unicode character. Member variables of the **integer** primitive type are initialized to zero by default.

Table 2.2 Numeric primitives and their ranges.			
Type	**Contains**	**Size**	**Range of Values**
byte	Signed integer	8 bits	−128 through 127
short	Signed integer	16 bits	−32768 through 32767
char	Unsigned Unicode character	16 bits	\u0000 through \uFFFF
int	Signed integer	32 bits	-2^{31} through $2^{31}-1$
long	Signed integer	64 bits	-2^{63} through $2^{63}-1$

Character Primitives

Note that when a **char** primitive literal value is used in code, it is enclosed in single quotation marks. For example, the following line declares and initializes a **char** variable with the Unicode value for the Greek pi character:

```
char pi = '\u03c0' ;
```

Floating-Point Primitives

Table 2.3 summarizes the characteristics of the floating-point primitives. Questions about these primitives tend to be related to the initialization and manipulation of floating-point variables. Member variables of the floating-point types are initialized to zero by default.

Boolean Primitive Variables

The two possible values for a boolean are, of course, **true** and **false**. Member variables of the boolean type are initialized to **false** by default. Unlike integers in C, integers in Java can never be interpreted as boolean values, so expressions used for flow control must evaluate to boolean.

Arrays

You can think of a Java *array* as a special type of object that knows the data type it contains and the number of these items it can hold. Arrays can hold primitives, references to regular objects, and references to other arrays. Be sure to remember that addressing elements in an array start with zero. One of the major safety features of Java is that every attempt to address an array element is checked to ensure that the bounds are not exceeded.

Declaring an Array

Array variables may be declared separately from any initialization of the array elements. Here are some examples of array declarations:

```
1.  int[] counts ;
2.  String names[] ;
3.  boolean flags[][] ;
```

Table 2.3	Characteristics of floating-point primitives.		
Type	**Contains**	**Size**	**Approximate Maximum And Minimum Value**
float	Single precision IEEE standard	32 bits	$\pm\,3.4 \times 10^{38}$ to $\pm\,1.4 \times 10^{-45}$
double	Double precision IEEE standard	64 bits	$\pm 1.8 \times 10^{308}$ to $\pm 4.9 \times 10^{-324}$

Statement 1 declares that the variable **counts** is an array of **int** primitives. Statement 2 declares that the variable **names** is an array of references to **String** objects. Note that the square brackets can follow either the array name or the array type. Statement 3 declares that the variable **flags** is a two-dimensional array of **boolean** primitives. Note that in these statements, I have not set the size of the arrays, and no memory has been allocated for the array items.

Creating an Array

The size of an array is fixed when it is created with the **new** operator or with special combined declaration and initialization statements. Here are examples of creating some arrays (note that lines 2 and 3 combine declaration and array creation):

```
1.  counts = new int[20] ; // assuming counts was declared int[]
2.  String names[] = new String[100] ;  // combines declaration
                                         // and creation
3.  boolean[][] flags = new boolean[8][8] ;
```

When arrays of primitives are created, they are filled with the default values: **zero** for numerics and **false** for booleans. Reference variable arrays, on the other hand, are filled with the special value **null**. After you have created an array, you can use the **length** variable to find out the number of elements the array has.

Initializing an Array

Arrays of primitives are automatically initialized to the default values, but reference variable arrays contain references to objects only after you create each individual object. In other words, there is no way to "bulk" initialize. In the following code, statement 1 declares and creates an array of **Point** objects, but there are no objects in the array until statement 2 runs. Statement 3 illustrates use of the **length** variable belonging to the array.

```
1.  Point spots[] = new Point[20];
2.  for(int i = 0 ; i < 20 ; i++){spots[i] = new Point(i,0);}
3.  int count = spots.length ;
```

Program Conventions

You will probably see some questions that involve the conventions for starting a Java application. The command line to start a Java application consists of the name of the Java interpreter, the name of the starting class (just the name—the class file type is assumed), and zero or more parameters. The JVM expects to find a method named **main** with the signature as follows:

```
public static void main(String[] args )
```

This method will be the first one executed by the JVM. The command-line parameters are turned into an array of **String** objects that is passed to the **main** method. The array is typically named **args**, but it could be named anything. For example, the command to run an application named **MyApp** with a word and two numbers as input parameters would look like this:

```
>java MyApp Texas 1.03 200
```

The **main** method would get an array of **String** objects with three elements, which you would address as **args[0]**, **args[1]**, and **args[2]**. The array is still generated if there are no parameters, but it will have a length of zero. Note the differences from C: You find the number of parameters by looking at the length of the array, and the first element is not the name of the class but the first command-line parameter.

*Note: You can have methods named **main** that have other signatures. The compiler will compile these without comment, but the JVM will not run an application that does not have the required signature. Furthermore, most compilers will not object if the **main** method in an application is not declared **public**; however, if the question comes up on the exam, you better say **public**.*

Applet Conventions

Java programs running in a Web browser environment are called *applets* and have a different set of conventions for program initialization and argument passing than applications. Instead of providing a **main** method in an arbitrary class, the programmer must derive a class from **java.applet.Applet**. The JVM in the browser creates an instance of this class and expects to find the following methods:

➤ *public void init()*—This method is called once, just after the applet object has been created and before anything has been shown on the screen.

➤ *public void start()*—This method is called when the applet is first shown and whenever it becomes visible after being hidden.

➤ *public void stop()*—This method is called whenever the applet is hidden.

➤ *public void destroy()*—This method is called when the JVM is about to permanently dispose of the applet.

Instead of the **args[]** array of **Strings**, an applet has access to named parameters that are supplied in the HTML tags that define the Web page containing the applet.

Utilization of Javadoc Format API Documentation

Java has an automatic documentation feature that, as far as I know, is not duplicated in any other language. If source code comments are formatted with a few simple rules, the Javadoc utility provided with the SDK can create HTML files, which are automatically linked to the rest of the API documentation. The great advantage of this approach is that if the rules are followed, keeping the documentation up-to-date is almost automatic. Although the exam will not require you to know how to create or use the Javadoc documentation, I strongly recommend that you become very familiar with it.

As an example of using the Javadoc documentation, suppose that you wanted to find out the variables and methods available for an **ActionEvent** object. (The **ActionEvent** class is part of the **java.awt.event** package.) Using a Web browser, you would open the documentation index, which lists the packages in alphabetical order.

On opening the link to the **java.awt.event** package, you would find an alphabetical listing of the classes in the package. Navigate to the correct package and then to the screen shown in Figure 2.1. It shows where the **ActionEvent** class fits in the object hierarchy.

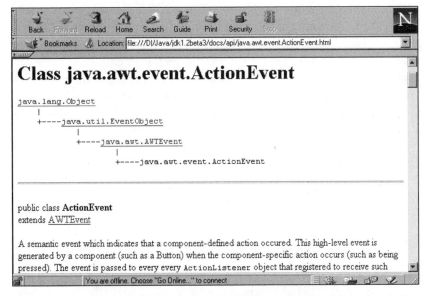

Figure 2.1 Browsing in the Javadoc-formatted Java API documentation at the main entry for the **ActionEvent** class.

Further down this page, you would find alphabetical listings of the variables and methods in the class. These are given in summary tables linked to more detailed explanations. However, this is not a complete picture of the variables and methods available to an **ActionEvent** object because, as shown in the figure, it inherits from **AWTEvent**, which inherits from **EventObject**, which inherits from **Object**. Note that although the primary organization of the documentation is by package, the parent classes of **ActionEvent** are in three other packages. By clicking on the links, you can navigate to the details of each of these classes.

In addition to the regular class details, there is documentation for Interfaces, Exceptions, and Errors that belong to a given package. The Javadoc documentation as distributed by Sun does have limitations in that only **public** and **protected** variables and methods are listed. However, the Javadoc utility has command-line parameters that can be set to include the **private** members.

Use the Source, Young Programmer

The SDK as downloaded includes the complete source code for the standard library classes in a single compressed file named src.jar. This file may be decompressed with the jar utility that comes with the SDK or with other zip tools. If you have the disk space, by all means extract the source code and study it.

Deprecated Classes and Other Items

In the transition from Java 1 to 1.1 and 1.2, and SDK 1.3, new naming conventions and other revisions to the standard library resulted in some classes, variables, and methods becoming outdated. Although they are still in the library to support older programs, their use is *deprecated*, meaning that they should not be used. The Javadoc API documentation provides a convenient listing of deprecated items and marks them in the class documentation. You can have every use of a deprecated method tagged by using the "-deprecation" option with the javac compiler.

Practice Questions

Question 1

Let's suppose you are writing a utility class and your company's policy is to keep utility classes in a package named **conglomo.util**. Select the correct code fragment to start a class file for a class that uses classes in the **java.awt** and **java.util** standard library packages.

○ a.

```
1. package java.conglomo.util
2. import java.awt.*
3. import java.util.*
```

○ b.

```
1. package conglomo.util ;
2. import java.awt.* ;
3. import java.util.* ;
```

○ c.

```
1. import java.awt.* ;
2. import java.util.* ;
3. import conglomo.util.* ;
```

Answer b is correct. Note that the package statement must be the first compiler-usable statement. It can follow comment lines and blank lines but must precede all **import** statements. Answer a is incorrect because the fragment has several errors. Line 1 tries to put your package in with the Java standard library, which is not allowed, and none of the lines is terminated properly with a semicolon. Answer c is incorrect because the fragment fails to declare the package. These are the statements other classes would use to import from the **conglomo.util** package.

Question 2

In a Java application, what are the appropriate modifiers and return type for the **main** method declaration? Write down the keywords in the correct order, choosing from the following keyword list:

```
private      protected     public     abstract
static       boolean       void       synchronized
final        Object        native     transient
```

The correct form for the **main** method in an application is as follows:

```
public static void main(String[] args)
```

or

```
static public void main(String[] args)
```

The **main** method must be a **static** member of the class so it is available when the class is loaded. The return type is **void** by convention. If you want to return an error code to the system, use **System.exit()**. **Main** must be public by convention.

Note that the question asks only for the modifiers and return type, not the complete declaration. It is a common error with this type of question to write down more than is asked for, causing you to lose credit.

Question 3

What will be the result of trying to compile and run an application in which the following is the only declaration of a **main** method? (Assume the rest of the class is correct.)

```
1.  public static void main(){
2.     System.out.println("hello world");
3.  }
```

○ a. The class will compile without error but the program will not run.

○ b. The class will compile and run, writing "hello world" to the standard output.

○ c. The compiler will report an error.

Answer a is correct; therefore, answers b and c are wrong. The code compiles, but the runtime system will report an error because it is expecting the exact method signature:

```
public static void main(String args[])
```

The compiler looks for only the correct syntax. It does not know how this class will be used, so it cannot enforce the method signature.

Question 4

Assume that the following program has been compiled and the **Demo.class** file is in the current directory:

```
1.   public class Demo {
2.       public static void main(String args[]
                )  {
3.           int n = 1 ;
4.           System.out.println("The word is " +
                 args[ n ] );
5.       }
6.   }
```

Select the correct command line to execute the program and produce "The word is gamma" as the output line.

- O a. Demo alpha beta gamma delta
- O b. java Demo alpha beta gamma delta
- O c. java Demo beta gamma delta
- O d. java Demo.class beta gamma delta
- O e. java Demo.class alpha beta gamma delta

Answer c is correct; "gamma" will be the second string in the **args** array, which has the index 1. Answer a is wrong because it does not start the Java interpreter. Answer b is wrong because "gamma" is the third string in the **args** array. Answers d and e are wrong because you don't use the class file type when starting the Java interpreter.

Question 5

Which of the following are not reserved words in Java? [Check all correct answers]

☐ a. **transient**

☐ b. **include**

☐ c. **goto**

☐ d. **union**

Answers b and d are correct. **include** and **union** are not reserved words in Java. C programmers should pay particular attention to learning which familiar C terms are not Java keywords. The Java keyword **transient** is used to label variables that should not be saved during serialization of an object. Therefore, answer a is incorrect. Java reserves **goto** but does not currently use it. Therefore, answer c is incorrect.

Question 6

What is the range of values that can be stored in a byte primitive variable?

○ a. 0 through 255

○ b. -127 through 128

○ c. -128 through 127

The correct answer is c. Byte variables use 8 bits and are signed.

Question 7

What is the range of values that can be stored in a long primitive?

○ a. 0 through 232 -1

○ b. -232 through 232 -

○ c. -263 through 263 -1

The correct answer is c. Long variables use 64 bits and are signed.

Question 8

Which of the following would be illegal identifiers for a Java variable?
[Check all correct answers]

❑ a. **my_stuff**

❑ b. **_yourStuff**

❑ c. **$money**

❑ d. **%path**

❑ e. **2enchantedEvening**

Answers d and e are correct. The illegal identifiers are **%path** and **2enchantedEvening**. The only leading punctuation characters allowed are $ and underscore, so **%path** causes an error. The leading numeral in **2enchantedEvening** leads Java to expect a number and causes a compiler error. **my_stuff**, **_yourStuff**, and **$money** are legal identifiers. Therefore, answers a, b, and c are incorrect.

Question 9

After the following code has been executed, what will the first element of the array contain?

```
String[] types = new String[ 20 ] ;
```

○ a. An empty String

○ b. The **null** value

○ c. zero

The correct answer is b. All arrays of reference type variables such as **String** are initialized to the special **null** value.

Need to Know More?

 Flanagan, David. *Java in a Nutshell, Third Edition.* O'Reilly & Associates, Inc., Sebastopol, CA, 1999. ISBN 1-56592-487-8. This is the most compact desktop reference book documenting the Java language.

 http://java.sun.com/docs/books/tutorial/information/download. html is where you can download an excellent tutorial in HTML form. You can also view it online here.

 http://java.sun.com/docs/books/jls/second_edition/html/j.title. doc.html is where the definitive Java language specification document is maintained in HTML form. This document has also been published as ISBN 0-201-31008-2, but most programmers will find the online documentation to be sufficient.

 http://java.sun.com/j2se/1.3/ is where you can download the Java API documentation in Javadoc-generated form.

Java Operators with Primitives and Objects

Terms you'll need to understand:

✓ Assignment
✓ **instanceof**
✓ **equals**

Techniques you'll need to master:

✓ Constructing numeric literals in base ten, hexadecimal, and octal formats
✓ Constructing character literals in Java's Unicode format
✓ Constructing string literals in the quoted format
✓ Understanding the effect of assignment and mathematical operators on primitives and objects
✓ Understanding the operation of bitwise and logical operators in expressions
✓ Understanding the implications of the various forms of the **AND** and **OR** logical operators
✓ Understanding the correct usage of the **==** comparison operator with primitives and objects
✓ Predicting the operation of the **equals** method with combinations of various objects
✓ Declaring, constructing, and initializing arrays of any type

Java uses literals and operators in a style that will be very familiar to all C programmers. In this chapter, I will review the way Java uses literals to initialize primitive variables, create objects, and pass values to methods. I will then review all of the Java operators used in expressions with both primitives and objects. You should not assume that the behavior of operators will be the same in Java as in C. Pay particular attention to the difference between the == operator (double equals sign) and the **equals** method; this seems to confuse many programmers.

Using Literals

Literals are used to create values that are assigned to variables, used in expressions, or passed to methods. You will need to know the correct ways of creating integer, floating-point, character, string, and boolean literals.

Numeric Literals

Literal numbers can appear in Java programs in base ten, hexadecimal, and octal forms, as shown in the following sample code statements, which combine declaring a variable and initializing it to a value:

```
1.   int n = 42 ;
2.   long j =  4096L ; // appending L or l makes it a long
3.   long k =  0xFFFFFFFL ;
4.   byte b2 =  010 ;  // an octal literal
5.    double f2 = 1.023 ;  // double is assumed
6.    float f2 = 1.023F ;   // F or f makes it a float
```

Notice that an unmodified integer value is assumed to be the 32-bit **int** primitive, but a value containing a decimal point is assumed to be the 64-bit **double,** unless you append an F or f to indicate the 32-bit **float** primitive.

In line 1, an unmodified literal integer is assumed to be in base ten format. In line 3, a number starting with a leading zero followed by an upper- or lowercase X is interpreted as a hexadecimal number. In line 4, a number with a leading zero and no X is interpreted as an octal number. Appending an upper- or lowercase L indicates a **long** integer.

Tricky Literal Assignment Facts

The compiler does a variety of automatic conversions of numeric types in expressions, but in assignment statements, it gets quite picky as a defense against common programmer errors. In the following code, lines 1 and 3 would cause a compiler error:

```
1.  int n2 = 4096L ;   // would require a specific (int) cast
2.  short s1 = 32000 ;  // ok
3.  short s2 = 33000 ;  // out of range for short primitive
4.  int secPerDay = 24 * 60 * 60 ;
```

Although 4096 would fit in an **int** primitive, the compiler would object to line 1 because the literal is in the **long** format. It would require a specific cast to allow the statement. The compiler also pays attention to the known range of primitives, passing line 2 but objecting to line 3. You could force the compiler to accept line 3 with a specific (**short**) cast, but the result would be a negative number due to the high bit being set. In line 4, the compiler pre-computes the resulting value rather than writing code to perform the multiplication.

Numeric Wrapper Classes

Each of the primitive data types has a corresponding wrapper class in the Java standard library. Java uses these classes for several purposes. The static variables of a wrapper class hold various constants, and the static methods are used for convenient conversion routines, such as the **toString** method, which returns a **String** representing a primitive value. You can also create objects that contain a primitive value, using either literals or primitive variables as in the following examples:

```
1. Integer cmd = new Integer( 42 );
2. Boolean flag = new Boolean( false );
3. Character ch = new Character( '\u000a' );
4. Long lx = new Long( x ) ; // where x is a long variable
```

The values contained in a wrapper object cannot be changed, so they are not used for computation. Wrapper objects are useful when you want to store primitive values using Java's utility classes—such as **Vector, Stack,** and **Hashtable**—that work only with objects. The names of the wrapper classes are **Byte, Short, Character, Integer, Long, Float, Double,** and **Boolean.** As you can see, the names reflect the primitive values they contain but start with a capital letter.

 The most important thing to remember about the wrapper class objects is that the contained value cannot be changed. These objects are said to be *immutable.*

Character Literals

Even though typical Java code looks as if it is made up of nothing but ASCII characters, you should never forget that Java characters are, in fact, 16-bit Unicode characters. The following code shows legal ways to declare and initialize **char** type primitive variables:

```
1.  char c1 =  '\u0057' ; // the letter W
2.  char c2 = 'W' ;
3.  char c3 = (char) 87 ; // the letter W
4.  char cr = '\r' ; // carriage return
```

Line 1 illustrates the Unicode representation of a character indicated by the leading \u sequence. The numeric value is always a four-digit hexadecimal number in this format. Line 2 uses single quotation marks surrounding the literal character, and an integer is cast to the **char** primitive type in line 3. Line 4 shows a literal representing a nonprinting character with an escape sequence.

You can also mix in Unicode characters and special characters with ASCII strings using the \u escape sequence (as shown in the "String Literals" section later in this chapter). Table 3.1 summarizes Java escape sequences that can be used in strings or to initialize character primitives.

Special Precautions to Take with Unicode

Java translates Unicode characters as it reads the text, so you can't insert the code for carriage return or line feed characters using Unicode in program source code. The compiler sees the carriage return or line feed as an end-of-line character and reports an error. That's why you must use the escape sequences shown in Table 3.1 to insert these characters in String literals.

Table 3.1 Java escape sequences.	
Escape Sequence	**Character Represented**
\b	Backspace.
\t	Horizontal tab
\n	New line (line feed).
\f	Form feed.
\r	Carriage return.
\"	Double quotation mark.
\'	Single quotation mark.
\\	Backslash.
\xxx	A character in octal representation; xxx must range from 000 through 377.
\uxxxx	A Unicode character, where xxxx is a hexadecimal-format number. Note that this is the only escape sequence that represents a 16-bit character.

String Literals

Because Java does not deal with strings as arrays of bytes, but as objects, the compiler has to do a lot of work behind the scenes. The following sample code shows the declaration and initialization of **String** variables with literals:

```
1.  String name = "" ;  // an empty string, but still an object
2.  String type = ".TXT" ;
3.  String longtxt =  "A great long bunch of text \n"
4.         + "to illustrate how you break long lines." ;
```

At the end of line 3, you will notice the sequence \n; this is an example of an escape code sequence used to insert special characters—in this case, a line feed. Line 4 illustrates the special meaning of the + operator when used with strings; this is discussed in "String Objects and the + Operator" section later in this chapter. Here is an example of a **String** literal with the Unicode representation of a capital Greek letter delta inserted between two double quotation mark characters:

```
String tx = "Delta values are labeled \"\u0394\" on the chart.";
```

Remember that string literals create **String** objects, not byte arrays. Most of the things you are used to doing with strings in C will not work in Java.

Boolean Literals

Fortunately, boolean literals are simple. Only the Java reserved words **true** and **false** can be used. Note that these words are always all lowercase. If you write

```
boolean flag = True ;
```

the compiler goes looking for a boolean variable named **True**.

C programmers should remember that integer variables can never be interpreted as boolean values. You must leave behind all of your tricks that depend on zero being interpreted as **false**.

Table 3.2	Numeric operators in Java.	
Precedence	**Operator**	**Description**
1	++	Increment by 1 (or 1.0)
1	—	Decrement by 1 (or 1.0)
1	+	Unary plus
1	-	Unary minus
2	*	Multiplication
2	/	Division
2	%	Modulo
3	+	Addition
3	-	Subtraction
5	<	Less than
5	>	Greater than
5	<=	Less than/equal
5	>=	Greater than/equal
6	==	Equal (identical values)
6	!=	Not equal to
13	**op=**	op assignment (**+=, -=, *=,** and so on)

Numeric Operators

In the last section, I created and initialized some variables. Now I'll look at Java's facilities for numeric operations. They will look very familiar to C programmers, but there are some differences. Operators that perform arithmetic or numeric comparison are shown in Table 3.2. The precedence gives the order in which the compiler does operations, with 1 being the first.

Increment and Decrement

Java follows the C convention with the increment and decrement operators, which directly modify the value in a primitive variable by adding or subtracting 1. When this operator appears in a larger expression, the order in which the modification occurs depends on the position of the operator, as shown in the following code fragment:

```
1.  int x = 5 ;
2.  int y = x++  ; // y gets the value 5, before incrementing x
3.  int y2 = ++x  ;  // y2 gets the value 7, after incrementing
```

Unary + and - Operators

Distinct from the arithmetic add and subtract operators, the unary + and - operators affect a single operand. Unary - changes the sign of a numeric expression to the right of the operator. Unary + has no effect on an expression; it is included for completeness and because some programmers like to use it to emphasize that a number is positive.

Arithmetic Operators

In general, the arithmetic operators +, -, /, and * work as you would expect, but you will need to know the conventions that the compiler uses to convert various primitives before performing operations. As with C, the operator appears between its two operands.

Arithmetic Operators with Assignment

The operators that combine an arithmetic operator with the = assignment operator perform an operation on the contents of the variable on the left side and store the results in the variable. For example, in the following code, line 2 is the equivalent of line 3:

```
1. int x = 5 ;
2. x += 10 ; // x gets  5 + 10
3. x = x + 10 ;
```

The compiler makes some assumptions when it sees an operator with assignment. For instance, in the following sequence of statements, the compiler does not object to the fact that line 2 adds an **int** value to a **byte** because it performs an explicit cast, the equivalent of line 4; however, in line 3, which is the logical equivalent of line 2, it raises an objection:

```
1. byte b = 0 ;
2. b += 27 ;
3. b = b + 27 ;
4. b = (byte)(b + 27) ;
```

Widening Conversions

Widening conversions of a number are those that don't lose information on the overall magnitude. For instance, the integer primitives **byte, char,** and **short** can all be converted to an **int** primitive, and an **int** primitive can be converted to a **long** integer without loss of information. An **int** can be converted to a **float** primitive, but there may be some loss of precision in the least significant bits. This conversion is carried out according to the Institute of Electrical and Electronics Engineers (IEEE) standard.

When evaluating an arithmetic expression with two operands, the compiler converts primitives by widening according to these rules:

1. If either is of type **double**, the other is converted to **double**.

2. Otherwise, if either is a **float**, the other is converted to **float**.

3. Otherwise, if either is of type **long**, the other is converted to **long**.

4. Otherwise, both operands are converted to **int**.

Conversion with Casting

You can always direct the order and direction of number conversions with specific **casts**. As an example, consider the following code fragment:

```
1.  float x = 123 ;
2.  byte b = 23 ;
3.  float y = x + b ;
4.  b = (byte) y ;
```

In line 3, the compiler converts b to a **float** before performing the addition. However, you have to include the specific **cast** operation to get the compiler to accept line 4 because converting a **float** to an 8-bit **byte** involves potential loss of magnitude and precision.

The Modulo Operator

You can think of the % (modulo) operator as yielding the remainder from an implied division of the left operand (dividend) by the right operand (divisor). The result will be negative only if the dividend is negative. Note that if the operands are integers, the **ArithmeticException** can be thrown if the divisor is zero, just as in integer division.

Using % with floating-point primitives produces results similar to the integer operation, but note that the special floating-point values, such as **NaN** and **POSITIVE_INFINITY**, can result.

Numeric Comparisons

The numeric comparisons <, >, <=, >=, !=, and == work pretty much as expected with Java primitives. If the operands are of two different types, the compiler promotes one according to the rules for arithmetic operators. Remember that the result of a numeric comparison is a boolean primitive.

The <, >, <=, and >= operators are meaningless for objects, but the == and != operators can be used. When used with object references, == results in **true** only if the references are identical. I will return to this subject later in this chapter because it is very important.

Be sure you master the differences between the == comparison with primitives and with objects. In my experience, this difference has been one of the most frequent sources of errors.

Arithmetic Errors

In general, Java lets you make a variety of arithmetic errors without warning you. If your code conducts operations that overflow the bounds of 32-bit or 64-bit integer arithmetic, that's your problem. Division by zero in integer arithmetic is the only error that produces a runtime exception, namely, an **ArithmeticException**.

On the other hand, floating-point operations meet the requirements of the IEEE standard for representing values that are out of the normal range. These special values are defined for **float** primitives as constants in the **Float** class, as shown in Table 3.3. The string representation is what you would get from the **Float.toString** method. The **Double** class defines similar constants for double primitive values.

Not a Number

The special **NaN** value is particularly tricky to handle. **NaN** can result from mathematical functions that are undefined, such as taking the square root of a negative number. You cannot directly compare the **NaN** value with anything. You must detect it with the special **Float.isNaN** or **Double.isNaN** methods, as in the following example:

```
1. float x = (float) Math.sqrt( y ) ; // where y may be negative
2. if( x == Float.NaN ) x = 0.0 ;  // WRONG, always false
3. if( Float.isNaN( x ) ) x = 0.0 ;
         // the right way to detect NaN
```

This example shows the right way (line 3) and one of the many wrong ways (line 2) to detect the **NaN** value.

Table 3.3 Special floating-point values.		
Constant	**Interpretation**	**Corresponding String**
Float.MAX_VALUE	The largest number representable	3.40282e+038
Float.MIN_VALUE	The smallest number representable	1.4013e-045
Float.NEGATIVE_INFINITY	Negative divided by zero	-Infinity
Float.POSITIVE_INFINITY	Positive divided by zero	Infinity
Float.NaN	Not a Number	NaN

Floating-Point Math and **strictfp**

The **strictfp** modifier is related to the way floating-point calculations are carried out, as affected by specialized math coprocessors. You will recall that **float** and **double** primitives use 32 and 64 bits, respectively, to store values. However, some floating-point coprocessors can use internal representations of numbers that use more bits for the intermediate results of calculation. These processors produce results that are more accurate but differ slightly from what you would get if every intermediate calculation result were forced back to a 32- or 64-bit representation.

Normally, you would want to use the most accurate results possible, but this means that a calculation on one Java Virtual Machine (JVM) could produce a result that is slightly different from the same calculation on another JVM. Of course, this is contrary to the spirit of Java. Starting in Java 1.2, the **strictfp** modifier has been available so that you can force floating-point math to reduce all intermediate results to the standard 32- or 64-bit representation, ensuring that calculations produce the exact same results on all JVMs.

When used as a method modifier, **strictfp** ensures that all calculations in the method follow the strict calculation rules. When used as a class modifier, **strictfp** forces all methods in a class to follow strict calculation rules.

String Objects and the + Operator

For convenience in working with strings, Java also uses the + and += operators to indicate concatenation. When the compiler finds an expression in which a string appears in association with a + operator, it turns all items in the expression into strings, concatenates the strings, and creates a new **String** object. The compiler has a complete set of conventions used to turn primitives and objects into **Strings**, but the only operators that can be used are the + and += operators.

The methods used to turn primitives into strings are found in the wrapper classes that Java has for each primitive. (Wrapper classes are discussed in detail in Chapter 10.) For instance, in the following code fragment, the compiler knows to use the **toString** method in the **Float** class to create a **String** representation of the **pi** primitive, and it knows how to add the Unicode character for the Greek letter pi to the **String**:

```
1. float pi = 3.14159f ;
2. String tmp = "Pi = " + pi + " or " + '\u03c0' ;
```

Objects and **toString()**

The root of the Java object hierarchy, the **Object** class, has a **toString()** method that returns a descriptive string. Therefore, every object has a **toString** method by inheritance. This default **toString** method produces a rather cryptic result, so many of the standard library classes implement a **toString** method that is more appropriate for the particular class. The net result is that the compiler will always be able to use the + operator in any combination of **String**s and objects.

Strings Are Immutable

The contents of a **String** object cannot be changed. Take the following code:

```
1. String filename = "mystuff" ;
2. filename += ".txt" ;
```

It looks as if I am changing a **String** object. What is actually happening is that there is a **String** object created in line 1 with a reference in the variable named **filename**. In line 2, the contents of that **String** are concatenated with the literal ".txt" and a reference to the new **String** object is stored in the variable **filename**.

 Questions involving the immutability of **String** objects frequently cause trouble for beginning Java programmers. Chapter 10 contains more examples and practice questions on this subject.

The **null** Value and Strings

The Java mechanism that adds various items together to create **String**s is able to recognize that a reference variable contains the special value **null,** instead of an object reference. In that case, the string "null" is added.

Bitwise and Logical Operators

Table 3.4 summarizes the operators that can be used on individual bits in integer primitives and in logical expressions. Bitwise operators are used in expressions with integer values and apply an operation separately to each bit in an integer. The term *logical expressions* refers to expressions in which all of the operands can be reduced to boolean primitives. Logical operators produce a boolean primitive result.

Table 3.4 Bitwise and logical operators.			
Precedence	**Operator**	**Operator Type**	**Description**
1	~	Integral	Unary bitwise complement
1	!	Logical	Unary logical complement
4	<<	Integral	Left shift
4	>>	Integral	Right shift (keep sign)
4	>>>	Integral	Right shift (zero fill)
5	**instanceof**	Object, type	Tests class membership

(continued)

Table 3.4	Bitwise and logical operators *(continued)*.		
Precedence	**Operator**	**Operator Type**	**Description**
6	==	Object	Equals (same object)
6	!=	Object	Unequal (different object)
7	&	Integral	Bitwise **AND**
7	&	Logical	Logical **AND**
8	^	Integral	Bitwise **XOR**
8	^	Logical	Logical **XOR**
9	|	Integral	Bitwise **OR**
9	|	Logical	Logical **OR**
10	&&	Logical	Logical **AND** (conditional)
11	||	Logical	Logical **OR** (conditional)
12	?:	Logical	Conditional (ternary)
13	=	Variable, any	Assignment
13	<<=	Binary	Left shift with assignment
13	>>=	Binary	Right shift with assignment
13	>>>=	Binary	Right shift, zero fill, assignment
13	&=	Binary	Bitwise **AND** with assignment
13	&=	Logical	Logical **AND** with assignment
13	|=	Binary	Bitwise **OR** with assignment
13	|=	Logical	Logical **OR** with assignment
13	^=	Binary	Bitwise **XOR** with assignment
13	^=	Logical	Logical **XOR** with assignment

Bitwise Operations with Integers

Bitwise operators change the individual bits of an integer primitive according to the familiar rules for **AND, OR,** and **XOR** (Exclusive **OR**) operations (as summarized in Table 3.5). The operands of the &, |, and ^ operators will be promoted to **int** or **long** types if necessary, and the result will be an **int** or **long** primitive, not a boolean. Because each bit in an integer primitive can be modified and examined independently with these operators, they are frequently used to pack a lot of information into a small space.

In thinking about the action of bitwise operators, you may want to draw out the bit pattern for various values. To keep them straight, it helps to draw groups of 4 bits so the groups correspond to hexadecimal digits. Questions on the test will

Table 3.5	Bitwise logic rules.		
Operand	**Operator**	**Operand**	**Result**
1	AND	1	1
1	AND	0	0
0	AND	1	0
0	AND	0	0
1	OR	1	1
1	OR	0	1
0	OR	1	1
0	OR	0	0
1	XOR	1	0
1	XOR	0	1
0	XOR	1	1
0	XOR	0	0

not require you to remember all of the powers of two, but being able to recognize the first few helps. Here is an example of the use of the **&** or **AND** operator:

```
short flags = 20 ; // 0000 0000 0001 0100   or   0x0014
short mask  =  4 ; // 0000 0000 0000 0100
short rslt = (short)( flags & mask ) ;
```

Note that because operands are promoted to **int** or **long**, the **cast** to **short** is necessary to assign the value to a **short** primitive variable **rslt**. Applying the rule for the **AND** operator, you can see that the bit pattern in **rslt** will be "0000 0000 0000 0100," or a value of 4. C programmers who are used to checking the result of a bitwise operation in an **if** statement, such as line 1 in the following code, should remember that Java can use boolean values in logic statements only, as shown in line 2:

```
1.  if( rslt ) doSomething()   ; // ok in C, wrong in Java
2.  if( rslt != 0 ) doSomething() ; // this is ok in both
```

Table 3.6 shows the result of applying the various bitwise operators to sample operands. Note that in the last line of the table, the ~, or complement, operator sets the highest order bit, which causes the integer to be interpreted as a negative number. I am using **short** primitives here to simplify the table, but the same principles apply to all of the integer primitives.

Table 3.6	Illustrating bitwise operations on some short primitives (16-bit integers).		
Binary	**Operation**	**Decimal**	**Hex**
0000 0000 0101 0100	op1	84	0x0054
0000 0001 0100 0111	op2	327	0x0147
0000 0000 0100 0100	op1 & op2	68	0x0044
0000 0001 0101 0111	op1 | op2	343	0x0157
0000 0001 0001 0011	op1 ^ op2	275	0x0113
1111 1110 1011 1000	~op2	-328	0xFEB8

I can't emphasize this enough! If you have not done much bit manipulation in your programming experience and are not comfortable with the material just covered, you should stop right now and write some small Java programs to become familiar with the concepts. Note that the **Integer** and **Long** wrapper classes have the **toBinaryString** and **toHexString** methods, which will help with the output. Here is an example Java method to perform various bitwise operations on two integers and display the results:

```
void test( int a, int b ){
    int c = a & b ;
    System.out.println("Result AND & " +
        Integer.toBinaryString( c ) + " = " + c ) ;
    c = a | b ;
    System.out.println("Result OR  | " +
        Integer.toBinaryString( c ) + " = " + c ) ;
    c = a ^ b ;
    System.out.println("Result XOR ^ " +
        Integer.toBinaryString( c ) + " = " + c ) ;
    System.out.println("Complement of " + a + " = " +
        Integer.toBinaryString( ~a ) ) ;
    System.out.println("Complement of " + b + " = " +
        Integer.toBinaryString( ~b ) ) ;
}
```

The Unary Complement Operators

The ~ operator takes an integer type primitive. If smaller than **int**, the primitive value will be converted to an **int**. The result simply switches the sense of every bit. The ! operator is used with **boolean** primitives and changes **false** to **true** or **true** to **false**.

The Shift Operators: <<, >>, and >>>

These operators work with integer primitives only; they shift the left operand by the number of bits specified by the right operand. The important thing to note with these operators is that the value of the new bit is shifted into the number. For << (left shift), the new bit that appears in the low order position is always zero.

Sun had to define two types of right shift because the high order bit in integer primitives indicates the sign. The >> right shift propagates the existing sign bit, which means a negative number will still be negative after being shifted. The >>> right shift inserts a zero as the most significant bit. Table 3.7 should help you to visualize what is going on. Again, if you are not comfortable with these bit manipulations, stop right now and write some test programs.

 When doing bit manipulations on primitives shorter than 32 bits, remember that the compiler promotes all operands to 32 bits before performing the operation.

Two final notes on the shift operators: If the right operand is larger than 31 for operation on 32-bit integers, the compiler uses only the five lowest order bits, that is, values of 0 through 31. With a 64-bit integer as the right operand, only the six lowest order bits (that is, values of 0 through 63) are used. Therefore, in line 1 of the following code fragment, y is shifted by only one bit; this also means that the sign bit is totally ignored, so in line 2, the right shift is not turned into a left shift by the minus sign:

```
1. x = y << 4097 ;
2. x = z >> -1 ;
```

Table 3.7	The results of some bit-shifting operations on sample 32-bit integers.	
Bit Pattern	**Operation**	**Decimal Equivalent**
0000 0000 0000 0000 0000 0000 0110 0011	starting x bits	99
0000 0000 0000 0000 0000 0011 0001 1000	after x << 3	792
0000 0000 0000 0000 0000 0000 0001 1000	after x >> 2	24
1111 1111 1111 1111 1111 1111 1001 1101	starting y bits	-99
1111 1111 1111 1111 1111 1111 1111 1001	after y >> 4	-7
0000 0000 0000 1111 1111 1111 1111 1111	after y >>> 12	1048575

Shift and Bitwise Operations with Assignment

Note that the assignment operator = can be combined with the shift and bitwise operators, just as with the arithmetic operators. The result is as you would expect.

Operators with Logical Expressions

The &, |, ^ (AND, OR, and XOR) operators used with integers also work with **boolean** values as expected. The compiler generates an error if both operands are not **boolean**. The tricky part (which you're almost guaranteed to run into) has to do with the && and || "conditional AND" and "conditional OR" operators.

When the & and | operators are used in an expression, both operands are evaluated. For instance, in the following code fragment, both the (x >= 0) test and the call to the **testY** method will be executed:

```
if(( x >= 0 ) & testY( y ) )
```

However, the conditional operators check the value of the left operand first and do not evaluate the right operand if it is not needed to determine the logical result. For instance, in the following code fragment, if x is -1, the result must be **false** and the **testY** method is never called:

```
if(( x >= 0 ) && testY( y ) )
```

Similarly, if the || operator finds the left operand to be **true**, the result must be **true**, so the right operand is not evaluated.

These conditional logical operators, also known as *short circuit logical operators*, are used frequently in Java programming. For example, if it is possible that a **String** object reference has not been initialized, you might use the following code, where the test versus **null** ensures that the **equalsIgnoreCase** method will never be called with a **null** reference:

```
//  ans is declared to be a String reference
if( ans != null && ans.equalsIgnoreCase( "yes") ) {}
```

Logical Operators with Assignment

Only the &, |, and ^ logical operators can be combined with =, producing &=, |=, and ^= logical operators. Naturally, in a logical expression with these combined operators, the left operand must be a **boolean** primitive variable. Note that there are bitwise operators that look the same but that work with integer primitives.

The **instanceof** Operator

The **instanceof** operator tests the type of object the left operand refers to versus the type named by the right operand. The value returned is **true** if the object is of that type or if it inherits that type from a super type or interface implementation.

The right operand must be the name of a reference variable, such as a class, an interface, or an array reference. Expressions using **instanceof** are unusual because the right operand cannot be an object. It must be the name of a reference type.

This operator is extremely handy in programming in cases in which an object reference may belong to several different classes. For example, suppose the following method could be called with several types of event objects descended from **AWTEvent**; the **instanceof** operator ensures that the correct method is called:

```
public void myEventProcess( AWTEvent evt ){
  if( evt instanceof ActionEvent )  processAction( evt );
  if( evt instanceof AdjustmentEvent ) processAdjustment(evt);
}
```

Remember that the **instanceof** operator can be used with interfaces and arrays as well as classes.

The Conditional Assignment Operator

The conditional assignment operator is the only Java operator that takes three operands. It is essentially a shortcut for a structure that takes at least two statements, as shown in the following code fragment (assume that **x**, **y**, and **z** are **int** primitive variables that have been initialized):

```
1.  // long way
2.  if( x > y ) z = x ;
3.  else z = y ;
4.  //
5.  // short way
6.  z = x > y ? x : y ;
```

The operand to the left of the **?** must evaluate as **boolean**, and the other two operands must be of the same type, or convertible to the same type, which will be the type of the result. The result will be the operand to the left of the colon if the **boolean** is true; otherwise, it will be the right operand.

More about Assignment

You have seen the use of the = operator in simple assignment such as x = y + 3. You should also note that the value assigned can be used by a further assignment operator, such as in the following statement, which assigns the calculated value to all four variables:

```
a = b = c = x = y + 3 ;
```

Testing Object Equality

It is a source of great confusion to novice programmers that Java has two ways of thinking about the equality of objects. When used with object references, the == operator returns **true** only if both references are to the same object. This is illustrated in the following code fragment in which I create and compare some **Integer** object references:

```
1.  Integer x1 = new Integer( 5 ) ;
2.  Integer x2 = x1 ;
3.  Integer x3 = new Integer( 5 ) ;
4.  if( x1 == x2 ) System.out.println("x1 eq x2" );
5.  if( x2 == x3 ) System.out.println("x2 eq x3" );
```

Executing this code will print only "x1 eq x2" because both variables refer to the same object. To test for equality of content, you have to use a method that can compare the *content* of the objects.

The equals Method

In the Java standard library classes, the method that compares content is always named **equals** and takes an **Object** reference as input. For example, the **equals** method of the **Integer** class (paraphrased from the original for clarity) works like this:

```
1. public boolean equals(Object obj){
2.   if( obj == null ) return false ;
3.   if( !( obj instanceof Integer ) ) return false ;
4.   return this.value == ((Integer)obj).intValue() ;
5. }
```

Note that the **equals** method does not even look at the value of the other object until it has been determined that the other object reference is not **null** and that it refers to an **Integer** object.

The **equals** method in the **Object** class (the root of the entire Java hierarchy of classes) returns **true** only if

```
this == obj
```

so in the absence of an overriding **equals** method, the == operator and **equals** methods inherited from **Object** are equivalent.

> Remember that the **equals** method compares content only if the two objects are of the identical type. For example, an **equals** test by an **Integer** object on a **Long** object always returns **false**, regardless of the numeric values. Also note that the signature of the **equals** method expects an **Object** reference as input. The compiler reports an error if you try to call **equals** with a primitive value.

The == with **Strings** Trap

One reason that it is easy to fall into the error of using == when you want **equals** is the behavior of **String** literals. The compiler optimizes storage of **String** literals by reusing them. In a large program, this can save a considerable amount of memory. Take the following code fragment:

```
1.   String s1 = "YES" ;
2.   String s2 = "YES" ;
3.   if( s1 == s2 ) System.out.println("equal");
4.   String s3 = new String( "YES" );
5.   String s4 = new String( "YES" );
6.   if( s3 == s4 ) System.out.println("s3 eq s4");
```

The **String** literal "YES" appears in both lines 1 and 2, but the compiler creates only one **String** object, referred to by both **s1** and **s2**. Thus, line 3 prints out "equal" and it appears to have been tested for equality of content with the == operator. However, the test in line 6 is always **false** because two distinct objects are involved.

> One of the most common mistakes that new programmers make is using the == operator to compare **String** objects instead of the **equals** method. At least one question involving understanding the difference is likely to appear on the test.

Array Initialization

An *array* in Java is a type of object that can contain a number of variables. These variables can be referenced only by the array index—a nonnegative integer. All of these contained variables, or elements, must be the same type, which is the type of the array. Every array has an associated **length** variable, established when the array is created, which you can access directly. If you try to address an element with an index that is outside the range of the array, an exception is generated. Java arrays are one-dimensional, but an array can contain other arrays, which gives the effect of multiple dimensions.

You can have arrays of any of the Java primitives or reference variables. The important point to remember is that when created, primitive arrays will have default values assigned, but object references will all be **null**.

Declaration

Like other variables, arrays must be declared before you use them. Declaration can be separate from the actual creation of the array. Here are some examples of declaring variables that are arrays of primitives (lines 1 through 3) and objects (lines 4 and 5):

```
1. int counts[] ;
2. int[] counts ; // 1 and 2 are equivalent
3. boolean flags [    ] ; // extra spaces are not significant
4. String names[] ;
5. MyClass[][] things ; // a two-dimensional array of objects
6. System.out.println( "counts = " + counts );
```

If lines 1 through 6 were in a method and the method was executed, line 6 would print "counts = null" because the array object has not yet been constructed.

Construction

You cannot do anything with an array variable until the array has been constructed with the **new** operator. The statement that constructs an array must give the size, as shown in the following code fragment, assumed to follow lines 1 through 6 in the previous code (the code in line 9 assumes that an integer primitive **nStrings** has been initialized):

```
7. counts = new int[20] ;
8. flags = new boolean[ 5 ] ;
9. names = new String[ nStrings ] ;
```

After this code executes, the array references will have array objects of known types, but exactly what is in the array depends on the type. Integer and floating-point primitive arrays will have elements initialized to zero values. Arrays of the **boolean** types will have elements of **false** values. Arrays of object types will have **null** references.

You can combine declaration of an array variable with construction, as shown in the following code examples:

```
1. float rates[] = new float[33] ;
2. String files[] = new String[ 1000 ] ;
```

 You must remember the distinction between the status of arrays of primitives and the status of arrays of object references after the array is constructed. Arrays of primitives have elements that are initialized to default values. Arrays of objects will have the value **null** in each element. You are practically guaranteed to have a related question on the exam.

Combined Declaration, Construction, and Initialization

Java allows a statement format for combined declaration, construction, and initialization of arrays with literal values, as shown in the following code examples (note that the **String** array defined in lines 2, 3, and 4 is two dimensional):

```
1. int[] fontSize = { 9, 11, 13, 15, 17 } ;
2. String[][] fontDesc  = {
3.    {"TimesRoman", "bold"}, {"Courier","italic"},
4.    {"ZapfDingBats", "normal"} } ;
```

Initialization

To provide initial object references or primitive values other than the default, you have to address each element in the array. In the following code, I declare and create an array of **Rectangle** objects, and then create the **Rectangle** objects for each element:

```
1. Rectangle hotSpots[] = new Rectangle[10];
2. for( int i = 0 ; i < hotSpots.length ; i++ ){
3.    hotSpots[i] = new Rectangle(10 * i, 0, 10, 10);
4. }
```

Object Array Sample Question

The following sample question is related to object arrays. This example caused many errors in my testing. I feel this difficulty illustrates two important points about taking the exam:

➤ Read the question carefully.

➤ Remember that the wrapper class names, although spelled like the primitives, always start with a capital letter.

Sample Question

What will happen when you try to compile and run the following application?

```
1. public class Example {
2.    public Boolean flags[] = new Boolean[4] ;
3.    public static void main(String[] args){
4.       Example E = new Example();
5.       System.out.println( "Flag 1 is " +
       E.flags[1] );
6.    }
7. }
```

○ a. The text "Flag 1 is true" will be written to standard output.

○ b. The text "Flag 1 is false" will be written to standard output.

○ c. The text "Flag 1 is null" will be written to standard output.

○ d. The compiler will object to line 2.

Answer c is correct. Most people forgot that **Boolean** is a wrapper class for **boolean** values and thus the array creation statement in line 2 merely created the array. All of the references in that array are initialized to **null**.

Practice Questions

Question 1

What will be the result of calling the following method with an input of 2?

```
1.  public int adder( int N ){
2.     return  0x100 + N++ ;
3.  }
```

○ a. The method will return 258.

○ b. The method will return 102.

○ c. The method will return 259.

○ d. The method will return 103.

Answer a is correct. The hexadecimal constant 0x100 is 256 decimal so adding 2 results in 258. The post increment of N will have no effect on the returned value. The method would return 102 if the literal constant were decimal, but it is not. Therefore, answer b is incorrect. Answers c and d are incorrect arithmetic.

Question 2

What happens when you attempt to compile and run the following code?

```
1. public class Logic {
2.    static int minusOne = -1 ;
3.    static public void main(String args[] ){
4.        int N = minusOne >> 31 ;
5.        System.out.println("N = " + N );
6.    }
7. }
```

○ a. The program will compile and run, producing the output "N = -1".

○ b. The program will compile and run, producing the output "N = 1".

○ c. A runtime **ArithmeticException** will be thrown.

○ d. The program will compile and run, producing the output "N = 0".

Answer a is correct. The `>>` operator extends the sign as the shift operation is performed. The program would have compiled and run, producing the output "N = 1" if the `>>>` operator, which shifts in a zero bit, had been specified, but it was not. Therefore, answer b is incorrect. An **ArithmeticException** is typically thrown due to integer division by zero, not by a shift operation. Therefore, answer c is incorrect. Answer d does not occur because the `>>` operator extends the sign as the shift is performed.

Question 3

What would be the result of running the following method with an input of 67?

```
1.  public int MaskOff( int n ){
2.      return n | 3 ;
3.  }
```

○ a. The method would return 3.

○ b. The method would return 64.

○ c. The method would return 67.

○ d. The method would return 0.

Answer c is correct. The bit pattern of 67 is 1000011, so the bitwise **OR** with 3 would not change the number. The method would have returned 3 if the bitwise **AND** operator & had been used, but this is the **OR** operator. Therefore, answer a is incorrect. The method would have returned 64 if the **XOR** operator ^ had been used, but it was not. Therefore, answer b is incorrect. Answer d cannot result from the **OR** of 67 with 3.

Question 4

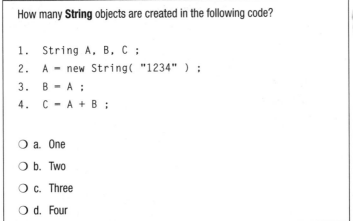

How many **String** objects are created in the following code?

```
1.   String A, B, C ;
2.   A = new String( "1234" ) ;
3.   B = A ;
4.   C = A + B ;
```

○ a. One

○ b. Two

○ c. Three

○ d. Four

The correct answer is b. Both **A** and **B** refer to the same **String** object, whereas **C** refers to a **String** created by concatenating two copies of **A**. Therefore, only two **String** objects have been created, and all other answers are incorrect.

Question 5

Which of the following versions of initializing a **char** variable would cause a compiler error? [Check all correct answers]

❑ a. char c = - 1 ;

❑ b. char c = '\u00FF' ;

❑ c. char c = (char) 4096 ;

❑ d. char c = 4096L ;

❑ e. char c = 'c' ;

❑ f. char c = "c" ;

Answers a, d, and f are correct. In answer a, the literal creates a negative **int** that the compiler recognizes as being outside the normal range of **char** (the only unsigned integer primitive). In answer d, an explicit cast would be required to convert the literal **long** into a **char**. In answer f, the string literal could be used only to initialize a **String** object. The other options are legal assignments to a **char** primitive. Therefore, answers b, c, and e are incorrect. Note that questions that ask you to identify statements that will not compile are likely to appear on the exam.

Question 6

What happens when you try to compile and run the following code?

```
1.  public class EqualsTest{
2.    public static void main(String args[]){
3.      Long LA = new Long( 7 ) ;
4.      Long LB = new Long( 7 ) ;
5.      if( LA == LB )
          System.out.println("Equal");
6.      else System.out.println("Not Equal");
7.    }
8.  }
```

○ a. The program compiles but throws a runtime exception in line 5.

○ b. The program compiles and prints "Equal".

○ c. The program compiles and prints "Not Equal".

Answer c is correct. When used with objects, the == operator tests for identity. Because **LA** and **LB** are different objects, the test fails. All other answers are incorrect.

Question 7

What happens when you try to compile and run the following code?

```
1.  public class EqualsTest{
2.    public static void main(String args[]){
3.      char A = '\u0005' ;
4.      if( A == 0x0005L ) {
5.          System.out.println("Equal");
6.      }
7.      else {
8.          System.out.println("Not Equal");
9.      }
10.   }
11. }
```

○ a. The compiler reports "Invalid character in input" in line 3.

○ b. The program compiles and prints "Not Equal".

○ c. The program compiles and prints "Equal".

Answer c is correct. The compiler promotes variable **A** to a **long** before the comparison. The compiler does not report "Invalid character in input" in line 3 because this is the correct form for initializing a **char** primitive. Therefore, answer a is incorrect. Because answer c is correct, answer b cannot possibly be the correct answer.

Question 8

In the following code fragment from an applet, we know that the **getParameter** call may return a **null** if there is no parameter named **size**:

```
1.  int sz ;
2.  public void init(){
3.      sz = 10 ;
4.      String tmp = getParameter("size");
5.      if( tmp != null X tmp.equals("BIG"))
            sz = 20 ;
6.  }
```

Which logical operator should replace **X** in line 5 to ensure that a **NullPointerException** is not generated if **tmp** is **null**?

○ a. **&**

○ b. **&&**

○ c. **|**

○ d. **||**

The correct answer is b, the "short-circuited" **AND** operator. All of the other operators would attempt to run the **equals** method on the **tmp** variable, even if it were **null**, causing a **NullPointerException**. Therefore, answers a, c, and d are incorrect.

Question 9

What would happen if you tried to compile and run the following code?

```
1.  public class EqualsTest{
2.    public static void main(String args[]){
3.      Long L = new Long( 7 );
4.      if( L.equals( 7L ))
           System.out.println("Equal");
5.      else System.out.println("Not Equal");
6.    }
7.  }
```

○ a. The program would compile and print "Equal".

○ b. The program would compile and print "Not Equal".

○ c. The compiler would object to line 4.

○ d. A runtime cast error would occur at line 4.

Answer c is correct. The compiler knows that the **equals** method takes an **Object** rather than a primitive as input. Because the program does not compile, answers a, b, and d are incorrect.

Question 10

What would happen if you tried to compile and run the following code?

```
1.  public class EqualsTest{
2.    public static void main(String args[]){
3.      Object A = new Long( 7 );
4.      Long  L = new Long( 7 ) ;
5.      if( A.equals( L ))
          System.out.println("Equal");
6.      else System.out.println("Not Equal");
7.    }
8.  }
```

○ a. The program would compile and print "Equal".

○ b. The program would compile and print "Not Equal".

○ c. The compiler would object to line 5.

○ d. A runtime cast error would occur at line 5.

Answer a is correct because the **Long** object created in line 3 does not lose its identity when cast to **Object A**, so the **equals** method knows the class is correct and compares the values. Because answer a is correct, answer b is obviously incorrect. Answers c and d do not occur because this is the correct form for comparing objects with the **equals** method. Therefore, they are incorrect.

Need to Know More?

 Flanagan, David. *Java in a Nutshell, Third Edition*. O'Reilly & Associates, Inc., Sebastopol, CA, 1999. ISBN 1-56592-487-8. This is the most compact desktop reference book documenting the Java language; operators and expression sytax are discussed in chapter 2.

 http://java.sun.com/docs/books/jls/second_edition/html/j.title. doc.html is where the definitive Java language specification document is maintained in HTML form. This document has also been published as ISBN 0-201-31008-2, but most programmers will find the online documentation to be sufficient. Operators are discussed in Chapter 3.

 http://java.sun.com/docs/books/vmspec/2nd-edition/html/ VMSpecTOC.doc.html is where the definitive JVM specification in the most current edition is maintained. It has detailed sections on the representation of primitive values such as interpretation of the **strictfp** modifier.

Creating Java Classes

Terms you'll need to understand:

✓ Access modifier

✓ **extends**

✓ **implements**

✓ Automatic variable

✓ Scope of variables

✓ Default constructor

Techniques you'll need to master:

✓ Constructing a class definition using the modifiers public, abstract, and final

✓ Constructing definitions of classes that implement interfaces

✓ Declaring methods using the modifiers public, private, protected, static, final, native, and synchronized, as well as understanding the consequences of using them

✓ Declaring variables using the modifiers public, private, protected, static, final, and transient

✓ Using variables declared inside code blocks

✓ Understanding the circumstances governing the use of default constructors

Classes are the core concept of the Java language. Because all programming in Java consists of defining classes, it is essential to understand how to create a class. Points that are likely to arise in exam questions include the visibility of methods and variables in a class and other program elements as controlled by access modifier keywords. You should also clearly understand the differences between instance variables, static variables, and variables declared inside code blocks.

Defining a Class

Java classes are always defined inside a single source code file. As discussed in Chapter 2, **package** and **import** statements at the start of the file tell the compiler which resources can be used to compile the class. A class is defined with a declaration followed by a block of code inside a bracket pair. At the start of the declaration, keywords describe where the class fits in the Java class hierarchy and control the accessibility of the class. The components of a class declaration are as follows:

➤ *Class modifiers*—An optional set of keywords.

➤ *Class keyword*—The word "class" must appear here.

➤ *Class name*—A Java name that must be unique within the package.

➤ *Superclass name*—Optionally, the word "extends" followed by the name of the parent class. If this does not appear, the class extends **java.lang.Object**.

➤ *Interfaces implemented*—Optionally, the word "implements" followed by a list of interface names.

➤ *Class body*—The code that declares the fields and methods of the class.

Table 4.1 summarizes the meaning of various Java keywords used in class declarations. You will have to be very familiar with this material.

Table 4.1 Summary of Java keywords used in class declarations.	
Keyword	Implication
public	This class will be visible to all classes in the program. If this word is not used, this class will be visible only within the package.
abstract	The **abstract** keyword *must* be used if a class contains one or more **abstract** method(s). However, a class *may* be declared **abstract** even if it does not contain any **abstract** method. A class declared **abstract** cannot be used to create an object.
final	This class cannot be subclassed. This word cannot be used with **abstract**.
extends	The class name following this keyword is the parent of this class. If this word is not used, the **Object** class will be the parent.
implements	This class provides for all the methods required by the interfaces that follow this keyword. Any number of interfaces can be implemented.

It is good practice for the test to work out the implications of various combinations of keywords in class declarations. Here are some examples to play with:

```
public abstract class ToneGenerator implements Runnable
class DataTable extends Observable
final class ErrorCodes
```

Abstract Classes

A class must be declared **abstract** if it has one or more methods declared **abstract**. Language designers use **abstract** classes to establish a pattern that can be filled out with concrete methods for a specific situation. For example, the **java.awt. Graphics** class is **abstract** because graphics methods depend on the specific hardware and operating system of a particular system. The Java Virtual Machine (JVM) supplies a specific class that is a subclass of **Graphics**, with methods suited to the specific system.

Final Classes

A class declared **final** cannot be used as a parent for another class. You may be wondering why anyone would declare a class as **final**. Frequently, this is done for security reasons. For example, the **java.lang.StringBuffer** class is declared **final** because experience has shown that the misapplication of string-manipulating methods in C has been at the root of hard-to-find security holes in network applications. Because **StringBuffer** is **final**, no hacker can slip in an object that is derived from **StringBuffer** and that does not have built-in security checks.

Class Modifier Restrictions

Classes cannot be **protected, private, native,** or **synchronized**. The words "abstract" and "final" cannot appear together because an **abstract** class, by definition, has declared methods that do not have implementations. Note that some compilers do not catch erroneous use of some keywords on class definitions.

The Class Body

The class body contains the declarations of the *members* of the class. These include fields (variables), methods, static initializers, instance initializers, and constructors. You can also have class definitions *inside* a class body. These *nested* classes are considered to be members of the enclosing class and have a special relationship with it. Nested classes are discussed in Chapter 5.

Class Members

Access to class members of all types is controlled by access modifier keywords as follows:

➤ *public*—A **public** member is accessible from any class in the program.

➤ *protected*—A **protected** member can be accessed only by classes in the same package and classes derived from the current class—no matter which package they are in.

➤ *private*—A **private** member can be accessed only from within the class.

➤ *default*—If none of the other access modifier keywords appears, the default of access only by classes in the same package applies. You may see the word "friendly" used in connection with the default access, but "friendly" is *not* a Java keyword.

Other keywords that can be applied to class members are **static, final, abstract, native, transient, volatile, strictfp,** and **synchronized.** The implications of these keywords are discussed in the following sections.

Fields

Fields are named variables, such as primitives and reference variables. Fields declared with the keyword **static** belong to the class and occur only once, as opposed to instance variables, which belong to class instances. Static variables are sometimes referred to as *class* variables. The **final** keyword means that the field cannot be changed once initialized.

The following code fragment illustrates the use of **static** and **final**; lines 2 and 3 define Java equivalents to what would be called constants in other languages:

```
1.  class Widget extends Object {
2.    public static final int TYPEA = 1 ;
3.    public static final int TYPEB = 2 ;
4.    private static int count = 0 ;
5.    static void addOne(){ count++ ; } // a static method
6.    static final String name = "Widget" ;
7.    static final Point varX ;
8.    static {  // start static initialization block
9.      varX = new Point( 0,0 ) ;
10.   } // end static initialization block
11.   // more code here
12. }
```

Note that if the word "final" is attached to a reference variable, the associated object must be created in the declaration statement, as in line 6, or in a static initialization block, as in lines 8 through 10.

 With reference variables, **final** means that the initial object reference cannot be replaced by another object reference—not that the object itself cannot be modified.

Classes with Only Static Members

It is quite feasible to have classes that have only static members, do not have constructors, and cannot be used to create an object. An example of this is the **Math** class in the Java standard library, which is used to provide typical mathematical functions. You address the static variables and methods with notation similar to that used with instance variables but with the name of the class instead of an instance reference, as shown in the following code:

```
1. area = Math.PI * rad * rad ; // addressing a static constant
2. root = Math.sqrt( area ) ; // addressing a static method
```

Variable Initialization

Both instance variables and class (static) variables have default initialization values that are used if the variable declaration statement does not include initial values. Class variables are initialized when the class is loaded by the JVM, and instance variables are initialized when an object is created. In contrast, there is no default initialization for variables that are declared inside the scope of methods or smaller code blocks.

It is essential to know the default initializations of static and instance variables. They are as follows:

➤ Integer primitives are initialized to 0.

➤ Floating-point primitives are initialized to 0.0.

➤ Boolean primitives are initialized to **false**.

➤ Reference variables are initialized to **null**.

More on Variable Modifiers

The modifiers **abstract, native,** and **synchronized** are not used with variables. The keyword **transient** is used to indicate variables that do not need to be saved when an object is saved using the object serialization methods. The keyword **volatile** is used to signal to the compiler that the designated variable may be changed by multiple threads and that it cannot take any shortcuts when retrieving the value in this variable.

Methods

Methods are defined with a method declaration. The elements in a method declaration are access modifier, additional modifiers, return type, method name, parameter list, and exceptions. The combination of name and parameter list constitutes the method *signature*. Table 4.2 summarizes the keywords that can be used in a method declaration. Note that if one of the access modifiers—**public, private,** or **protected**—does not appear, the default is visibility within the package.

Method Code

If the method is not declared **abstract,** the declaration is followed by a block of code enclosed in a bracket pair. An **abstract** declaration is followed by a semicolon. If the method is declared as returning a value, all paths through the code must terminate in a **return** statement that returns the correct type of value. If the method is declared with a **void** return type, **return** statements are optional; however, if they appear, they must not return a value.

Method Overloading

Java allows multiple methods in a class with the same name as long as they have different parameter input lists. This is called *overloading* a method. You can see

Table 4.2 Summary of Java keywords used with methods.	
Keyword	**Implication**
public	The method is visible to all classes in the program.
private	The method is visible only inside the class.
protected	The method is visible to classes inside the package and to subclasses.
final	The method cannot be overridden in subclasses.
abstract	The method is declared without an implementation.
static	The method is independent of any object of the class but can address only static variables.
native	The implementation must be provided in machine language for a specific system.
strictfp	All floating-point math in the method must reduce all intermediate results to the standard 32- or 64-bit form.
synchronized	A **Thread** entering this method obtains a lock on the object, which prevents other **Thread**s from entering any synchronized code for the object.
throws	This word introduces a list of checked exceptions that the method may throw. Exceptions are discussed in Chapter 7.
void	If the method does not return a value, the word "void" must appear as the return type.

many examples of overloading in the Java standard libraries. For instance, the **java.awt.Graphics** class has six different **drawImage** methods.

Method Overriding

When a method in a derived class has the same name and signature as a method in the parent class, we say that the parent class method is overridden. A good example of this in the Java standard library is the **toString** method defined in the **Object** class. Many classes override **toString** with more informative versions.

native Methods

Java provides the method modifier **native** to label a method that will be implemented in machine language by the JVM or by a user-supplied library. A **native** method is declared with a semicolon that represents the body of the method that will be provided by **native** code. Creating your own **native** methods by means of the Java Native Interface (JNI) is beyond the scope of the programmer's exam. However, here is a sample **native** method declaration from the Java **Thread** class:

```
public static native void yield();
```

Local Variables

Local variables, also known as "automatic" variables, are declared inside methods or small blocks of code. The storage for these variables does not exist in an object but in the environment of the **Thread** executing the method. The rules for initialization of and access to these variables are quite different from those for instance variables. My experiments with model tests have indicated that many people are weak on initialization and scope of local variables. The term *scope* refers to the section of code in which a variable can be referred to. A variable declared in a block of code, such as a method, has a scope within that block of code.

Initialization

Local variables are not initialized automatically; the programmer must provide a value for all variables before they are used. The compiler will report an error if there is any path through your code that does not initialize a variable before it is used, as illustrated in the following code fragment where **nameTable** is a **Hashtable** object:

```
1. public String lookup( String abrev ){
2.    String fullname ;
3.    if( nameTable.containsKey( abrev ) ) {
4.       fullname = (String) nameTable.get( abrev ) ;
5.    }
6.    return fullname ;
7. }
```

The purpose of the **lookup** method is to return the full name if the abbreviation is a key in the **nameTable**. However, the compiler detects that there is a path through the code in which **fullname** will not be initialized and reports an error. One solution to the problem is to initialize **fullname** in line 2; another is to provide an **else** branch that sets **fullname** after line 5.

Scope of Local Variables

Remember that the scope (visibility) of local variables is restricted to the code block in which they are declared. For instance, in the following code fragment, the compiler will object to the use of **val** in lines 5 and 7 because the scope of the variable is inside the **try** block:

```
1. public int parseParam( String s ){
2.   try {
3.     int val = Integer.parseInt( s );
4.   }catch(NumberFormatException e ){
5.     val = -1 ;
6.   }
7.   return val ;
8. }
```

Another common mistake related to scope is the attempt to use a loop variable outside the code block of the loop. For example, in the following code fragment, the loop counter **i** will be meaningless outside the loop, and the attempt to use it in line 5 will cause a compiler error:

```
1. public int findNdx( String name ){
2.   for( int i = 0 ; i < nameList.length ; i++ ){
3.     if( name.equals( nameList[i] ) break ;
4.   }
5.   return i ;
6. }
```

final Local Variables

The only modifier that can be applied to a local variable is **final**. The implication is the same as with other variables—once the variable has been set, it cannot be changed. Final local variables are of interest mainly in *inner classes*, which are discussed in Chapter 5.

Static Initializers

In addition to declaring and initializing a **static** variable in the same statement, you can create a special block of code that runs when the JVM loads the class. This is typically used to initialize complex structures. For instance, if you wanted to create a **Hashtable** for rapid lookup of state names from two-letter abbreviations, you could create and initialize the **Hashtable** with code like the following (and adding 47 more states):

```
static String[] states = { "Texas", "Florida", "Oklahoma" } ;
static String[] abrev = { "TX", "FL", "OK" } ;
public static Hashtable statesByAb ;
static {
  statesByAb = new Hashtable();
  for( int i = 0 ; i < abrev.length ; i++ ){
     statesByAb.put( abrev[i], states[i] );
  }
} // end of static initializer block
```

The **statesByAb Hashtable** would be available as soon as the class was loaded. Because it is declared **public**, any method in any class can use it.

Constructors

Constructors are chunks of code used to initialize a new object. All Java classes must have at least one constructor, either declared in the class or as an implicit default constructor. Although constructors look like methods, they are considered separately. Constructors always have the name of the class and no return type. You can control access to constructors with the access modifiers **public**, **protected**, and **private**, just as you can with other methods. Unlike methods, constructors cannot have the modifiers **abstract, static, final, native**, or **synchronized**. Constructor declarations can have a list of thrown exceptions.

Constructing a new object involves allocating the right amount of memory and initializing variables. Because your custom class may inherit from a long hierarchy of classes, constructing even a simple-looking object may involve a lot of work by the JVM. Fortunately, the compiler takes care of most of the details.

A class can have any number of constructors as long as they have different signatures. The restriction is that each constructor must have a different parameter list. Constructors are not inherited, so each derived class must specifically implement any constructors it needs; however, a derived class can make use of the constructors of its parent class using the **super** keyword. For example, the **java.awt.Rectangle** class has the following constructor:

```
public Rectangle( int x, int y, int width, int height )
```

If I wanted to write a class, **MyRect**, extending **Rectangle**, one possible constructor would be as follows:

```
public MyRect( int w, int h ){
   super( 0,0,w,h );
   // other initialization code here
}
```

If an invocation of the **super** constructor is used, it must be the first line of the constructor code. Any other use of the **super** constructor causes a compiler error.

The Implied **super** Constructor

The Java compiler does a lot of extra work in compiling constructor code. If the first line of the code body does not have an invocation of the **super** constructor, the compiler inserts "super()", an invocation of the *default* constructor that takes no parameters belonging to the parent class.

Default Constructors

If no other constructors are declared in a class, the compiler creates a default constructor that takes no parameters and simply calls the parent class constructor, which takes no parameters. This can lead to problems, as shown in the following simple example:

```
1. class Base extends Object {
2.    int type ;
3.    Base( int n ) { type = n ; }
4. }
5. class XBase extends Base {
6.    String X = "" ;
7. }
```

Because the **Base** class has a constructor that takes a parameter (line 3), the compiler does not create a default **Base** constructor. The **XBase** class is defined without a constructor, so the compiler attempts to provide a default constructor. However, there is no constructor without parameters in the **Base** class, so the compiler issues this error:

```
No constructor matching Base() found in Base
```

This rather odd-sounding error message has confused many beginning Java programmers. You will probably encounter one or more test questions related to default constructors.

Overloaded Constructors

A class can have any number of constructors as long as they have different parameter lists. One constructor can invoke another, but the statement has to be the first one in the code body. In the example shown in Listing 4.1, the constructor that takes a **String** and two **int** primitives invokes the constructor that takes two **int** primitives.

Listing 4.1   Code for a Java class that has two constructors.

```
import java.awt.* ;
  class Base extends Object {
    Point theP ;
    String str = "" ;
    Base( int x, int y ){
        theP = new Point( x, y );
    }
    Base( String txt, int x, int y ){
       this( x, y );
       str = txt ;
    }
  }
```

Constructors Throwing Exceptions

Because constructors don't have a return value, new Java programmers often wonder how to signal that a constructor has failed. The answer is that Java workhorse concept, the **Exception**. Chapter 7 discusses the use of **Exception**s, but the following sample constructor should give you the general idea:

```
public HelpFile( String filename ) throws IOException {
  File f = new File( filename );
  if( !f.exists() ) throw new FileNotFoundException( filename );
  // normal construction continues
}
```

Here are some points to keep in mind about constructors:

➤ If you don't define any constructor in the class code, the compiler provides a default constructor that takes no parameters.

➤ You can invoke constructors in the parent class, but this must be done in the first line of code in the constructor body.

➤ A class can have multiple constructors, but they must have different parameter lists.

➤ A constructor can invoke another constructor in the class, but this must be done in the first line of code in the constructor body.

➤ The only way to abort a constructor is to throw an exception.

Interfaces

Interfaces are reference types like classes but can have only **abstract** method declarations and constants as members. Interfaces are defined in the same way as classes, with a source code file that has a ".java" file type that is compiled to a class file. Interfaces are also members of packages, just like classes. Java uses interfaces extensively to provide a convenient alternative to multiple inheritance. A Java class can implement any number of interfaces.

A class that implements an interface must provide implementations for all of the methods that the interface defines. An object of this class then has a sort of alternate identity and can be referred to as being of the interface type. For example, the **Runnable** interface, a member of the **java.lang** package, defines only a single method with the following signature:

```
public void run();
```

Another simple interface is the **ActionListener** interface in the **java.awt.event** package. The single method required by this interface has the signature shown in the following code snippet:

```
public void actionPerformed( ActionEvent e );
```

The **CountDown** Demonstration Class

Listing 4.2 shows a Java class that demonstrates several of the features I have been talking about. The function of the **CountDown** class is to animate a countdown message after a user clicks a button. To do this, it implements the **Runnable** interface (so it can have a separate **Thread** to run a timer mechanism) and the **ActionListener** interface (so it can be notified when a button is clicked on).

Listing 4.2   Complete source for the CountDown class.

```
import java.awt.TextField ;
import java.awt.event.*;
public class CountDown extends java.lang.Object implements
     java.awt.event.ActionListener, java.lang.Runnable
{
  static int counters = 0 ;
  static synchronized int incCount(){ return ++counters; }
  TextField text ;
```

```
int myN ;
CountDown( TextField tf ){
  text = tf ; myN = incCount() ;
}

public void run()
{ for(int i = 10 ; i >= 0 ; i--){
    try{
       text.setText( Integer.toString( i ));
       Thread.sleep( 1000 );
    }catch(InterruptedException e ){}
  }
}
  // required by ActionListener interface
public void actionPerformed(ActionEvent e)
{ Thread t = new Thread( this );
  System.out.println("Start counter " + myN );
  t.start();
}
}
```

The CountDown Constructor

Note that the constructor for **CountDown** takes a reference to a **TextField** object. **TextField** objects are used in Java applications and applets with graphical user interfaces (GUIs) to show a single line of changeable text. The constructor saves this reference in the instance variable named **text**.

Every time a new **CountDown** object is created, the counter is incremented in the **static incCount** method, and a unique number is returned to the constructor. Because the **incCount** method is synchronized, only one **Thread** at a time can use it to obtain a serial number; thus, every **CountDown** object has a unique **myN**.

If you are sure that only one **Thread** will be creating **CountDown** objects, you can leave off the **synchronized** keyword. If you browse through the source code for Java standard library components, such as **java.awt.TextField**, you will see that many classes use this technique to create a unique serial number.

The ActionListener Interface

The **CountDown** class has an **actionPerformed** method to satisfy the requirements of the **ActionListener** interface. In the **java.awt.Button** class, there is a method that has the following signature:

```
public synchronized void addActionListener( ActionListener a );
```

Note that the input parameter is a reference to an interface, not to a specific class. Any object that wants to get **ActionEvents** from a **Button** needs only implement the **ActionListener** interface and register with the **Button**.

The Runnable Interface

To satisfy the **Runnable** interface, **CountDown** has a **run** method. When a **Thread** is attached to an object that has a **run** method and the **Thread** is started, it automatically executes the **run** method. I will cover **Threads** and the **Runnable** interface in more detail in Chapter 9.

References to Interfaces

You can have variables declared interface types, as illustrated in the following code from an applet using **CountDown** objects:

```
CountDown cd1 = new CountDown( textField1 );
Runnable rcd1 = cd1 ;
ActionListener acd1 = cd1 ;
button1.addActionListener( acd1 );
```

Here you see three reference variables of three different types that all refer to the same object. You can also use the **instanceof** operator to see if a given object implements an interface.

Defining an Interface

Defining an interface is just like defining an **abstract** class with all **abstract** methods. Interfaces can have access modifiers of **public** or *blank*, just like classes. An interface can be defined as extending another interface, in a hierarchy similar to the class hierarchy, but there is no base interface analogous to the **Object** class.

Defining Constants in an Interface

The closest Java comes to a "constant" is a variable declared as **static** and **final**. For convenience, Java lets you define **static final** variables in interfaces as well as in normal classes.

Practice Questions

Question 1

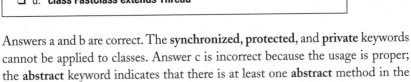

Which of the following class declarations use modifier keywords incorrectly? [Check all correct answers]

❏ a. **public synchronized class FastClass extends Thread**

❏ b. **private protected class FastClass**

❏ c. **public abstract class FastClass**

❏ d. **class FastClass extends Thread**

Answers a and b are correct. The **synchronized, protected,** and **private** keywords cannot be applied to classes. Answer c is incorrect because the usage is proper; the **abstract** keyword indicates that there is at least one **abstract** method in the class. Answer d is incorrect because it shows a legal class declaration.

Question 2

Take the following class:

```
1. class Widget extends Thingee{
2.    static final int maxWidgetSize = 40 ;
3.    static String Title ;
4.    public Widget( int mx, String T  ){
5.       maxWidgetSize = mx ;
6.       Title = T ;
7.    }
8.       // other code
9. }
```

What will happen when you try to compile this code and run a program that creates a **Widget** as follows?

```
10.   Widget myWidget =
              new Widget( 50, "Bigger");
```

○ a. The program compiles and runs fine.

○ b. The program compiles but gets a runtime error in line 5.

○ c. The compiler objects to line 5.

○ d. The compiler objects to line 6.

Answer c is correct. The compiler knows that a variable declared as **static final** cannot be modified, so it generates an error. Answers a and b are incorrect because a compiler error occurs. Answer d is incorrect because line 6 is perfectly reasonable; objects are allowed to access and modify **static** (class) variables as long as they are not also declared **final**.

Question 3

Take the following listing of the **Widget** class:

```
1. class Widget extends Thingee{
2.    static private int widgetCount = 0 ;
3.    public String wName ;
4.    int wNumber ;
5.
6.    static synchronized int
         addWidget(){ widgetCount++ ;
7.        wName = "I am Widget # " +
             widgetCount ;
8.        return widgetCount ;
9.    }
10.   public Widget(){
11.       wNumber = addWidget();
12.   }
13. }
```

What happens when you try to compile the class and use multiple **Widget** objects in a program?

○ a. The class compiles and each **Widget** gets a unique **wNumber** and **wName** reflecting the order in which the **Widget**s were created.

○ b. The compiler objects to line 7.

○ c. The class compiles, but a runtime error related to the access of the variable **wName** occurs in the **addWidget** method.

Answer b is correct; the static method **addWidget** cannot access the member variable **wName**. Static methods can refer to static variables such as **widgetCount**, only. Answers a and c are incorrect because a compiler error is generated by line 7. Another reason answer c is incorrect is that the compiler catches the incorrect use of access modifiers, such as **static**.

Question 4

Take the following listing of the **Widget** class:

```
1. class Widget extends Thingee{
2.    static private int widgetCount = 0 ;
3.    public String wName ;
4.    int wNumber ;
5.
6.    private static synchronized int
         addWidget(){
7.        return ++widgetCount ;
8.    }
9.    public Widget(){
10.       wNumber = addWidget();
11.   }
12. }
```

What happens when you try to compile the class and use multiple **Widget** objects in a program that uses multiple **Threads** to create **Widget** objects?

○ a. The class compiles and each **Widget** gets a unique **wNumber** reflecting the order in which the **Widgets** were created.

○ b. The compiler objects to the **addWidget** call of a static method in line 10.

○ c. A runtime error occurs in the **addWidget** method.

○ d. The class compiles and each **Widget** gets a **wNumber**, but you cannot guarantee that the number will be unique.

The correct answer is a. The use of **synchronized** in line 6 ensures that number assignment will not be interrupted, no matter how many **Threads** are trying to create **Widget** objects. Answer b is incorrect because line 10 is in the correct form, although **Widget.addWidget()** could also be used. Answer c is incorrect because the **addWidget** method has no code that can generate a runtime error. Answer d is incorrect because the use of **synchronized** in line 6 ensures that number assignment will not be interrupted, no matter how many **Threads** are trying to create **Widget** objects.

Question 5

When you try to compile the following source code produces a compiler warning to the effect that the variable **tmp** may not have been initialized:

```
1. class Demo{
2.    String msg = "Type is " ;
3.    public void showType( int n ) {
4.       String tmp ;
5.       if( n > 0 ) tmp = "positive";
6.       System.out.println( msg + tmp );
7.    }
8. }
```

Which of the following changes would eliminate this warning? [Check all correct answers]

❏ a. Make line 4 read:

```
4.     String tmp = null ;
```

❏ b. Make line 4 read:

```
4.     String tmp = "" ;
```

❏ c. Insert a line following line 5:

```
6.     else tmp = "not positive" ;
```

❏ d. Remove line 4 and insert a new line after 2 so **tmp** becomes a member variable instead of a local variable in **showType**:

```
3.     String tmp ;
```

Answers a, b, c, and d are correct. All of these changes will eliminate the warning. Both answers a and b provide for initializing the reference when it is declared. Answer c ensures that **tmp** gets initialized no matter what the value of n. Answer d makes **tmp** a member variable that will be initialized to **null** by default.

Question 6

The following method definition is designed to parse and return an integer from an input string that is expected to look like "nnn,ParamName" (in the event of a **NumberFormatException**, the method is to return -1):

```
1. public int getNum( String S ){
2.    try {
3.       String tmp =
             S.substring( 0,S.indexOf(','));
4.       return Integer.parseInt( tmp );
5.    }catch(NumberFormatException e){
6.       System.out.println("Problem in "
                    + tmp );
7.    }
8.    return -1 ;
9. }
```

What happens when you try to compile this code and execute the method with an input string that does not contain a comma separating the number from the text data?

○ a. A compiler error in line 6 prevents compilation.

○ b. The method prints the error message to standard output and returns -1.

○ c. A **NullPointerException** is thrown in line 3.

○ d. A **StringIndexOutOfBoundsException** is thrown in line 3.

Answer a is correct because the scope of the **tmp String** is confined to the **try** block; thus, it cannot be used in line 6. The situation in answer b does not occur because of the compiler error related to the scope of the **tmp** variable. Answer c would not occur even if the scope of the **tmp** variable were fixed. Answer d would occur only if the scope of the **tmp** variable were fixed by declaring and initializing **tmp** in the first line of the method.

Question 7

Take the following class definition:

```
1. public class DerivedDemo extends Demo{
2.    int M, N, L ;
3.    public DerivedDemo( int x, int y ){
4.      M = x ; N = y ;
5.    }
6.    public DerivedDemo( int x ){
7.      super( x );
8.    }
9. }
```

Which of the following constructor signatures *must* exist in the **Demo** class for **DerivedDemo** to compile correctly? [Check all correct answers]

❑ a. **public Demo(int a, int b)**.

❑ b. **public Demo(int c)**.

❑ c. **public Demo( )**.

❑ d. There is no requirement for a constructor in **Demo**.

The correct answers are b and c. The code in answer b is required because it is called in line 7. The code in answer c is required because a default (no arguments) constructor is needed to compile the constructor starting in line 3. The code in answer a is not required because no constructor with that signature is explicitly called. Answer d is incorrect because the constructor in c is required.

Need to Know More?

 Flanagan, David. *Java in a Nutshell, Third Edition.* O'Reilly & Associates, Inc., Sebastopol, CA, 1999. ISBN 1-56592-487-8. This is the most compact desktop reference book documenting the Java language. Chapter 3, "Object-Oriented Programming in Java," is pertinent to this chapter.

 http://java.sun.com/docs/books/tutorial/information/download.html is where you can download an excellent tutorial in HTML form. The trail titled "Learning The Java Language" is pertinent to this chapter.

 http://java.sun.com/docs/books/jls/second_edition/html/j.title.doc.html is where the definitive Java language specification document is maintained in HTML form. This document has also been published as ISBN 0-201-31008-2, but most programmers will find the online documentation sufficient.

 http://java.sun.com/j2se/1.3/docs.html is the Java application programming interface (API) documentation in Javadoc-generated form; you can download it from Sun Microsystems here. Although this site changes a lot, the last time I looked, it was a good starting point to locate the current documentation.

 http://java.sun.com/docs/books/jls/strictfp-changes.pdf documents the changes to the Java language specification necessitated by the addition of the strictfp modifier.

Nested Classes

Terms you'll need to understand:

✓ Nested class
✓ Inner class
✓ Member class
✓ Local class
✓ Anonymous inner class
✓ **final** local variable

Techniques you'll need to master:

✓ Distinguishing the various types of nested classes and what they are used for
✓ Writing a constructor for each of the different types of nested class
✓ Distinguishing the characteristics of variables that nested classes are allowed to use
✓ Writing inner classes to handle events

The designers of Java decided at an early stage that Java classes would have single inheritance—in other words, each class has only one parent class. Sometimes in object-oriented programming, you wish a class could partake of the methods of more than one parent. In Java 1, this was supplied to some extent by the concept of interfaces, but in Java 1.1, the designers found it necessary to add the concept of nested classes.

Nested and Inner Classes

The main driving force for this change in the language was a major change in the way user interface events are handled. In Java 1, user interface events could be delivered only to classes in the user interface hierarchy. As Java applications got larger, this method was found to be slow and inflexible.

Starting with Java 1.1, events can be delivered to any object, but this implies great duplication of code in every class that needs to handle an event. Nested classes are the solution to avoiding this duplication of code and simplifying the process of adding an event handler to a class. Although nested classes can be used for a variety of purposes, you are most likely to see them as inner classes in connection with event handling.

What Is a Nested Class?

Generally speaking, a nested class is a member of another class. However, it is common to speak of the static members as nested and the nested classes that are members of instances of the enclosing class as inner classes. Indeed, you are most likely to read about inner classes only, but the more general term is nested classes.

The basic idea is simply that a top-level Java class, in addition to having member variables and member methods, can have a member class. This member class can inherit from any top-level class and implement any interface, independent of the object hierarchy of the enclosing class. Just as member methods in a class have unlimited access to all private and other variables and methods in the class, nested classes have unlimited access.

Why Make a Nested Class?

You would want to create a nested class for two main reasons:

➤ You might need to make use of the special functionality of class A from within class B without complicating the inheritance hierarchy of either class. This is the reason for the use of inner classes to support the Java 1.1 event model.

➤ From the point of view of programming philosophy, if class A exists solely to help work with class B, you might as well make class A a member of class B. This helps to keep all of the code related to class B in a single source code file.

When You Shouldn't Make a Nested Class

Nested classes are not a cure-all, and some Java programmers find them down-right ugly. Large nested classes make reading Java code harder than it already is, so keep your nested classes small for easy maintenance. If you find your nested class getting larger than the normal class it lives in, consider redesigning it as a normal class. Inner classes simplify automatic code generation for event handling with the Java graphical user interface (GUI) model, and your encounters with inner classes will probably be in the context of event handling.

How to Make a Nested Class

From a programmer's standpoint, you create a nested class by simply declaring a class inside the declaration of a top-level class or inside a block of code. From the Java compiler's standpoint, a lot of work has to be done. The Java compiler has to create a class file for both the enclosing class and the nested class. The name of the nested class is created by the compiler, starting with the name of the enclosing class. From the Java Virtual Machine (JVM) standpoint, only a slight change in the format of class files was needed to add nested classes; otherwise, the JVM treats a nested class just like any other.

Here is a summary of the different configurations of nested classes:

➤ *Nested static class*—A named class declared **static**. It can directly access only static variables and methods. It is considered a top-level class.

➤ *Nested interface*—A named interface, declared as a static member of a class, typically used for defining methods used to access the enclosing class.

➤ *Inner class (member)*—A named class defined as a member of the enclosing class. It must be associated with an instance of the enclosing class. There can be multiple member inner classes in an enclosing class. Member inner classes can be declared as **public, private, protected, final,** or **abstract,** but they cannot have the same name as any enclosing class.

➤ *Inner class (local)*—A named class defined in a code block in a method of the enclosing class. The inner class can access local variables in the method and parameters passed to the method only if the variables are declared **final.** As with a local variable, the inner class cannot be accessed outside the code block; in other words, the scope of the class is confined to the code block.

➤ *Inner class (anonymous)*—A class defined inside a single expression, having no name or constructor method. These classes can access local variables in the method and parameters passed to the method only if they are declared **final.**

Static Nested Classes

A static nested class is simply one that is declared inside another class and is declared with the **static** modifier. Like static methods, a static nested class can refer to static variables and methods only directly. It can refer to instance variables and methods only when given a reference to an object of the enclosing class type. The following code is a rough outline of the way a static class is declared:

```
class NormalClass {
    static class NestedClass {
        // methods and variables of NestedClass
    }
    // methods and variables of NormalClass
}
```

A Static Nested Class Example

Most of the examples of static nested classes I have seen have been a little forced, but I've found a more realistic example, one related to experiments in computer-based artificial life (ALife). In typical ALife experiments, the programmer creates a class representing an organism, then provides for creation of lots of individuals and lets them roam an artificial environment.

One approach to giving each individual a slice of CPU time is to give each one a **Thread**, but this has disadvantages, such as excessive overhead. In the following example, the static nested class is used to portion out execution time to each "live" object, using only one thread and taking advantage of the access the static nested class has to the enclosing top-level class static variables.

The **Bubble** class, as shown in Listing 5.1, creates a simple object that has a color, a radius, an x and y position, and an x and y rate of change variables. A **Bubble** object knows how to move and how to paint itself on the screen, but it is the **BubTimer** class that provides the **Thread** to execute the **move** method and time the calls to **repaint**.

The **BubTimer** class (emphasized in the listing with shading) also provides for creating new **Bubble** objects and adding them to the **Vector** of active objects. Note that the **BubTimer.addBub** method can directly access the static variables and private methods of the **Bubble** class. In fact, to emphasize the special relationship of the nested class to the enclosing class, all of the instance variables and methods of the **Bubble** class are **private**, so only **BubTimer** can access them.

Listing 5.1   The Bubble class with the static nested BubTimer class.

```
import java.lang.*;
import java.awt.* ;
import java.util.* ;
```

```java
public class Bubble extends java.lang.Object
{
    static Vector allBub = new Vector();
    static Dimension size ;
    public static class BubTimer extends Thread {
      Panel P ;
      BubTimer(Panel p ){ P = p ;
      }
      public void addBub(int x, int y ){
        allBub.addElement(
            new Bubble( Color.red, 20, x, y ) );
      }
      public void run(){
        while( true ){
          if( allBub != null && allBub.size() > 0 ){
            Enumeration e = allBub.elements();
            while(e.hasMoreElements()){
                ((Bubble)e.nextElement()).move();
            }
            P.repaint();
          }
          try {
            Thread.sleep(100);
          }catch(InterruptedException e){}
        }
      }
      public void paintAll(Graphics g ){
        if( allBub == null || allBub.size() == 0 ) return;
        Enumeration e = allBub.elements();
        while(e.hasMoreElements()){
            ((Bubble)e.nextElement()).paint( g );
        }
      }
    }

    // Bubble instance variables
    private Color clr ;
    private int radius, x, y, dx, dy ;
    private Bubble( Color c, int r, int xx, int yy ){
      clr = c ; radius = r ; x = xx ; y = yy ;
      dx = dy = r/2 ;
    }
    private void move(){
      x += dx ; y += dy ;
      if( x > size.width ) dx = -dx ;
      else if( x < 0 ) dx = -dx ;
      if( y > size.height) dy = -dy ;
```

```
    else if( y < 0 ) dy = -dy ;
  }
  private void paint(Graphics g){
    g.setColor( clr );
    g.fillOval( x, y, radius, radius );
  }
}
```

A Member Inner Class Example

Listing 5.2 shows a typical example of the use of an inner class (the shaded code) to implement an interface (in this case, the **ActionListener** interface) that requires only a single method: **actionPerformed**. (The role of **ActionListener**s in Java event handling is covered in Chapter 13.) This code was originally generated with Symantec's Visual Café development environment, so the inner class is named **SymAction**. **SymAction** extends **Object** (by default) and implements **ActionListener**.

In the **init** method, I create an instance of the **SymAction** class and connect it to the **button1** and **button2** objects with the **addActionListener** method. The sole functions of **SymAction** are to receive events generated when a button is clicked, and to perform an appropriate method. In this example, **button1** clears a text field and **button2** sends data from the text field using the **doSend** method:

Listing 5.2   A Java applet that makes use of a named inner class to handle events.

```
import java.awt.*;
import java.awt.event.* ;
import java.applet.*;
public class Applet1 extends Applet{
.../ / variables
  public void init(){
    button1 = new Button("Clear");
    button2 = new Button("Send");
    textField1 = new TextField();
    // various initialization statements to create
    // the rest of the interface
    SymAction lSymAction = new SymAction();
    button1.addActionListener(lSymAction);
    button2.addActionListener(lSymAction);
  }
  class SymAction implements java.awt.event.ActionListener
  {
    public void actionPerformed( ActionEvent event)
    {
```

```
    Object object = event.getSource();
    if (object == button1) textField1.setText("");
    if( object == button2) doSend( textField1.getText() );
    }
} // end of inner class definition
    // code left out to save space
} // end of enclosing class definition
```

If you were to compile the code in Listing 5.2, you would find that the compiler has created both an **Applet1.class** and an **Applet1$SymAction.class**. The formal name of the inner class would be **Applet1.SymAction**, but the extra period would confuse some operating systems, so the compiler uses a dollar sign instead.

Because the **SymAction** object is created in the context of an instance of **Applet1**, it has access to all variables and methods—both static and instance members. Even if **textField1** were declared **private**, the inner class object would have access to it.

A Local Inner Class Example

A local inner class is defined inside the scope of a code block—typically, the code block of a method, but it could be any code block. In the following method code, the purpose is to return a **Hashtable** object containing a subset of names and keys derived from two **String** arrays—**keys** and **names**—in the enclosing class:

```
Hashtable makeHash( String start ){
    class myHash extends Hashtable {
        public myHash(){
            super(10);
        }
        public void buildHash( String str ){
            for( int i = 0 ; i < keys.length ; i++ ){
                if( names[i].startsWith( str ) ){
                    put( keys[i], names[i] );
                }
            }
        }
    } // end inner class definition
    myHash h = new myHash();
    h.buildHash( start );
    return h ;
}
```

Access to Local Variables

The introduction of local inner classes (classes declared inside the scope of a code block or statement) produced a problem for Java's designers. An object created in an inner class may live long after the code block has been exited and any local variables have been discarded. The inner class declaration could see these variables, but how could an inner class method refer to them? The solution was to provide a new meaning for the word "final." When the compiler finds a local variable declared **final**, it creates a special hidden copy of the variable that the inner class can refer to safely. This also applies to parameters that are input to the method in which the inner class is declared.

 Local inner classes and anonymous classes can refer to local variables only if they are declared **final**.

An Anonymous Inner Class Example

In Listing 5.2, the **SymAction** object was connected to two buttons. If you needed to connect only to a single button, you could use the even simpler anonymous-style inner class for **Applet2**, as shown in Listing 5.3. The class is defined and a single instance of it is created entirely within a single Java statement. It is anonymous because the class does not have a name and no named variable holds a reference to it. The only reference to the object is in the list of **ActionListeners** that **button1** holds.

Listing 5.3   A Java applet making use of an anonymous inner class.

```
import java.awt.* ;
import java.awt.event.* ;
import java.applet.* ;
public class Applet2 extends Applet{
...// variables
  public void init()
  {
     button1 = new Button("Clear");
     textField1 = new TextField();
     // various initialization statements to create
     // the rest of the interface
     button1.addActionListener(
        new ActionListener()
        { // start inner class definition
           public void actionPerformed( ActionEvent evt )
           { textField1.setText("");
           }
        }
     ); // end of addActionListener statement
  } // end of init method
  // code left out to save space
} // end of enclosing class definition
```

With anonymous inner classes, the compiler names the compiled class file sequentially. Therefore, in the example in Listing 5.3, it would create **Applet2$1.class**. In this example, the anonymous inner class had only one method because that is all that is required for the **ActionListener** interface. There is no limit on the number of methods and variables it could declare, but such code gets harder and harder to read as the number of variables and methods expands.

The observant student would have noticed the curious thing about the inner class declaration. It used the name of an interface, **ActionListener**, where a named class would have a class name and "implements ActionListener." In this case, the anonymous class extends **Object** by default and the compiler supplies the necessary code.

An anonymous inner class can also be declared as extending a class, but the syntax does not use the word "extends". In the following sample code fragment, which provides for handling **FocusEvents** in the **panel1** object, the parent class is **FocusAdapter**:

```
panel1.addFocusListener(
  new FocusAdapter()
  { public void focusGained( FocusEvent evt ) // override parent
    { // do something here
    }
  } // end anonymous inner class definition
) ; // end addFocusListener statement
```

Accessing Nested Classes from Outside

Now that you have seen examples of the various types of nested classes, let's look at how a nested class can be accessed from outside the enclosing class.

A Static Nested Class Example

Listing 5.4 shows an example of how to create an instance of the static nested class **BubTimer**, defined in Listing 5.1, in an Applet **start** method (shaded in the code listing). Notice how the statement that creates the **BT** object addresses **BubTimer** as a member of the **Bubble** class. This code also illustrates the use of a named inner class, which extends the **MouseAdapter** class to capture mouse-click events.

Listing 5.4   An applet using the **BubTimer** class.

```
import java.awt.*;
import java.applet.*;
```

```
public class BubApplet extends Applet
{
  Bubble.BubTimer BT ;
  public void init()
  {
    setLayout(null);
    setSize(426,266);
    Bubble.size = getSize();
    SymMouse aSymMouse = new SymMouse();
    this.addMouseListener(aSymMouse);
  }
  public void start(){
    BT = new Bubble.BubTimer((Panel)this );
    BT.addBub( 0,0 );
    BT.start();
  }
  public void paint(Graphics g){
    BT.paintAll( g );
  }
  class SymMouse extends java.awt.event.MouseAdapter
  {  public void mouseClicked(java.awt.event.MouseEvent evt)
    {  BT.addBub(evt.getX(), evt.getY());
    }
  } // end inner class
}
```

Using a Member Inner Class Object

The important thing to remember about inner classes is that an inner class object must always be associated with an instance of the enclosing class. Let's consider the following outline of a class:

```
public class NormClass {
  public class NestedClass {
      // methods and variables of NestedClass
  }
  // methods and variables of NormClass
}
```

It is possible for another class to create references to objects of these classes, as follows:

```
NormClass nc = new NormClass() ;
NormClass.NestedClass nnc = nc.new NestedClass();
```

You can also create an instance of the inner class without specifically keeping a reference to an instance of the enclosing class. Of course, there has to be an enclosing class instance, but you don't have to keep a reference to it, as shown in the following code:

```
NormClass.NestedClass nnc = new NormClass().new NestedClass();
```

The new instance of **NormClass** will not be garbage collected because the **NestedClass** object, **nnc**, keeps a reference to it. If the instance of **NestedClass** has to refer to the associated instance of **NormClass**, the following syntax is used:

```
NormClass myPartner = NormClass.this ;
```

As another example, if both **NormClass** and **NestedClass** had a **String** variable "name", the **NestedClass** object could refer to them as follows:

```
System.out.println("My name is " + name ) ; // nested class name
System.out.println("My partner is " + NormClass.this.name ) ;
```

 You should know the correct ways to define various types of nested classes. Also, be aware of which variables and methods of the enclosing class each type of nested class has access to.

Practice Questions

Question 1

You need to write code in an applet that will call the **submitData** method when **button1** is clicked. To do this, connect **button1** with an object that implements the **ActionListener** interface. Which of the following anonymous class declarations is the correct way to do this?

○ a.

```
button1.addActionListener(
      new ActionListener()
      { public void
          actionPerformed( ActionEvent evt )
        {  submitData() ;
        }
      }
    );
```

○ b.

```
button1.addActionListener(
      new Object implements ActionListener()
      { public void
          actionPerformed( ActionEvent evt )
        {  submitData() ;
        }
      }
    );
```

○ c.

```
button1.addActionListener(
      new ActionListener()
      { submitData() ;
      }
    );
```

Answer a is correct. This block of code will call the **submitData** method when **button1** is clicked. Answer b is incorrect because the "Object implements" terminology is wrong. An anonymous inner class implementing an interface does extend **Object**, but the compiler provides the default. Answer c is incorrect because it does not have a method declaration for **actionPerformed**, the method required by the **ActionListener** interface.

Question 2

Why would a responsible Java programmer want to use a nested class? [Check all correct answers]

❏ a. To impress the boss with his/her knowledge of Java by using nested classes all over the place

❏ b. To keep the code for a very specialized class in close association with the class it works with

❏ c. To support a new user interface that generates custom events

Answers b and c are correct; they are both good reasons to use a nested class. Although answer a has a certain attraction, the question specified a *responsible* programmer. Inappropriate use of nested classes can result in code that is hard to read and maintain. Therefore, answer a is incorrect.

Question 3

When you are programming a local inner class inside a method code block, which of the following statements is true?

○ a. The inner class will have access only to static variables in the enclosing class.

○ b. The inner class can use any variables declared in the method.

○ c. The inner class can use only local variables that are declared **final**.

○ d. The inner class can use only local variables that are declared **static**.

Answer c is correct. Only local variables declared **final** can be used by the inner class. The inner class can have access to any static or instance variables. Therefore, answer a is incorrect. Inner classes cannot use any non-final variables declared in the method, even if they are declared **static**. Therefore, answers b and d are incorrect.

Question 4

The following is an outline of code for a top-level class (assume that both classes have correct constructors that take no parameters):

```
class NormalClass {
   static class NestedClass {
     // methods and variables of NestedClass
     }
   // methods and variables of NormalClass
}
```

Which of the following code fragments shows the correct way to declare and initialize a reference to a **NestedClass** object from outside **NormalClass**?

◯ a.

```
NormalClass.NestedClass myNC = new
   NormalClass.NestedClass();
```

◯ b.

```
NestedClass myNC = new NormalClass().new
   NestedClass();
```

◯ c.

```
NestedClass myNC =
          new NormalClass.NestedClass();
```

Answer a shows both a correct reference variable declaration and a correct constructor. Answers b and c have an incorrect declaration of the reference variable because the name of a nested class starts with the enclosing class name.

Question 5

You have been given a programming problem with respect to a Java application. An existing class called **AB** now needs some additional functionality.
It has been proposed that this additional functionality be provided using a
nested or inner class, **ABC**. You have been able to establish the following
requirements:

1. There will probably be more than one **AB** instance active in the
   application, so the solution has to work no matter how many **AB**
   instances there are.

2. **ABC** will need to have access to instance methods and variables
   as well as static variables.

3. More than one method in **AB** must have access to a method of
   ABC.

Which configuration of a nested class is the best bet for this problem?

○ a. A static class

○ b. A member inner class

○ c. An inner class defined in an **AB** method

○ d. An anonymous inner class

Answer b is the best approach because a member inner class can easily take care
of all three requirements. Answer a is incorrect because of the requirement to
access instance variables. Answers c and d are incorrect because of the requirement that more than one method in AB will need to use ABC.

Question 6

The following is an outline of code for a top-level class (assume that both classes have correct constructors that take no parameters):

```
class BaseClass {
    public class NestedClass {
      // methods and variables of NestedClass
      }
    // methods and variables of BaseClass
}
```

Which of the following code fragments shows the correct way to declare and initialize a reference to a **NestedClass** object from outside **BaseClass**?

○ a.

```
BaseClass.NestedClass myNC = new
   BaseClass.NestedClass();
```

○ b.

```
NestedClass myNC = new BaseClass().new
   NestedClass();
```

○ c.

```
NestedClass myNC = new BaseClass.NestedClass();
```

○ d.

```
BaseClass.NestedClass nbc = new
   BaseClass().new NestedClass();
```

Answer d shows both a correct reference variable declaration and a correct constructor. This statement creates a **BaseClass** object, which the **NestedClass** must have. Answer a is incorrect because it does not create a **BaseClass** object for the **NestedClass** to be associated with. Answers b and c have an incorrect declaration of the reference variable because the name of a nested class starts with the enclosing class name. Therefore, answers b and c are incorrect. Compare this question with question 4, where the nested class is a static member. It is essential that you master the distinction.

Question 7

In the following code for a class in which **methodA** has an inner class, which variables would the statement in line 8 be able to use in place of **XX**? [Check all correct answers]

```
1. public class Base {
2.    private static final int ID = 3 ;
3.    private String name;
4.    public void methodA( final int nn ){
5.      int serialN = 11 ;
6.      class inner {
7.        void showResult(){
8.          System.out.println("Rslt= " + XX);
9.        }
10.     } // end class inner
11.     new inner().showResult();
12.   } // end methodA
13. }
```

❑ a. The **int ID** in line 2

❑ b. The **String** in line 3

❑ c. The **int nn** in line 4

❑ d. The **int serialN** in line 5

Answers a, b, and c are correct. Answers a and b are correct because inner classes can access any static or member variable in the enclosing class. Answer c is correct because, although the **int nn** in line 4 is a local variable, it is declared **final**. Answer d is incorrect because the variable is not declared **final**.

Question 8

> Which of the following statements is true?
>
> ○ a. An inner class can have the same name as its enclosing class.
>
> ○ b. An instance of a nonstatic inner class always has an associated instance of the enclosing class.
>
> ○ c. An anonymous inner class is always assumed to directly extend **Object**.

Only answer b is correct. It is true that an instance of a nonstatic inner class always has an associated instance of the enclosing class. Answer a is incorrect because inner classes are prohibited from having the same name as the enclosing class. Answer c is incorrect because an anonymous inner class can extend any class; however, the declaration syntax does not use the word "extends".

Need to Know More?

 Flanagan, David. *Java in a Nutshell, Third Edition*. O'Reilly & Associates, Inc., Sebastopol, CA, 1999. ISBN 1-56592-487-8. This is the most compact desktop reference book documenting the Java language. Chapter 3, "Object-Oriented Programming in Java," is pertinent to this chapter.

 http://java.sun.com/docs/books/tutorial/information/download.html is where you can download an excellent tutorial in HTML form. The "Implementing Java Classes" subsection of the trail titled "Learning The Java Language" is pertinent to this chapter.

 http://java.sun.com/docs/books/jls/second_edition/html/j.title. doc.html is where the definitive Java language specification document is maintained in HTML form. Parts of the document are also available in PDF form. This document has also been published as ISBN 0-201-31008-2, but most programmers will find the online documentation to be sufficient.

 http://java.sun.com/j2se/1.3/docs.html is the Java application programming interface (API) documentation in Javadoc-generated form; you can download it from Sun Microsystems here. Although this site changes a lot, the last time I looked, it was a good starting point to locate the current documentation.

6

Converting and Casting Primitives and Objects

. . . .

Terms you'll need to understand:

✓ Narrowing conversion

✓ **instanceof**

✓ Object hierarchy

✓ Widening conversion

✓ Interface references

Techniques you'll need to master:

✓ Understanding how primitive data types are converted and cast

✓ Understanding how object references are converted and cast

✓ Understanding when an object reference cast is necessary

✓ Understanding which cast operations are legal

You have already encountered some of Java's rules for converting between various primitive types in the discussions of initializing variables (Chapter 2) and mathematical expressions (Chapter 3). In this chapter, I will cover these conversions and the use of cast operations with primitives more formally. Java reference variables can refer to classes, interfaces, or arrays. This chapter covers the rules that govern how they can be converted and cast.

Converting and Casting Primitives

Every Java expression—whether arithmetic, a literal, or a method call—has a type. When the result of an expression has to be assigned to a variable or used in another expression, a different type may be required. The Java compiler is allowed to perform some type conversions automatically but rejects others unless the programmer provides a specific cast. In this section, I'll discuss the rules the compiler uses.

Widening Conversions

Generally speaking, the Java compiler is allowed to perform primitive conversions that do not lose information about the magnitude of the value. It is also allowed to perform some conversions of integers to floating-point values that lose some precision due to the impossibility of representing all integers in floating-point formats.

Signed Integer Conversion

Signed integer conversions proceed by simply extending the sign bit, so a byte with a value of minus 1 can become a **short, int,** or **long** with a value of -1. Of course, if the integer is positive, the zero sign bit is extended, so the value stays positive.

Integers of **int** (32-bit) size or smaller can be converted to floating-point representation, but because a **float** also uses only 32 bits and must include exponent information, there can be a loss of precision. Integer types smaller than 32 bits are first converted to a 32-bit **int** and then to a **float**. In a similar fashion, when integer values are converted to **double**, the integer is first converted to a **long** and then to a **double**.

Unsigned **char** Conversion

The **char** primitive type is the only integer that Java treats as unsigned. When a **char** type is converted to **int** or **long**, the value is always positive. Because the **short** primitive is a signed integer, you cannot simply convert a **char** to a **short** with code such as line 2 in the following:

```
1. char ch = '\u8243' ;
2. short s = ch ;  // compiler objects
3. short x = (short) ch ; // ok
```

A specific cast is required, as shown in line 3. In this case, the high bit of the **char** is set; therefore, the **short** value is negative.

Float to Double Conversion

As you might expect, the compiler is free to convert **float** primitives to **double** whenever it wants to. This conversion does not cause the loss of any precision. If the **float** has one of the special values, **NaN** (Not a Number), POSITIVE_INFINITY, or NEGATIVE_INFINITY, the **double** ends up with the corresponding **double** special values.

When Are Conversions Done?

In addition to performing conversions when assigning a value to a primitive variable and when evaluating arithmetic expressions, the Java compiler makes conversions as necessary to match the signature of methods. Consider the following code fragment, which makes use of the Java standard library **Math** class **static sin** method:

```
int x = 1 ;
double sinx = Math.sin( x );
```

The Java compiler looks up the signature of the method and finds that there is only one **sin** method in the **java.lang.Math** class:

```
public static native double sin( double d );
```

Because this requires a **double** as input, the compiler produces code that is the equivalent of the following (naturally, without any actual temporary variables):

```
int i = 1 ;
long tempL = i ;
double tempD = tempL ;
double sin = Math.sin( tempD );
```

Here's another example of the method signature controlling conversion of primitives:

```
1. int m = 93 ;
2. long n = 91 ;
3. long x = Math.max( m, n );
4. int y = Math.max( m, (int)n );
```

The **Math max** and **min** methods come in several different versions, one each for **int, long, float,** and **double.** Therefore, in the code that calls **Math.max** with one **int** and one **long** in line 3, the compiler converts the **int** primitive to a **long** value. The alternative in line 4 forces the compiler to cast the value of **n** to an **int** and calls the version of **max** that uses two **int** primitives.

Method Signatures and Return Values

Here are the signatures of some of the **Math** class methods:

```
public static int max( int a, int b );
public static long max( long a, long b );
public static float max( float a, float a );
public static double max( double a, double b );
```

The compiler chooses a method to use based on the input parameters, not on the **return** value. If you need to put the maximum of two **int** primitives in a **double** variable, the compiler uses the version of **max** that returns an **int** and converts the **return** value just before assigning it to the **double** variable.

Impossible Conversions

The following conversions with primitives are not allowed, although some of them might appear plausible to the C programmer:

➤ Any primitive type to any reference type

➤ The **null** value to any primitive type

➤ Any primitive to **boolean**

➤ A **boolean** to any primitive

Casting Primitives

When a Java expression calls for conversion of a primitive type to another type with a smaller range (*narrowing conversion*), the compiler insists on a specific cast. At runtime, casts that lose information do not cause a runtime exception. It is up to the programmer to think through all the implications of the cast.

Casts between Integer Types

Narrowing conversion of integer types simply lops off the excess bits. The sign of the converted primitive depends on the value in the sign bit position, and this result is independent of the original sign of the original value.

Note that a conversion of a **byte** to a **char** loses information despite the fact that a **char** uses 16 bits (whereas a **byte** uses 8) because **char** is unsigned and does not allow negative values. Therefore, the compiler requires a specific cast to convert **byte** to **char**.

Casts from Floating-Point to Integer Types

The first step in converting a **float** or **double** to an integer type is conversion to either a **long**, if the destination is **long**, or **int** for all other integer types. The final step is dropping any excess bits. You can get some surprising results from these conversions because all special floating-point values, such as **NaN** and **POSITIVE_INFINITY**, turn into integer values without any complaint from the compiler or an exception. For example, the following code prints "Value = 0":

```
double d = Math.sqrt( -1.0 ); // i.e. Double.NaN
int x = ( int) d ;
System.out.println("Value = " + x ) ;
```

Casts from **double** to **float**

Because a **double** can represent a much wider range of magnitudes than a **float**, the cast may produce some unexpected results. Java follows the Institute of Electrical and Electronics Engineers (IEEE) 754 standard for these conversions, as follows:

➤ A **double** value too small to be represented as a **float** becomes a positive or negative zero.

➤ A **double** value too large to be represented as a **float** becomes positive or negative infinity.

➤ A **double** with the special **NaN** value becomes the float **NaN** value.

Compiler Casts

In many cases, the compiler handles casts of literal values for you. For example, in the following, **int** literal values are accepted as initial values for **byte** variables:

```
byte crn = 13 ;
byte lf = 0x000A ;
```

Presumably, the compiler is smart enough to realize that the values can be cast to **byte** without loss of information.

Converting and Casting Reference Types

Java has three kinds of *reference* type variables: class type, interface type, and array type. A variable of type **Object** can hold a reference to any of these three types because **Object** is the root of the Java object hierarchy. This point is important because a Java method that is passed an **Object** reference may have a reference to just about anything.

 In contrast to converting and casting primitives, converting and casting a reference to a variable does not change the object being referred to. Once created, an object can be referred to in a variety of ways, but the object type is not changed. However, the reference type determines the way in which Java expressions can use the reference.

The **instanceof** Operator

Objects always "know" what type they are. The programmer can use the **instanceof** operator to check the type of any object reference. For example, the following method can detect a class type (**String**), interface type (**Runnable**), and an array type (**long[]**) reference:

```
public int checkRefType(Object ref ){
  if( ref instanceof String ) return 1 ;
  if( ref instanceof Runnable ) return 3 ;
  if( ref instanceof long[] ) return 4 ;
  return 0 ;
}
```

instanceof with Two Objects

Suppose you have two objects, **objA** and **objB**, and you want to see if they are of the same class. You cannot use

```
if( objA instanceof objB )
```

because the **instanceof** operator expects a type as a right operand. The solution is to use the **Object** method **getClass()**, as shown in the following code:

```
if( objA.getClass() == objB.getClass() )
```

This statement determines whether the same **Class** object was used to create **objA** and **objB**.

The Special **null** Value

Note that any reference variable can be set to the special **null** value, but **null** is not an instance of anything. All **instanceof** tests with a **null** reference produce **false**.

. . . .

Conversion and Object Hierarchy

The conversions of object references that are allowed depend on the object hierarchy. Consider the following diagram showing the family tree of the **java.awt. FileDialog** class:

```
java.lang.Object
   |- java.awt.Component
         |- java.awt.Container
               |- java.awt.Panel
               |- java.awt.ScrollPane
               |- java.awt.Window
                     |- java.awt.Dialog
                           |- java.awt.FileDialog
```

A reference to a **FileDialog** object can be assigned to a variable of any type higher in the hierarchy without a specific cast, as shown in the following code fragment:

```
Dialog myDialog = new FileDialog( this, "Open" );
Component tc = myDialog ;
```

This is called a *widening conversion* of a reference. Because the compiler can assure itself that this is a legal conversion, there is no runtime checking of this conversion. Widening conversions can also be performed when calling a method. For instance, the **add** method of the **Container** class has this signature:

```
public Component add( Component cmp );
```

This means that a call to this method can use a reference to a **Panel**, a **Window**, or a wide variety of other objects that inherit from **Component** without a specific cast or runtime check.

instanceof and the Object Hierarchy

The **instanceof** operator returns **true** for any type in the operand's parentage. For instance, consider the hierarchy shown in the diagram of the family tree of the **FileDialog** class shown in the previous section; if **testObj** were created as a **Panel**, the following expressions would return **true**:

```
testObj instanceof java.awt.Panel
testObj instanceof java.awt.Container
testObj instanceof java.awt.Component
testObj instanceof java.lang.Object
```

The freedom that the programmer has to convert any reference to an **Object** reference is the reason for the design of the Java utility classes for manipulating collections of objects. For example, the **Vector** and **Stack** classes can accept and return any reference as an **Object** reference. If you were writing a calculator program working in reverse Polish notation, you might keep a stack of operands with the following code, where **opStack** is a **java.util.Stack** object:

```
1. public void pushD( double d ){
2.    opStack.push( new Double( d ) );
3. }
4. public double popD(){
5.    Double dt = (Double) opStack.pop();
6.    return dt.doubleValue();
7. }
```

In line 2, a **Double** object with the **double** value **d** is created because **Stack** works with objects, not primitives. Note how line 5 has a specific cast of the reference returned by the **pop** method to type **Double** because **pop** returns an **Object** reference. If line 5 had been written

```
Double dt = opStack.pop() ;
```

a compiler error would have resulted. A specific cast is required for this narrowing conversion of a reference. As far as the compiler is concerned, the reference returned by **pop** is to an **Object** until proven otherwise. The compiler inserts a check of the type of the reference returned by **pop**. If this type is not compatible with a cast to **Double**, a **ClassCastException** is thrown.

 The specific cast is necessary only when you are converting from a superclass to a subclass reference type. Conversions from a subclass to superclass are allowed anywhere.

Conversion with Interface References

Essentially, interface reference types can be converted only to interface types or **Object** references. For example, if your class **MyPanel** derived from **Panel** implements **Runnable**, you could use the following statements:

```
MyPanel  p = new MyPanel() ;
Panel tmp = p ;  // conversion up class hierarchy
Runnable runp = p ; // conversion to an interface reference
Object obj = p ; // conversion to the root of the hierarchy
MyPanel p2 = (MyPanel) obj ; // conversion with a cast
Runnable runp2 = (Runnable) obj ;
```

Interface Complications

Interfaces can have subinterfaces, just as classes have subclasses. However, you should be aware of one difference: An interface can be defined as extending more than one interface. This follows from the fact that a class can *implement* more than one interface. One example of an interface inheriting from more than one interface is as follows:

```
public interface RunObs extends Runnable, Observer
```

Any class implementing this interface must provide methods required by both **Runnable** and **Observer**, and, of course, you could cast a reference to an object implementing **RunObs** to either a **Runnable** or **Observer** interface reference. The following expressions using **instanceof** would return **true** if **rx** were a reference to an instance of a class implementing **RunObs**:

```
1. rx instanceof RunObs
2. rx instanceof Runnable
3. rx instanceof Observer
```

The Special Case of Arrays

Arrays are a special kind of reference type that do not fit in the class hierarchy but can always be cast to an **Object** reference. Arrays also implement the **java.io. Serializable** and the **java.lang.Cloneable** interfaces and inherit the **Clone** method from **Object**. This means that an array reference can be cast to a **Cloneable** interface or **Serializable** interface reference.

Cloning an array creates a new array with the same size and contents as the original. Here is an example of array cloning code (note that the **clone** method is declared as returning **Object**, so a cast to the specific array type is required):

```
int[] nnn = new int[1000] ;
int[] xxx = (int[]) nnn.clone();
```

Two kinds of arrays exist: arrays of primitives and arrays of references.

Primitive Arrays

Primitive arrays have no hierarchy, and you can cast a primitive array reference only to and from an **Object** or **Cloneable** reference. Converting and casting primitive array elements follow the same rules as converting and casting simple primitive variables. Although the syntax for casting to an array type, as shown in line 3 in the following code, may look a little strange, it is perfectly legal:

```
1. int sizes[] = { 4,6,8,10,14,20 };
2. Object obj = sizes ;
3. int x = (( int[] ) obj )[2] ;
```

As with other runtime casts, if the **obj** reference in line 3 is not to an **int** array, a **ClassCastException** is thrown.

It is a common mistake to think that because an **int** can be cast to a **long**, you should be able to cast an **int** array to a **long** array. Remember that an array object controls access to memory storage set up for a particular variable type and can deal with only that type.

Arrays of Reference Types

Casting of arrays of reference types follows the same rules as casting single references. Note that an array reference can be converted independently of whether or not the array has been populated with references to real objects. For example, suppose you have a class named **Extend** that extends a class named **Base**. You could then use the following code to manipulate a reference to an array of **Extend** references:

```
Extend[] exArray = new Extend[ 20 ];
Object[] obj = exArray ;
Base[] bArray = exArray ;
Extend[] temp = ( Extend[] ) bArray ;
```

Summary of Reference Conversion Rules

The rules for reference conversions (conversions that the compiler will not throw out) that can be coded legally in Java are summarized in the following list; to pass the runtime check, the actual reference will have to be of the proper type:

➤ An **Object** reference can be converted to:

  ➤ An **Object** reference

  ➤ Any class reference with a runtime check

  ➤ Any array reference with a runtime check

  ➤ Any interface reference with a runtime check

➤ A class reference can be converted to:

  ➤ Any superclass type, including **Object**

  ➤ Any class reference with a runtime check

  ➤ An interface reference if the class implements the interface

  ➤ Any interface reference with a runtime check

➤ An interface reference can be converted to:

   ➤ An **Object** reference

   ➤ An interface that it implements

   ➤ Any interface reference with a runtime check

➤ A primitive array reference can be converted to:

   ➤ An **Object** reference

   ➤ A **Cloneable** reference

   ➤ A primitive array reference of the same type

➤ A reference array can be converted to:

   ➤ An **Object** reference

   ➤ An **Object** array reference

   ➤ A **Cloneable** reference

   ➤ Any superclass array reference

   ➤ Any class array with a runtime check

Practice Questions

Question 1

What will happen when you try to compile the following code?

```
1. public void printArray( Object x ){
2.    if( x instanceof int[] ){
3.       int[] n = (int[]) x ;
4.       for( int i = 0 ; i < n.length ; i++ ){
5.          System.out.println("integers = " +
                 n[i] );}
6.    }
7.    if( x instanceof String[] ){
8.       System.out.println("Array of Strings");
9.    }
10. }
```

○ a. It compiles without error.

○ b. The compiler objects to line 2 comparing an **Object** with an array.

○ c. The compiler objects to line 3 casting an **Object** to an array of **int** primitives.

○ d. The compiler objects to line 7 comparing an **Object** to an array of **Objects**.

Answer a is correct. This is perfectly good code. Answers b, c, and d are incorrect because array references are treated like other **Objects** by the **instanceof** operator.

Question 2

Here are three proposed alternatives to be used in a method to return **false** if the object reference **x** has the **null** value. Which statement will work?

○ a.   **if(x == null) return false ;**

○ b.   **if(x.equals(null)) return false ;**

○ c.   **if(x instanceof null) return false ;**

Answer a is the only correct way to check a reference for the **null** value. Answer b is incorrect because if **x** is **null**, there will not be an object whose **equals** method can be called. This statement would cause a **NullPointerException** at runtime when **x** is **null**. Answer c is incorrect because only a reference type, such as a class, interface, or array, can be the right operand of the **instanceof** operator.

Question 3

Here is the class hierarchy showing the **java.awt.event.ActionEvent** class family tree:

```
java.lang.Object
  |- java.util.EventObject
        |- java.awt.AWTEvent
              |- java.awt.event.ActionEvent
```

Suppose you have the following code to count events and save the most recent event:

```
1. int evtCt = 0 ;
2. AWTEvent lastE ;
3. public void saveEvent( AWTEvent evt ){
4.   lastE = evt ;
5.   evtCt++ ;
6. }
```

Which of the following calls of **saveEvent** would run without causing an exception? [Check all correct answers]

❑ a. An **AWTEvent** object reference

❑ b. An **ActionEvent** object reference

❑ c. An **EventObject** object reference

❑ d. A **null** value

Answers a, b, and d are correct. Answer a is correct because it matches the method signature. Answer b is correct because a subclass reference can always be cast up the hierarchy. Answer d is correct because any reference can be set to **null**. Answer c is incorrect because the reference cannot be cast to a subclass down the hierarchy.

Question 4

Suppose you have two classes defined as follows:

```
class ApBase extends Object implements
    Runnable
class ApDerived extends ApBase implements
    Observer
```

Also suppose you have two variables created as follows:

```
ApBase aBase = new ApBase() ;
ApDerived aDer = new ApDerived();
```

Which of the following Java statements will compile and execute without error? [Check all correct answers]

❑ a. **Runnable rn = aDer ;**

❑ b. **Runnable rn2 = (Runnable) aBase ;**

❑ c. **Observer ob = aBase ;**

❑ d. **Observer ob2 = (Observer) aBase ;**

Answers a and b are correct. Answer a is correct because the **ApDerived** class inherits from **ApBase,** which implements **Runnable.** Answer b is correct because the inserted cast (**Runnable**) is not needed but it does not cause a problem. Answer c fails to compile because the compiler can tell that the **ApBase** class does not implement **Observer.** Therefore, answer c is incorrect. Answer d is incorrect because it compiles but fails to execute. Because of the specific cast, the compiler thinks you know what you are doing, but the type of the **aBase** reference is checked when the statement executes and a **ClassCastException** is thrown.

Question 5

Suppose you have an **ApBase** class declared as:

```
class ApBase extends Object
                 implements Runnable
```

The following code fragment takes a reference to an **ApBase** object and assigns it to a variety of variables:

```
1. ApBase aBase = new ApBase();
2. Runnable aR = aBase ;
3. Object obj = aR ;
4. ApBase x = (ApBase)obj ;
```

What will happen when you try to compile and run this code?

○ a. The compiler objects to line 2.

○ b. The compiler objects to line 3.

○ c. The code compiles but when run throws a **ClassCastException** in line 4.

○ d. The code compiles and runs without a problem.

Answer d is correct. These casts and assignments are all legal. Answer a is incorrect because an object reference can be assigned to an interface reference as long as the compiler knows that the object implements the interface. Answer b is incorrect because an interface reference can be assigned to a reference to **Object** because **Object** is the base of the Java class hierarchy. Answer c is incorrect because the object referred to has not lost its identity, so it passes the runtime cast check.

Question 6

> You have a method, **scale,** defined as follows, where **scalex** and **scaley** are
> **int** constants:
>
> ```
> 1. public Point scale( long x, long y ){
> 2.    return new Point((int)(x / scalex),(int)
>          (y / scaley));
> 3. }
> ```
>
> Keeping in mind that the signature of the **scale** method specifies **long** integer inputs, what will happen when you call this method with **int** primitives as in the following fragment?
>
> ```
> 4. int px = 100 ;
> 5. int py = 2000 ;
> 6. Point thePoint = scale( px, py );
> ```
>
> ○ a. A compiler error is caused.
>
> ○ b. The program compiles but a runtime cast exception is thrown.
>
> ○ c. The program compiles and runs.

Answer c is correct because promotion of the **int** primitives to **long** values is handled automatically by the compiler. Answer a is incorrect because of this promotion. Answer b is incorrect both because the promotion is legal and because cast exceptions are thrown only by reference variable casts.

Question 7

> Which of the following casts of primitive values will *not* lose information?
> Keep in mind that **long**s are 8 bytes, **int**s are 4 bytes, and **short**s and **char**
> are 2 bytes. [Check all correct answers]
>
> ❏ a.
> ```
> long lx = 0x05544332211L ;
>           // that is 366216421905 decimal
> int ix = (int) lx ;
> ```
> ❏ b.
> ```
> short sx = (short) 0x7654 ; // 30292 decimal
> char cx = (char) sx ;
> ```
> ❏ c.
> ```
> long lx = 0xOFFFFL ; // 65535 decimal
> short sx = (short) lx ;
> ```
> ❏ d.
> ```
> int ix = (int) 37 ;
> byte bx = (byte) ix ;
> ```

Answers b and d are correct. They do not lose information. In answer a, the bits
representing the hex digits 55 are lost. Therefore, answer a is incorrect. In answer
c, the high order bit in **sx** is set; because a **short** is a signed integer, this represents
-1. Therefore, answer c is incorrect.

Question 8

Suppose you have two classes defined as follows:

```
class ApBase extends Object
                    implements Runnable
class ApDerived extends ApBase
                    implements Observer
```

Also suppose two variables have been created as follows:

```
ApBase aBase = new ApBase() ;
ApDerived aDer = new ApDerived();
```

Which of the following Java code fragments compiles and executes without error?

○ a.
```
Object obj = aBase ;
Runnable rn = obj ;
```

○ b.
```
Object obj = aBase ;
Runnable rn = (Runnable) obj ;
```

○ c.
```
Object obj = aBase ;
Observer ob = (Observer)aBase ;
```

○ d.
```
Object obj = aDer ;
Observer ob2 = obj ;
```

Answer b is correct; it compiles and runs. The compiler assumes you know what you are doing with the cast to **Runnable**. Answer a is incorrect because it fails to compile. As far as the compiler is concerned, **obj** is a plain **Object**, so it objects to the assignment to a **Runnable** reference. Answer c is incorrect because it compiles but fails to run. Because of the specific cast, the compiler thinks you know what you are doing, but the type of the **aBase** reference is checked when the statement executes, and a **ClassCastException** is thrown. Answer d is incorrect because it fails to compile. As far as the compiler is concerned, **obj** is a plain **Object**, so it objects to the assignment to an **Observer** reference.

Question 9

What will be the result of trying to compile the following class?

```
1.  import java.io.* ;
2.  public class Test extends Object{

3.    public static void main(String args[] ){
4.      String[] names = new String[10] ;
5.      if( names instanceof Object[] )
            System.out.println("Obj[] true");
6.      if( names instanceof Object )
            System.out.println("Obj true ");
7.      double d = Math.sqrt( -1.0 );
                    // creates Double.NaN
8.      int x = (int) d ;
9.      System.out.println("d= " + d +
            " cast to int Value = " + x ) ;
10.     long lx = Long.MAX_VALUE ;
11.     float f = lx ;
12.     int[] nnn = new int[1000] ;
13.     Object obj = nnn ;
14.     Cloneable clobj = nnn ;
15.     Serializable sb = nnn ;
16.     int[] xxx = (int[])nnn.clone();
17. }
18. }
```

○ a. A compiler error is caused by the conversion from **long** to **float** in line 11.

○ b. A compiler error is caused by the conversion from **int[]** to **Object** in line 13.

○ c. A compiler error is caused by the conversion from **int[]** to **Serializable** in line 15.

○ d. The program compiles without error.

Answer d is correct. All of the casts and conversions in this code are allowed by the compiler. Because the program compiles without error, answers a, b, and c are incorrect.

Need to Know More?

 Joy, Bill, et al. *The Java Language Specification, Second Edition*. Addison-Wesley, Reading, MA, 2000. ISBN 0-201-31008-2. This is the most authoritative source on the Java language. Chapter 5 covers casting and converting.

 Venners, Bill. *Inside the Java Virtual Machine, 2nd edition*. McGraw-Hill, New York, NY, December, 1999. ISBN 0-07-135093-4. If you want the bit-twiddling details of how the Java Virtual Machine (JVM) interprets Java bytecodes, this is a good source. Chapter 11 covers the bytecodes that convert numeric primitives.

 http://java.sun.com/docs/books/jls/second_edition/html/j.title. doc.html is where the definitive Java language specification document is maintained in HTML form. Parts of the document are also available in PDF form. This document has also been published as ISBN 0-201-31008-2, but most programmers will find the online documentation to be sufficient.

Flow Control and Exceptions

. . . .

Terms you'll need to understand:

✓ break

✓ continue

✓ try

✓ catch

✓ finally

✓ throws

✓ throw

Techniques you'll need to master:

✓ Recognizing the legal forms for **if** and **switch** statements

✓ Predicting the flow of control through complex nested control structures

✓ Using **break** and **continue** with statement labels in loops

✓ Understanding when to use **throws** in method declarations

✓ Writing code that creates and throws exceptions

Many of the aspects of Java flow control are familiar to programmers who have worked with other languages, particularly C. The **if, else, switch, do,** and **while** statements behave the same way in Java as they do in C. The **for** loop in Java is also similar to that in C. As far as the concept of exceptions, which vastly simplify the task of designing programs that gracefully handle errors and exceptional conditions, Java has a highly developed improvement over C for controlling program flow when errors or other exceptional conditions occur.

Basic Flow Control

You should already be familiar with the basics of Java flow control, so the following sections concentrate on areas that have caused people trouble in my online testing of proposed questions for this book.

Boolean Expressions

The first point to stress is that Java requires expressions that evaluate to a **boolean** primitive result in flow control statements. C programmers who are used to using integer values of zero for **false** and nonzero for **true** will have to watch out for this.

Another important point has to do with the sequence of evaluation in complex logical expressions. Although you can control the sequence with parentheses, you should also study the precedence of the various arithmetic and logical operators (as shown in Chapter 3, Tables 3.2 and 3.4). For example, given the following statement

```
if( a + b > aMax | c + d < cMin )
```

you should recognize that operator precedence causes the compiler to evaluate the additions first, followed by the arithmetic comparisons. Finally, the two **boolean** primitive results are ORed together.

 Watch out for **boolean** expressions that use the **&&** and **||** "short circuiting" or "conditional" logical operators. These were discussed in the "Operators with Logical Expressions" section in Chapter 3.

No goto in Java Flow Control

Note that although **goto** is a reserved word in Java, it is not currently used. Java does not allow arbitrary jumps to labeled statements. However, statement labels can be used with the **break** and **continue** statements in loops, discussed later in this chapter.

The **if-else** Structure

The **if** statement simply evaluates an arbitrary expression that results in a **boolean** primitive value. If the value is **true**, the code block attached to the **if** is executed. This code block can be a single statement, which for simplicity does not have to be enclosed in braces, or it can be an arbitrarily long block of code in braces. The programmer has the option of putting an **else** statement immediately following the **if** code block to provide an alternate block of code that will be executed if the value is **false**.

Whether or not to enclose a single statement in braces is a matter of style. A good reason to always use braces is that debuggers will not let you set breakpoints on a single statement following **if** or **else** unless it is in its own code block. If you have any doubts about which **if** an **else** statement goes with, the rule is that it is considered to go with the innermost **if** to which it could legally belong.

 Programming problems frequently involve a complex nested set of **if-else** constructs. The first step in solving one of these is figuring out which code blocks go with which **if** and **else** statements. The questions at the end of the chapter include some examples of nested **if** statements.

The **switch-case** Structure

Java provides the extremely handy **switch-case** construct to facilitate selecting between multiple alternatives. This is such a common programming situation that the Java Virtual Machine (JVM) has bytecodes designed to speed this operation. Within the block of code controlled by a **switch** statement, the programmer can place **case** statements and (optionally) a **default** statement. In the following example, a **String** variable gets set according to the value of the integer variable x:

```
switch( x ) {
  case 0 : str = "none" ; break ;
  case 1 :
    str = "single" ; break ;
  case 2 :
    str = "pair" ;
    break ;
  default :  str = "many" ;
}
```

Each **case** keyword is followed by an integer constant, followed by a colon. Notice that the code block belonging to each **case** can immediately follow the colon on the same line or on separate lines. If the value of x is not one of the values provided for in **case** statements, the **default** statement code is executed. If there is no **default** statement and no exact match, execution resumes after the **switch** block of code.

The Fall-Through Trap

The preceding example uses **break** statements, which terminate the code for each **case** and cause execution to continue after the **switch** code block. If a break does not appear, execution "falls through" to execute code in subsequent **cases**. For example, in the following code fragment, a value of 0 would cause output of "A, B, ":

```
switch( x ){
    case 0 : System.out.print("A, ");
    case 1 : System.out.print("B, "); break ;
    default : System.out.println("huh?");
}
```

 Most errors that occur when you work with **switch** structures seem to be related to forgetting about fall-through. Make it a habit to check for the **break** statements on any question that involves **switch**.

The block of code associated with each **case** can be as simple as a single statement or it can be hundreds of lines of code. In addition, this code block can have another **switch** statement. However, for optimum readability, you should consider turning any complex code into a separate method and simply calling that method from the **case** statement.

What a switch Must Have

The expression in a **switch** statement must evaluate to one of the 32-bit or smaller integer types: **byte, char, short,** or **int.** The compiler checks that the legal range of the integer type covers all of the constants used in **case** statements in the **switch** code block.

 Apparently, this fact regarding **switch** statements is not well known among Java programmers, so it's probably worth repeating. The compiler throws an error if the legal range of the integer type in the **switch** statement does not cover all of the constants used in **case** statements.

What a case Statement Cannot Have

Each **case** statement must have a literal constant or a value the compiler can evaluate as a constant of a 32-bit or smaller integer type. It cannot have a **float** constant, a **long** constant, a variable, an expression, a **String,** or any other object. Furthermore, the compiler checks that the constant is in the range of the integer type in the **switch** statement. In other words, if you are using a **byte** variable in the **switch** statement, the compiler objects if it finds **case** statement constants outside the -128 through 127 range that a **byte** primitive can have.

The code block associated with a **case** must be complete within the **case**. In other words, you can't have an **if-else** or loop structure that spreads across multiple **case** statements.

What a case Statement Can Have

Constants in **case** statements can be integer literals, or they can be variables defined as **static** and **final**. For example, the **java.awt.event.KeyEvent** class defines a bunch of "public static final int" variables, such as **VK_F1**, **VK_F2**, and so on. The compiler can use these values in **case** statements because it can look up the integer value at compile time.

Using **break** and **continue** with **switch**

In addition to the plain **break** statement, which simply causes execution to continue after the **switch** code block, you can use a **break** with a statement label. This is typically done to terminate a loop that encloses the switch code block, as in the following code fragment:

```
1. int state = 0 ;
2. lab: for( int x = 0 ; x <100 ; x++ ){
3.        switch( state ){
4.          case 0 :
5.            state = tryX( x ); break ;
6.          case 1 :
7.            state = tryAgain(x); break ;
8.          case 2 :
9.            System.out.println("Found key");
10.           break lab ;
11.        }
12.        System.out.println("tried " + x );
13.    }
```

Think of the label in line 2 as labeling the entire **for** loop. When the **break** in line 10 is executed, execution breaks out of that loop and continues after line 13.

If the statement in line 10 read

```
10.           continue lab ;
```

execution would skip line 12 and resume the loop with the next value of *x*.

Label Rules

Identifiers used for labels on statements do not share the same namespace as the variables, classes, and methods of the rest of a Java program. The naming rules, as far as legal characters, are the same as for variables except that labels are always terminated with a colon. You can reuse the same label name at multiple points in a method as long as one usage is not nested inside another. Labels cannot be freestanding—they must always be associated with a statement.

The **for** Loop Structure

Java provides the **for** loop to let you repeat blocks of code under control of a loop counter variable. The general form of the **for** loop is a **for** statement followed by a loop body. The **for** statement consists of three sections, as shown in the following code:

```
for( initialization ; logical test ; update )
```

When a **for** statement is executed, the first thing that happens is that the initialization expressions, if any, are executed. Next, the logical test expression, if present, is executed—if the result is **false**, the loop is exited immediately. If there is no logical test or the result is **true**, the loop body statement(s) is/are executed. Finally, the update expression(s), if present, is/are executed and the logical test is repeated.

Initialization

The initialization section can be empty, have a single expression, or have multiple expressions separated by commas. This section is typically used to set the initial value of a loop counter. For example:

```
1.  for( int i = 0 ; i < iMax ; i++ )
2.  for( i = 0, j = 100 ; ; j -= i )
```

If the expression both declares and initializes a variable as in line 1, it must be the only expression in the section. For example, the following statement will not compile:

```
for(int i = 0, int j = 0 ; i < x ; i++, j++ ){
```

You should be aware that a loop counter declared in the initialization section has a scope restricted to the loop. A common error is to attempt to use a loop counter declared inside the **for** statement outside the loop.

Logical Test

If a logical test is present, it must be a single expression that results in a boolean value. Expressions that don't result in a boolean value cause a compiler error. If no logical test is present, as in line 2 of the preceding example, the only ways a programmer can stop the loop are by using a **break** statement or by throwing an exception.

Update

The update section can be empty, have a single expression, or have multiple expressions separated by commas. Typically, this section is used to increment or decrement the loop counter.

Using **break** and **continue** in Loops

In addition to the logical test, you can control the operation of a loop with **break** and **continue** statements, with and without labels. The plain **break** statement immediately terminates the loop code block, whereas the **continue** statement skips any remaining code in the block and continues with the next loop iteration. The following code fragment illustrates both uses:

```
1. for( int i = 0 ; i < iMax ;i++ ){
2.    if( toDo[i] == null ) continue ;
3.    if( processToDo( toDo[i] ) ) break ;
4.    System.out.println( "Still looking");
5. }
```

The statement in line 2 uses **continue** to skip the code in lines 3 and 4. If the array element is **null**, the loop continues with the next iteration of the loop counter. In contrast, the **break** statement in line 3 terminates the loop entirely. The limitation of **break** and **continue**—which is that they can affect only the loop they reside in—is overcome with labeled statements. The following example shows the same code embellished with an inner loop (note that the outer loop now has a label, "labA", on the starting statement):

```
1. labA: for( int i = 0 ; i < iMax ;i++ ){
2.        for( int j = 0 ; j < jMax ; j++ ){
3.            if( toDo[i][j] == null ) continue labA ;
4.            if( processToDo( toDo[i][j] ) ) break labA ;
5.        } // end loop over j values
6.        System.out.println( "Still looking");
7.    }
```

Now, the **continue** statement in line 3 jumps out of the loop over the values of j and continues with the next value for i, as generated by the **for** statement in line 1. The **break** statement in line 4 terminates the outer loop, and execution resumes after line 7.

Optional Parts of a **for** Loop

Actually, just about everything in a **for** loop is optional. The following statement represents the bare minimum **for** loop, with "{}" representing an empty code block:

```
for(;;){}
```

Naturally, any **Thread** starting this loop would never be heard from again. Here are two more practical examples of **for** loops with missing parts:

```
1.  int x ;
2.  for( x = 0 ; testX( x ) ; x++ ){}
```

In the preceding example, all of the work is done in the **testX** method, which, of course, has to return a boolean value. The following example skips the initialization section because the variable *x* is already initialized:

```
1.  int x = 199 ;
2.  for( ; x >= 0 ; x- ) {
3.    // calculations go here
4.  }
```

Common Mistakes with for Loops

Here are some common mistakes that programmers make with **for** loops:

➤ *Variable scope*—Remember that a variable declared in a **for** statement can be referred to only inside the loop. Watch out for accidentally declaring a variable in a loop with the same name as an instance variable. The compiler will let you get away with this and will use the local variable inside the loop. The results can be very confusing.

➤ *Loop counter problems*—Watch out for paths through the loop that fail to increment or decrement the loop counter.

Using while and do

The other loop constructs in Java are provided by **while** and **do**. The general form of a **while** loop is as follows:

```
while( logical_test ){
   code block
}
```

The logical test is performed first. If the result is **true**, the code block is executed. If the result is **false**, the code block is skipped and execution continues after the closing brace. You can also combine a **while** test with an expression in a single statement, as follows:

```
while( i < ans.length() && ans.charAt( i ) != '*') i++ ;
```

If you want a loop that continues indefinitely, you can use a boolean literal value of **true** in the **while** statement.

The **do** loop construct moves the position of the logical test to the end of the code block; therefore, the code is always executed at least once, as shown in this code fragment:

```
do {
    code_block
}while( logical_test );
```

break and **continue** statements with and without labels work with **while** and **do** loops just as they do with **for** loops. The **break** statement exits the loop entirely, and **continue** skips to the end of the loop.

Exceptions

In the best of all possible worlds, nothing would ever go wrong in a Java program. In reality, your program may have to deal with many unexpected problems, such as missing files, bad user input, dropped network connections, and (unfortunately) programming errors. Java provides an elegant approach to handling these problems with the exception mechanism. This mechanism uses exception and error objects to handle everything from an end-of-file condition to an out-of-memory error.

The Hierarchy of **Throwable** Things

Java exceptions are objects that are instances of classes derived from the **java.lang. Throwable** class, as shown in the following diagram:

```
java.lang.Object
   ← java.lang.Throwable
           ← java.lang.Error
           |        ← a whole bunch of errors
           |
           ← java.lang.Exception
                    ← java.lang.RuntimeException
                    |        ← various unchecked exceptions
                    ← various checked exceptions
```

A **Throwable** exception or error is said to be "thrown" at the point where it is generated and "caught" at the point where execution continues. When an exception or error is thrown, the JVM works back through the chain of method calls that led to the error, looking for an appropriate handler to "catch" the object. If no handler is found, the **Thread** that created the error or exception dies.

The **Throwable** class provides methods that can trace the "stack" of method calls that a **Thread** has executed to get to the point at which the error occurred. This provides one of the main tools for debugging Java programs after an error or exception has occurred. **Throwable** objects can also have a **String** message attached to them. Typically, this is used to explain the cause of the exception or error. For example, the following code prints any message attached to the exception and then prints the stack trace:

```
} catch( Exception  e) {
  System.out.println("Message: " + e.getMessage() );
  e.printStackTrace( System.out ) ;
}
```

The **Error** Classes

As you can see, the first major division in the hierarchy is between errors and exceptions. Subclasses of **Error** are used to signal errors that are usually fatal and are not caught by **catch** statements in the program. Their function is to provide some information before the program has to terminate. As a programmer, you will usually be concerned with the **Exception** branch of the **Throwable** hierarchy only.

Catching Exceptions

Programmers can provide for the handling of exceptions using the Java keywords **try** and **catch**, with or without **finally**. I will first consider how exceptions are handled in a method that uses **try** and **catch** only.

How **try** and **catch** Work

A **try** statement is used to enclose a block of code in which an exception may occur. Each **try** statement can have one or more associated **catch** "clauses" that provide for handling exceptions. A **catch** clause declares a variable that must be of the class **Throwable** or a subclass of **Throwable**. This variable can be used in the code block associated with the **catch**. The general form is as follows:

```
1. try {
2.   code_block
3. }catch( ExceptionType varname ){
4.   optional code which can use varname
5. }
```

When an exception is thrown in the code block, the JVM looks at the type of the exception in the first **catch** clause. If the thrown exception can legally be assigned to that variable, it is assigned and the **catch** code block is executed. You can think of the **catch** clause as the *exception handler* for a particular exception type. The scope of the variable named in the **catch** clause is restricted to the **catch** code block.

Multiple **catch** Clauses

A succession of **catch** clauses can be attached to a **try** statement. If the thrown exception cannot be assigned to the variable in the first **catch** clause, the JVM looks at the second, and so on. If the thrown exception cannot be caught by any of the **catch** clauses provided, and there is no **finally** clause, the JVM looks for a handler in the calling method. If the code block in the **try** statement executes without throwing an exception, all of the **catch** clauses are ignored and execution resumes after the last **catch**.

The order of the **catch** clauses must reflect the exception hierarchy, with the most specific exception first. Obviously, if the first **catch** was the most general, none of the others could be reached. The compiler does not warn you if your **catch** statements are out of order.

How **try** and **catch** Work with **finally**

The principal idea behind **finally** is that programmers need to have a way to correctly dispose of system resources, such as open files, no matter which exceptions are thrown by the code in a **try** block. If a **try** statement has a **finally** clause attached, the code block associated with **finally** is *always* executed unless the **Thread** executing the **try** dies. To illustrate this, consider the following code:

```
public int testX( String x){
  try {
    return someMethod( x );
  }catch( NullPointerException nex ){
    System.out.print("NullPointer, " );
    return -1 ;
  }catch( RuntimeException rex){
    System.out.print("Runtime ");
    return -2;
  }finally{
    System.out.println("Finally");
  }
}
```

The **someMethod** method can throw a **NullPointerException**, which is a subclass of **RuntimeException**, or several other kinds of **RuntimeException**, such as **ArithmeticException**. Note that the **catch** for **NullPointerException** has to come before that for **RuntimeException** because **NullPointerException** is a subclass of **RuntimeException**.

Here are some examples of possible results from executing this code:

➤ No exception is thrown in **someMethod**. "Finally" is printed, and the method returns the value from **someMethod**.

➤ A **NullPointerException** is thrown in **someMethod**. "NullPointer, Finally" is printed, and –1 is returned.

➤ An **ArithmeticException** is thrown in **someMethod**. "Runtime Finally" is printed, and –2 is returned.

➤ An uncaught exception is thrown in **someMethod**. "Finally" is printed, and nothing is returned because the JVM now treats the exception as if it were thrown directly by the **testX** method.

 In my online testing of questions related to exceptions, many errors were made regarding the operation of **try** and **catch** with **finally** clauses. I suggest you experiment with test programs until you are confident that you can predict the program flow under various conditions.

How **try** and **finally** Work without **catch**

Just because most examples you see use **try**, **catch**, and **finally** together, you should not assume there will always be a **catch** with a **try** block. A **try** with **finally** is a perfectly reasonable way to ensure that a particular piece of code will always be executed no matter what happens inside the **try** block, as shown in the following code:

```
try {
  // lots of possible returns and exceptions here
} finally {
  // statements that must be executed here
}
```

Checked and Unchecked Exceptions

The most important division in the exception branch of the **Throwable** hierarchy is between checked and unchecked exceptions. All classes that descend from **RuntimeException** are called "unchecked" because the compiler does not require an explicit provision in the code for catching them.

All other classes that descend from **Exception** are called "checked" exceptions because the compiler insists on provisions in the code for catching them.

 Be prepared to distinguish between checked and unchecked exceptions in a variety of programming circumstances. It's easy to overlook this distinction on the test.

The design philosophy that the Java designers used to place various exceptions in the checked or unchecked categories was an attempt to balance the likelihood of an exception being generated, with a desire to avoid cluttering the code with **try** and **catch** statements. Some overhead is involved in setting up a **try** statement, so considerations of performance also entered into the design decisions.

Using throws

The alternative to using **try** and **catch** wherever a checked exception might occur in a method is simply to declare that the method throws the exception. For instance, if you have a method that opens a file, reads some data, and closes the file, you will be calling many library methods that **throw IOException** or one of its subclasses. You might declare the method as follows:

```
public int readMyData(String filename) throws IOException
```

Note that the Java keyword **throws** comes after the method parameter list. If the method can throw more than one kind of exception, you simply list them separated by commas after the **throws** keyword. For example:

```
public int readMyData(String filename) throws EOFException,
    FileNotFoundException, InterruptedIOException
```

Because these are checked exceptions, the compiler insists on their being handled by any method that calls **readMyData**. On the other hand, if you have a method that declares that it throws a list of unchecked exceptions, the compiler does not insist on their being handled.

Throwing an Exception

Throwing an exception involves two things: creating an object from an exception class by calling a constructor and using it in a **throw** statement. In general, exceptions can be constructed with or without an explanatory message. However, nothing prevents you from creating a custom exception class that carries more information than a single **String**. I'll look at a custom exception class in the "Creating Your Own Exception" section later in this chapter. Here is an example of a statement to create and throw an exception:

```
throw new ArithmeticException("Out of Range");
```

Rethrowing Exceptions

In some cases, you may want to catch an exception, do some processing, and then *rethrow* the exception so the calling method can also do some processing. This is accomplished with the **throw** statement, as shown in the following code fragment:

```
try {
   readMyData("booklist.txt");
}catch(FileNotFoundException ex){
   System.out.println("book list not found!");
   throw ex ;
}
```

 Be sure you remember the distinctly different meanings of the two keywords **throw** and **throws**. **throw** is used to throw an exception object inside a method, whereas **throws** appears in method declarations.

Exceptions in Overriding Methods

When you have a method in a subclass that has the same name, parameter list, and return type as a method in the parent class, the subclass method is said to *override* the parent class method. Let's suppose the parent class method is defined as follows:

```
public boolean readTest( String x) throws IOException
```

The Java compiler allows the overriding subclass method to be defined as throwing **IOException**, throwing one or more subclasses of **IOException**, or not throwing any exceptions. It does not allow the overriding subclass to be declared as throwing a more general checked exception or a checked exception from another hierarchy.

A moment's reflection will reveal why this requirement exists. If an overriding method in a derived class could throw a more general exception, then code that called the parent class method would not work correctly with the derived class.

Program Design with Exceptions

Designing with exceptions can greatly simplify programming and in some cases speed it up. For example, try the following suggestion for speeding up iteration through a large array. Because Java performs an array bounds check with every array access, you do not need to use a loop counter when iterating through an array. Instead, just catch the exception that results when the bounds check fails, as in the following code fragment:

```
int i = 0, sum = 0 ;
try {
for(;;) sum += count[i++] ;
}catch( IndexOutOfBoundsException e ){}
```

Although it is true that this is faster than using a loop counter as long as the array is large enough that the overhead of setting up the **try** is relatively small, this approach is not necessarily a good idea in all situations. For one thing, it prevents the use of "stop on exception" logic in a debugger.

Creating Your Own Exception

In this section, I'll illustrate some of the considerations involved in creating and using your own exception class. The example I have chosen has been reinvented a number of times by programmers who miss the "assert" construct in C, which is frequently a big help in debugging. The custom exception is **AssertionException**, and the class needed to make use of it is **Assertion**. Both classes are shown in Listing 7.1, but because they are both public, they would have to be defined in separate files.

 To really understand programming with exceptions, you can't beat hands-on experience. I suggest you add the classes in Listing 7.1 to a real Java project and experiment with ways to use them.

Listing 7.1   The two classes needed to implement AssertionExceptions.

```
1. public class AssertionException extends RuntimeException {
2.    // this constructor assures that there will always be a
      // message
3.  public AssertionException(){
4.    super("AssertionException");
5.  }
6.
7.  public AssertionException(String msg ){
8.    super( msg ) ;
9.  }
10. }
11.
12. /* a class with only static methods to check assertions */
13.
14. public class Assertion {
15.   public static boolean ASSERTION_ON = true ;
16.   private Assertion() {} ; // no public constructor
17.   // method without a message
18.   public static void assert( boolean validFlg )
19.       throws AssertionException {
20.     if( ASSERTION_ON && !validFlg ) {
21.       throw new AssertionException();
```

```
22.     }
23.   }
24.  // method with a message
25.   public static void assert( boolean validFlg, String msg )
26.        throws AssertionException {
27.     if( ASSERTION_ON && !validFlg ) {
28.        throw new AssertionException(msg);
29.     }
30.   }
31. }
```

Using the Assertion Class

The idea behind assertions is that at critical points in your program, you can insert a single statement that can check for a required condition and produce a custom informative message if the condition does not exist. For example, suppose you need to ensure that the value of X does not exceed a given maximum. You could use code like this:

```
Assertion.assert( X <= xMax, "X too large" );
```

Such code would throw an **AssertionException** if the test expression evaluated to **false**. The exception is created with an attached message in the code on line 28 of Listing 7.1. If you had a **catch** clause in a position to catch this exception, such as the following

```
catch(AssertionException ex ){
   System.out.println( ex );
}
```

you would get the following message on the standard output:

```
AssertionException: X too large
```

Exception vs. RuntimeException

In line 1 of Listing 7.1, you can see that I derived **AssertionException** from the class **RuntimeException**. This means that the compiler does not check for the appropriate exception-handling mechanism in the surrounding code. You can put in the **try-catch** structure to catch an **AssertionException,** but the compiler does not insist on it. The following example would compile without a problem:

```
public void checkName(String tmp){
   Assertion.assert( tmp != null && tmp.length() > 1, "Name");
   // more code here
}
```

However, if you changed the parent of **AssertionException** from **RuntimeException** to **Exception**, the same code would cause the compiler to report the following error: "Exception **AssertionException** must be caught or it must be declared in the **throws** clause of this method." In other words, if **AssertionException** were a checked exception, the compiler would require either an explicit **try-catch** structure in the **checkName** method or a declaration of the method, as follows:

```
public void checkName(String tmp) throws AssertionException{
    Assertion.assert( tmp != null && tmp.length() > 1, "Name");
    // more code here
}
```

Practice Questions

Question 1

A method to compute the sum of all elements in an array of **int** is needed.
The following proposed method is incomplete:

```
1. public int total( int[] x ){
2.    int i, t = 0 ;
3.    -select statement to go here
4.    { t += x[ i++ ] ;
5.    }
6.    return t ;
7. }
```

What is the correct statement for line 3?

- ○ a. **for(int i = 0 ; i < x.length ;)**
- ○ b. **for(i = 0 ; i < x.length ;)**
- ○ c. **for(i = 0 ; i < x.length ; i++)**
- ○ d. **for(i = 1 ; i <= x.length ; i++)**

Answer b is correct because it avoids the errors of the other options. Answer a results in a compiler error because *i* is already declared in line 2. Therefore, answer a is incorrect. Answer c is incorrect because the loop counter *i* is incremented twice, thus skipping alternate array elements. Answer d is incorrect for several reasons: The first element of the array is missed, and the final cycle of the loop causes an **ArrayIndexOutOfBoundsException**; also, the loop counter is incremented twice.

Question 2

The following method takes a **char** input and returns an **int** value:

```
1. public int maze( char d ){
2.    if( d <= 'N' ){
3.      if( d == 'E' ) return 2 ;
4.      return 1 ;
5.    }
6.    else if( d == 'S' ) return 3;
7.    else if( d == 'W' ) return 4;
8.    return 0 ;
9. }
```

Which of the following statements about this method are true? [Check all correct answers]

☐ a. The input of 'A' produces an output of 1.

☐ b. The input of 'X' produces an output of 0.

☐ c. The input of 'D' produces an output of 0.

☐ d. The method fails to compile due to syntax errors.

Answers a and b are correct. The method in this code sample will produce outputs of 1 and 0 for the inputs of A and X, respectively. Answer c is incorrect because with a value of 'D', the statements at lines 3 and 4 are executed. Answer d is incorrect because this code compiles without problems.

Question 3

You want the following method to print a message when the input value is in the range equal to or greater than **xMin** and less than or equal to **xMax**:

```
1. public void chkRange( int x ){
2.   if(XXXX) System.out.println("In Range");
3. }
```

What alternate expressions could be substituted for **XXXX** in line 2 of the code? [Check all correct answers]

☐ a. **(x <= xMax) && (x >= xMin)**

☐ b. **xMin <= x <= xMax**

☐ c. **!(x < xMin II x > xMax)**

Answers a and c are correct. Answer a works fine. Note that the **&&** form "shortcuts" the evaluation if the first test fails. Answer c also works fine. Note that the || form "shortcuts" the evaluation if the first term is **true**. The ! (NOT) operator is then applied to the result. Answer b is incorrect. It causes a compiler error because the result of the first test "xMin <= x" is a **boolean** primitive. A **boolean** primitive cannot be combined with the remaining arithmetic expression.

Question 4

Take the following method that will be called with various input values:

```
1. public void soundOff( int x ){
2.    switch(x){
3.      case 1: System.out.print("One ");
4.      case 2:
              System.out.print("Two "); break ;
5.      case 3: System.out.print("Three ");
6.      default: System.out.print("Do What?");
7.    }
8. }
```

Which of these input and output pairs will be observed? [Check all correct answers]

❑ a. Input = 1, Output = "One"

❑ b. Input = 0, Output = "One Two"

❑ c. Input = 3, Output = "Three Do What?"

❑ d. Input = 4, Output = "Do What?"

Answers c and d are correct. Answer c is correct because case 3 "falls through" to the **default** statement. Answer d is correct because any value not in a **case** statement executes the **default** statement. Answer a is incorrect because case 1 does not have a **break** statement, so the following case would execute also, producing "One Two". Answer b is incorrect because any value not in a **case** statement executes the default. The **switch-case** structure does not care about the numerical order in which cases appear.

Question 5

Take the following code fragment:

```
1. switch( x ) {
2.    case 100 : System.out.println(
         "One hundred");break ;
3.    case 200 : System.out.println(
         "Two hundred");break ;
4.    case 300 : System.out.println(
         "Three hundred");break ;
5. }
```

Which declarations of *x* will *not* cause a compiler error? [Check all correct answers]

☐ a. **byte x = 100 ;**

☐ b. **short x = 200 ;**

☐ c. **int x = 300 ;**

☐ d. **long x = 400 ;**

Answers b and c are correct. As far as answer b, the variable *x* can be a **short** because all of the cases can be accommodated. As far as answer c, *x* can be an **int** because all of the cases can be accommodated in the **int** range. Answer a is incorrect because the variable *x* cannot be a **byte** type because the values 200 and 300 are not compatible (the byte range is -128 through 127). The type used in the **switch** statement must accommodate all of the values in the **case** statements. Answer d is incorrect because **switch** statements cannot use **long** values. You would have to have a specific **cast** for *x* to be a **long**, as follows:

```
1.  switch((int)x) {
```

Question 6

Take the following code fragment with a break to a labeled statement:

```
1. int i, j ;
2. lab: for( i = 0 ; i < 6 ; i++ ){
3.         for( j = 5 ; j > 2 ; j- ){
4.            if( i == j ) {
5.              System.out.print(" " + j );
                    break lab ;
6.           }
7.         }
8.      }
```

What will the printed output be?

○ a. 3 4 5

○ b. 3 4

○ c. 3

Answer c is correct. The statement on line 5 executes with a value of 3, and then the **break** terminates the loop started on line 2. Answers a and b are incorrect because the statement on line 5 executes only once, and the **break** terminates the loop started on line 2.

Question 7

The following method is designed to convert an input string to a floating-point number while detecting a bad format:

```
1. public boolean strCvt( String s ){
2.   try {
3.     factor =
            Float.valueOf( s ).floatValue();
4.     return true ;
5.   }catch(NumberFormatException e){
6.     System.out.println("Bad number " + s);
7.     factor = Float.NaN ;
8.   }finally { System.out.println("Finally");
9.   }
10.   return false ;
11. }
```

Which descriptions of the results of various inputs to the method are correct? [Check all correct answers]

❏ a. Input = "0.234" - Result: factor = 0.234, "Finally" is printed, **true** is returned.

❏ b. Input = "0.234" - Result: factor = 0.234, "Finally" is printed, **false** is returned.

❏ c. Input = null - Result: factor = NaN, "Finally" is printed, **false** is returned.

❏ d. Input = null - Result: factor = unchanged, "Finally" is printed, **NullPointerException** is thrown.

Answers a and d are correct because these inputs cause these results. Answer b is incorrect because the return value in line 4 is used. Answer c is incorrect because a **NullPointerException** is thrown in line 3 and is not caught in the method. Line 7 is never reached.

Question 8

Here is the hierarchy of exceptions related to array index and string index errors:

```
Exception
  +— RuntimeException
      +— IndexOutOfBoundsException
          +— ArrayIndexOutOfBoundsException
          +— StringIndexOutOfBoundsException
```

Suppose you had a method *X* that could throw both array index and string index exceptions. Assuming that X does not have any **try-catch** statements, which of the following statements are correct? [Check all correct answers]

☐ a. The declaration for *X* must include "throws ArrayIndexOutOfBoundsException, StringIndexOutOfBoundsException".

☐ b. If a method calling *X* catches **IndexOutOfBoundsException**, both array and string index exceptions are caught.

☐ c. If the declaration for *X* includes "throws IndexOutOfBoundsException", any calling method must use a **try-catch** block.

☐ d. The declaration for *X* does not have to mention exceptions.

Answers b and d are correct. Answer b is correct because exceptions obey a hierarchy just like other objects. Because these exceptions descend from **RuntimeException**, they do not have to be declared. Therefore, answer d is correct. The significant word here is "must." Because these exceptions descend from **RuntimeException**, they do not have to be declared. Therefore, answer a is incorrect. Answer c is incorrect for a similar reason, because these exceptions descend from **RuntimeException**. They do not have to be caught even if declared by method *X*.

Question 9

You are writing a set of classes related to cooking and have created your own exception hierarchy derived from **java.lang.Exception** as follows (note that both **BitterException** and **SourException** descend from **BadTasteException**):

```
Exception
    ┼─ BadTasteException
          ┼─ BitterException
          ┼─ SourException
```

Your base class, **BaseCook**, has a method declared as follows:

```
int rateFlavor(Ingredient[] list) throws
    BadTasteException
```

A class, **TexMexCook**, derived from **BaseCook** has a method that overrides **BaseCook.rateFlavor()**. Which of the following are legal declarations of the overriding method? [Check all correct answers]

❑ a. **int rateFlavor(Ingredient[] list) throws BadTasteException**

❑ b. **int rateFlavor(Ingredient[] list) throws Exception**

❑ c. **int rateFlavor(Ingredient[] list) throws BitterException**

❑ d. **int rateFlavor(Ingredient[] list)**

Answers a, c, and d are correct. Answer a is correct because overriding methods can throw the same exception. Answer c is correct because the overriding method can throw an exception that is a subclass of the original. Answer d is correct because the overriding method does not have to throw an exception at all. Answer b is incorrect because if the overriding method throws an exception, it must throw the same exception or a subclass.

Question 10

You are writing a set of classes related to cooking and have created your own exception hierarchy derived from **java.lang.Exception**, as follows:

```
Exception
    ← BadTasteException
          ← BitterException
          ← SourException
```

Your custom exceptions have constructors taking a **String** parameter. You have a method declared as follows:

```
int rateFlavor(Ingredient[] list)
              throws BadTasteException
```

Which of the following shows a correct complete statement to throw one of your custom exceptions?

- ○ a. **new SourException("Ewww!") ;**
- ○ b. **throws new SourException("Ewww!");**
- ○ c. **throw new SourException("Ewww!");**
- ○ d. **throw SourException("Ewww!");**

Answer c is correct. This statement creates and throws the exception. Answer a is incorrect because this statement is missing the keyword **throw**. Answer b is incorrect because the keyword needed is **throw; throws** is used in method declarations. Answer d is incorrect because it does not create an exception object with the **new** keyword.

Question 11

Take the following code for the **test** method:

```
1.   public int test(String x, int n ){
2.     if( n == 0 ) return n ;
3.     else if( n == 1 ){
4.       if( x != null ) return 5 ;
5.     }
6.     else if( n == 2 && x != null ){
7.       if( x.equals("YES") ) return 3;
8.       else if( x.equals("NO") return 4 ;
9.     }
10.    return -1 ;
11. }
```

Which of the following statements are true? [Check all correct answers]

❑ a. If the input n = 1, line 6 will always be executed.

❑ b. If the input string *x* is "NO" and n is 2, the method returns 4.

❑ c. If the input n is 1 and the input string is "YES", the method returns 3.

❑ d. The **else** on line 6 goes with the **if** on line 3.

Answers b and d are correct. Answer a is incorrect because if *x* is not null, the method returns from line 4. Answer c is incorrect because if n is 1, lines 7 and 8 are not executed.

Question 12

Here is a **test** method:

```
String test( int n ){
   String tmp = "?" ;
   if( n < 3 ) n- ;
   switch( n ){
     case 1 :
        return "one" ;
     case 2 :
        n = 3 ;
     case 3 :
        break ;
     case 4 :
     default :
        return tmp ;
   }
   return "Result " + n ;
}
```

Which of the options correctly describes the input and returned value from this method? [Check all correct answers]

❑ a. Input 1 - Return = "one"

❑ b. Input 2 - Return = "Result 3"

❑ c. Input 3 - Return = "Result 3"

❑ d. Input 4 - Return = "?"

❑ e. Input 5 - Return = "?"

Answers c, d, and e are correct. Answer c is correct because 3 is not decremented, and it executes case 3, leaving n unchanged. Answer d is correct because 4 is not decremented, and case 4 falls through to the default, returning "?". Answer e is correct because 5 is not decremented, and the default case returns. Answer a is incorrect because the value 1 is decremented to 0, causing the default case to execute and return "?". Answer b does not occur because 2 is decremented to 1 and "one" is returned.

Need to Know More?

 Joy, Bill, et al. *The Java Language Specification, Second Edition.* Addison-Wesley, Reading, MA, 2000. ISBN 0-201-31008-2. This is the most authoritative source on the language. See Chapter 11 for information on exceptions and Chapter 14 for material on flow control.

 Venners, Bill. *Inside the Java Virtual Machine, 2nd edition.* McGraw-Hill, New York, NY, December, 1999. ISBN 0-07-135093-4. If you want the bit-twiddling details of how the JVM interprets Java bytecodes, this is a good source. See Chapters 16 and 17 for details on how flow control and exceptions are implemented in bytecodes.

 http://java.sun.com/docs/books/jls/second_edition/html/j.title. doc.html is where the definitive Java language specification document is maintained in HTML form. Parts of the document are also available in PDF form. This document has also been published as ISBN 0-201-31008-2, but most programmers will find the online documentation to be sufficient.

Working with Java Classes and Objects

. . . .

Terms you'll need to understand:

✓ Polymorphism

✓ Extending

✓ Overloading

✓ Overriding

✓ Garbage collection

✓ Finalizer methods

Techniques you'll need to master:

✓ Recognizing the distinction between "is a" and "has a" in Java class design

✓ Understanding the difference between overloading and overriding a method, and the limitations of each technique

✓ Understanding how Java manages memory recycling with garbage collection

✓ Understanding how Java finalizer methods are used

This chapter covers some topics related to programming with Java objects. I will examine some basic aspects of designing classes to fit various programming problems. I also review Java's built-in mechanisms for freeing and reusing memory and other system resources used by objects after they are no longer needed.

Object-Oriented Design

I am certainly not going to be able to cover all of object-oriented design in a single chapter. It's not a subject you can master overnight. In addition to reading this book, I recommend that you study good object-oriented code—such as the Java standard library classes—and books, such as the *Design Patterns*, cited at the end of the chapter.

To gain a complete understanding of object-oriented design, you need to be comfortable with some of the basics, such as the object relationships expressed as the phrases "is a" and "has a". You will also need to be comfortable with the implications of class hierarchies, overloading, and overriding.

A Class Hierarchy

To facilitate this discussion, I'll outline the class hierarchy that you might use to represent a book, such as this one. The parent of my specialized set of classes is **BookElement**, descended directly from **Object**. For simplicity's sake, I'll ignore any consideration of which package these classes should be in. The **BookElement** class has some variables and methods that are common to all parts of a book, and the subclasses have some specialized variables and methods, as shown in the following outline:

```
Object
    +—BookElement
            +—TableOfContents
            +—Introduction
            +—Chapter
            +—Appendix
            +—Index
```

The class declarations for these classes might look like this:

```
public class BookElement extends Object
public class TableOfContents extends BookElement
public class Chapter extends BookElement
...[etc.]
```

In the terminology I want to emphasize, a **BookElement** object "is an" **Object**. A **Chapter** object "is a" **BookElement** and of course, it also "is an" **Object** by virtue of inheritance. Recalling the **instanceof** operator, which was discussed in Chapter 6, you can see that in the following code fragment, the logical test would result in "true" being printed:

```
Chapter chap1 = new Chapter();
if( chap1 instanceof BookElement ) System.out.println("true")
```

A class to represent a book would require member variables to hold each of the possible **BookElement**-related components, as suggested by the following code fragment:

```
public class Book extends Object {
  TableOfContents toc;
  Introduction  intro ;
  Chapter[] chapt ;
...[etc.]
```

I would then say that a **Book** object "has a" **TableOfContents** member variable.

Polymorphism

Looking at the **Book** class described in the "A Class Hierarchy" section earlier in this chapter, consider the **TableOfContents** object that **toc** refers to. Because this object can also be referred to as a **BookElement** object or an **Object** class object, it is said to exhibit *polymorphism* (the generic term for having many forms).

If there were a method that operated on **BookElement** objects, you could call it with an **Introduction** object, a **Chapter** object, or any of the other classes that extend **BookElement**. These objects behave like **BookElement** objects because they inherit from **BookElement**, but they never lose their original identity.

Model, View, and Controller Aspects

One of the most useful object-oriented design concepts involves separating the elements of a problem into *model, view,* and *controller* aspects. Model elements are responsible for holding data and performing elementary operations. The **Book** class described in the "A Class Hierarchy" section earlier in this chapter would be a model of a book and would hold the **BookElement** objects that are models of pieces of the book. However, **BookElement**s would not display themselves or interact directly with users—that is the responsibility of views and controllers.

You can see the virtue of separating these functions when you consider the number of different views you might want to have of a single model. For example, you might want an outline view, a page layout view, and an editing view. Controller functions would handle interaction with the user, for example, interpreting a scrollbar movement into a change in a view. The controller aspects of a problem are frequently linked closely with a particular view, so you should not expect a model/view/controller approach to always neatly yield separate classes for each aspect.

 If you have not already done so as part of your Java experience, you should experiment with setting up your own hierarchy of classes to represent something in which you are interested. Reading about object-oriented design is no substitute for experience.

When Inheritance Is Not Possible

Programmers who are new to Java frequently run into the problem of inheritance not being possible. They have planned a class hierarchy but find that Java will not allow them to extend the class they wanted to use as a base. For example, the following class declaration won't compile because **String** is declared as a **final** class:

```
public BookElement extends String
```

In other words, **BookElement** cannot possibly "be a" **String**. The solution is simple: Let the class have a **String** member variable; thus, **BookElement** "has a" **String**.

Generally speaking, the designers of Java have chosen to make **final** those classes that could create a security risk if a derived class was allowed. Because character buffer manipulation is a classic hacker route, **String** and **StringBuffer** are **final** classes.

Overloading and Overriding

The terms *overloading* and *overriding* are applied to situations in which you have multiple Java methods with the same name. Within a particular class, you can have more than one method with the same name as long as they have different input parameter types. This is described as overloading the method name. To continue the book example, the **BookElement** class might have methods declared as follows:

```
public void addText( String txt )
public void addText( String[] lines )
```

You would say that **addText** has been overloaded. The Java compiler can distinguish between calls to these two methods because they have different *signatures*. The number, type, and order of the input parameters plus the method name determine the signature. The overloaded methods can have different return types and can throw different exceptions.

As far as Java is concerned, the two **addText** methods are entirely different. The duplicate names are really just a convenience for programmers. If one method were declared in the **BookElement** class and the other in the **Chapter** class, you would still describe these as overloaded method names. The compiler does not allow a class to have two methods with identical signatures but different return types, even if one method is declared in a parent class and is inherited.

Overriding Methods

If a subclass method has the same name, parameter list, and return type as a superclass method, you say that the subclass method overrides the superclass method. Continuing with the book example, if **BookElement** has a method declared as

```
public void addText( String txt )
```

the **Chapter** class can declare a method that overrides **addText**, as follows:

```
public void addText( String s )
```

Now consider the following code fragment in which a **Chapter** object is created but the reference is cast to a **BookElement** variable:

```
Chapter ch = new Chapter();
BookElement b = ch ; // casting to the parent class
b.addText("If a subclass has "); // which method is called?
```

The question is: Which method is executed, the one in the **Chapter** class or the one in the **BookElement** class? The answer is related to the fact that objects always know what type they are; just being cast to a **BookElement** reference does not change the object type. Because the Java Virtual Machine (JVM) resolves method calls at runtime using the actual object, the **Chapter** version of **addText** is executed. The ability to do this is part of what makes Java so flexible, but there is a price to pay in the restrictions you must observe when writing an overriding method. These restrictions can be summarized as follows:

➤ *Access modifiers*—An overriding method cannot be made more private than the method in the parent class.

➤ *Return type*—The return type must be the same as in the parent class method.

➤ *Exceptions thrown*—Any exception declared must be of the same class as that thrown by the parent class or of a subclass of that exception.

You should know how to distinguish between overloaded and overridden methods.

Overriding Methods and the **abstract** Keyword

Java allows the class designer to declare a method as **abstract**. This essentially nails down the access, parameter list, and return type for a particular method name but does not provide a code body. Any class with such a method must also be declared **abstract**. This is done so that all classes extending the **abstract** class and overriding the **abstract** method are compatible.

In the sample hierarchy, **BookElement** could be declared as follows:

```
public abstract class BookElement extends Object
```

A good candidate for an **abstract** method might be:

```
public abstract void addText( String s );
```

Every class that extends **BookElement** must now either override **addText** with a *concrete* definition or must be declared **abstract**.

When You Can't Override a Method

Methods that are declared **final** cannot be overridden—that's the meaning of the word *final*. Methods that are declared **private** cannot be seen outside the class and therefore cannot be overridden. However, because the private method name cannot be seen, you can reuse the method name in a subclass. This is not the same as overriding because you do not have access to the overridden method.

Calling the Overridden Method

In many cases, a programmer overrides a method in a base class simply to add some embellishments. When doing this, you do not need to repeat code that already exists in the parent class method. You can call that method using the **super** keyword. For example, suppose the **BookElement** class has a **setFont** method declared as follows:

```
public void setFont(Font f, int size)
```

If your **Chapter** class, which extends **BookElement**, needs to do some additional computation every time the **setFont** method is called, the overriding method could follow the following scheme:

```
public void setFont( Font f, int size){
    super.setFont( f, size );
    // more calculations here
}
```

Note that the **super** notation can be used only to execute a method in the immediate superclass. A class derived from **Chapter** could not execute the **setFont** method in the **BookElement** class. Furthermore, a class outside the **BookElement** hierarchy has no way of using a reference to a **Chapter** object to execute the setFont method in **BookElement**.

 It's important to understand how overriding works, including how to use **super** to execute an overridden method. Another important topic is the restrictions placed on the signature and return type of both overloaded and overridden methods. In my online testing, many programmers were weak on these restrictions, so study up!

Can You Override a Variable?

Yes, you can override a variable. This is the short answer. A subclass can have a variable with the same name as a variable in the parent class. In this case, if the parent class variable is not private, the subclass variable is said to *shadow* the parent class variable. However, there is a significant difference between the way the Java compiler treats methods and the way it treats variables. Because of the way variables are stored in the memory allocated to an object, references to variables can be computed at compile time based on the type of the variable.

Suppose that the **BookElement** class defines a variable named **lineCt** and the subclass **Chapter** defines another variable named **lineCt**. Which value would be printed by the following code fragment?

```
Chapter ch = new Chapter();
BookElement b = ch ; // casting to the parent class
System.out.println( b.lineCt );
```

If you guessed that the compiler would use the **lineCt** variable found in the **BookElement** class because **b** is a **BookElement** reference, you would be correct.

 Remember that references to member variables are computed at compile time using the type of the reference. References to member methods are resolved at runtime using the type of the object.

Object Garbage

I looked at the creation of objects using constructors in Chapter 4. Now I'll look at how objects are destroyed. Unlike C, Java does not allow for explicit destruction of objects. Instead, the memory space used by an object that is no longer reachable by the program is reclaimed by a method quaintly called "garbage collection." It could be more appropriately named memory recycling. For an excellent detailed description of how the inner workings of Java accomplish this, see the book *Inside the Java Virtual Machine* by Bill Venners (see the "Need to Know More?" section for more information).

The JVM can maintain control of all available memory because all object creation goes through the same mechanism. The Java programmer cannot pull any sneaky C-like tricks of getting memory directly from the operating system. JVMs typically run the garbage collection as a low-priority **Thread**, which is activated when the JVM feels that it is running short of available memory. The programmer can also *suggest* to the JVM that now is a good time to run garbage collection with one of the following method calls, but there is no guarantee that the JVM will do it:

```
System.gc() ;
Runtime.getRuntime().gc();
```

As a programmer, you cannot control when garbage collection is run, which can be annoying because garbage collection is CPU intensive. You can make delays less obvious by calling one of the **gc** methods when you know the user is unlikely to be demanding an instant response (for example, just after your program shows a new data screen).

The design decision to remove object destruction from the control of the programmer and place it under the control of the JVM vastly simplifies the programmer's job, but you still need to know how it works. Despite automatic garbage collection, you can still write code that runs out of memory when it shouldn't.

How Is Garbage Collected?

Strange as it may seem, the Java language specification does not lay down the law on how garbage is to be collected. It does not even say that every JVM must provide garbage collection. Because garbage collection was left unspecified, every designer who implements the JVM gets to try to come up with the optimum **gc** method for a particular system.

Basically, garbage collection works by locating objects that no longer have references in active **Thread**s that execute in the current program. To detach an object from your program, just set all references to that object to **null**. For example, in the following code fragment, a **String** object is created with a reference stored in **str**:

```
1. String str = new String("Size = " + x );
2. System.out.println( str );
3. str = null ;
```

Assuming that the **System.out** object does not keep a copy of the reference, the **String** object will be eligible for garbage collection after line 3 is executed.

All objects created as local variables in a block of code, such as a method, become eligible for garbage collection when the **Thread** exits the block of code. It is not necessary to set them to **null**.

Memory Traps for the Unwary

Suppose you have an object that represents some data to which you attach a scrollbar as an **AdjustmentListener**. You might set your reference variable to **null**, but the data object will still be attached to the scrollbar and thus will not be garbage collected. (That is why Java provides a **removeAdjustmentListener** method.)

Normally, all objects created for local variables in a method become eligible for garbage collection when the method exits. Exceptions would be if an object were added to a collection somewhere or returned to the calling method.

Garbage Collection and **String** Objects

It seems convenient when you are talking about garbage collection to use examples with **String** objects; however, there are complications. To save memory, **String** literal values are "interned" so that a single instance can be shared by multiple classes. In the following code, there is only one instance of the **String** with the value "yes" due to this sharing:

```
String a = "yes" ;
String b = "yes" ;
String c = "yes" ;
```

The **intern** method in the **String** class makes the system search for a preexisting **String** object with a given content and returns that reference. In the following code, the **substring** method creates a new **String**, but if the call to **intern** finds a **String** with the "yes" content, the new **String** is discarded and **d** refers to the preexisting version:

```
String d = "yes or no".substring(0,3).intern() ;
```

This optimization makes talking about garbage collection with **String** objects rather tricky.

Garbage Collection and Finalizers

Because Java objects may use other system resources besides memory, Java provides for *finalizer* methods. The **Object** class defines a do-nothing **finalize** method, as shown in the following code:

```
protected void finalize() throws Throwable{
}
```

If your class definition declares an instance method that overrides the **finalize** method, the JVM runs the method after it has decided that an object is eligible for reclamation, but before reclaiming the memory used by the object. This is your last chance (as a programmer) to clean up after yourself! However, because you cannot be sure when the JVM will run the **finalize** method, you should not rely on it to be run at any particular time. Also, you cannot ensure that one object's finalizer is run before another's.

The JVM may identify an object as being available for garbage collection and finalization but not run the **finalize** method at that time. Instead, it keeps a list of objects to be finalized. The Java language specification says that the **System.runFinalization** method call "suggests" that the JVM expend effort toward running the finalization methods of objects that have been found to be discarded but whose finalization methods have not yet been run. Other books suggest that the call *will* run the finalization methods. I believe that the major JVM implementations do respond at once to **runFinalization**, but it is not required by the language specification.

You should be concerned with file handles as a system resource. Even if you close all files after you are finished with them (which is a good programming practice), you might be concerned that exceptions or other problems could skip your normal file closing. You could write a **finalize** method that would check to see if a file has been closed and close it if necessary; however, the Java standard library file classes generally already have **finalize** methods that do this, but you get the idea.

Remember that the Java programmer has no direct control over when garbage collection is done. After you remove the last reference to an object, it is up to the JVM to decide when to recycle the memory involved. You cannot force the JVM to run object **finalize** methods at a particular time or in a particular order.

Practice Questions

Question 1

You are working on an aquarium simulation class named **Aquarius**. You already have a method that adds a **Fish** object to the aquarium and returns the remaining fish capacity. This method has the following declaration:

```
public int addFish( Fish f )
```

Now you want to provide for adding a whole school of fish at once. The proposed method declaration is:

```
protected boolean addFish( Fish[] f )
```

The idea is that it will return **true** if there is more room in the tank or **false** if the tank is now too full. Which of the following statements about this proposal is true?

○ a. This technique is called overloading.

○ b. This technique is called overriding.

○ c. The compiler will reject the new method because the return type is different.

○ d. The compiler will reject the new method because the access modifier is different.

Answer a is correct. This is overloading the method named **addFish**. Answer b is incorrect because overriding means that a method with the exact same signature and return type was created in a subclass. Answer c is incorrect because overloading methods can have any return type. Answer d is incorrect because overloading methods can have any access modifier.

Question 2

The **GenericFruit** class declares the following method:

```
public void setCalorieContent( float f )
```

You are writing a class **Apple** to extend **GenericFruit** and want to add methods that overload the method in **GenericFruit**. Which of the following would constitute legal declarations of overloading methods? [Check all correct answers]

- ❑ a. **protected float setCalorieContent(String s)**
- ❑ b. **protected void setCalorieContent(float x)**
- ❑ c. **public void setCalorieContent(double d)**
- ❑ d. **public void setCalorieContent(String s) throws NumberFormatException**

The correct answers are a, c, and d. Answer a is a valid overloading method declaration because the parameter list differs from the method in **GenericFruit**. Answer c is a valid overloading method declaration because the parameter list differs from the method in **GenericFruit**. Answer d is a valid overloading method declaration because the parameter list differs from the method in **GenericFruit**. Answer b is incorrect. It overrides, not overloads, the parent class method because it has the same parameter list. Note that answer b would cause a compiler error because it is more private than the method it overrides.

Question 3

You are designing an application to give dietary advice. To maximize the advantage of working in an object-oriented language, you have created a **GenericFruit** class that will be extended by classes representing different kinds of fruit. The following code fragment shows the class declaration and all of the instance variables in the **GenericFruit** class:

```
1. public class GenericFruit extends Object {
2.    protected float avgWeight ;
3.    protected float caloriesPerGram ;
4.    String varietyName ;
5.// class definition continues with methods
```

Which of the following would be a reasonable variable declaration for the **Apple** class that extends **GenericFruit**?

○ a. **Image picture ;**

○ b. **private float avgWeight ;**

○ c. **private GenericFruit theFruit ;**

Answer a is correct; you would then say that **Apple** "has an" **Image**. Answer b is incorrect because shadowing the base class **avgWeight** variable would only cause trouble. Answer c is incorrect because there is no need for **Apple** to "have a" **GenericFruit** because it "is a" **GenericFruit** by inheritance.

Question 4

You are taking over an aquarium simulation project. Your predecessor cre-ated a generic **Fish** class that includes an **oxygenConsumption** method declared as follows:

```
public float oxygenConsumption( float
    temperature )
```

The aquarium simulation sums oxygen consumption for all fish in the tank with the following code fragment, where **fishes** is an array of **Fish** object references:

```
1. float total = 0 ;
2. for( int i =0 ; i < fishes.length ;i++ ){
3.    total +=
          fishes[i].oxygenConsumption( t );
4. }
```

You are writing a subclass for a particular fish species. Your task is to pro-vide a method with species-specific metabolism data that will transpar-ently fit into the simulation. Do you want to overload or override the **oxygenConsumption** method?

○ a. Overload it.

○ b. Override it.

Answer b is correct; if you *override* the **oxygenConsumption** method, the Java runtime calls the overriding method for all fish where a specific method is pro-vided or the generic method if there is none. Answer a is incorrect because if you *overloaded* the **oxygenConsumption** method using a different method signature, the Java runtime would not call the specific method for **Fish** where a specific method was provided. It would always call the generic method.

Question 5

The **GenericFruit** class declares the following method to return a **float** number of calories in the average serving size:

```
public float aveCalories( )
```

Your **Apple** class, which extends **GenericFruit**, overrides this method. In a **DietSelection** class that extends **Object**, you want to use the **GenericFruit** method on an **Apple** object. What is the correct way to finish the statement in the following code fragment so the **GenericFruit** version of **aveCalories** is called using the **gf** reference?

```
1. GenericFruit gf = new Apple();
2. float cal = // finish this statement
                  // using gf
```

○ a. **gf.aveCalories();.**

○ b. **((GenericFruit)gf).aveCalories();.**

○ c. **gf.super.aveCalories();.**

○ d. There is no way to call the **GenericFruit** method.

Answer d is correct. There is no way for a class outside the **GenericFruit** hierarchy to call the **GenericFruit** method using an **Apple** reference. Answer a is incorrect because the runtime resolution of the method calls the **Apple** method. Answer b is incorrect because this extra cast does not change the object type. Answer c is incorrect because it does not create a valid Java statement.

Question 6

You have a **BuildDB** class that has a method for opening a local file declared as:

```
public InputStream openFile(String filename)
    throws FileNotFoundException
```

Now you want to extend **BuildDB** with a new class, **BuildNetDB**, and override **openFile** as follows:

```
public InputStream openFile(
        String urlstring ) throws IOException
```

Note that **FileNotFoundException** is a subclass of **IOException**. Which of the following statements are true? [Check all correct answers]

❑ a. The compiler will consider the **BuildNetDB** method to be an overloading of the base class method.

❑ b. The compiler will object to the **BuildNetDB** method because **FileNotFoundException** is a subclass of **IOException**.

❑ c. The compiler will object to the method in **BuildNetDB** because of the different name in the parameter list.

❑ d. Changing the exception thrown by the method in **BuildDB** to **IOException** will make the compiler happy.

Answers b and d are correct. Answer b is correct because an overriding method cannot throw an exception that is more general than the original method. Answer d is correct because if the overriding method and original method throw the same exception, there is no problem. Answer a is incorrect because the name and parameter list match, so the compiler considers this an overriding method. Answer c is incorrect because the compiler considers only the number, type, and order of parameters, not the name used in the parameter list.

Question 7

Here is a method that takes an array of **Object** references, adds them to a **Vector**, and calls the **doSomething** routine (assume that the **doSomething** method does not keep a reference to any of the objects involved):

```
1. public void test( Object[] obj ){
2.    Vector v = new Vector() ;
3.    for(int i =0 ; i < obj.length ;i++ ){
4.       v.addElement( obj[i] );
5.    }
6.    doSomething(v);
7. }
```

Which of the following statements is correct?

○ a. The **Vector** object can be garbage collected after line 7.

○ b. The references from **obj** prevent the **Vector v** from being garbage collected after the method exits.

○ c. The **obj** array can be garbage collected after line 7.

○ d. The extra reference in **v** to the objects in the **obj** array will prevent them from ever being garbage collected.

Answer a is correct. There will be no reference to the **Vector** object after the method returns. Answers b and d are incorrect because they have things backward: When there are no references to **v**, it makes no difference what references **v** is storing. Answer c is incorrect because the method that called **test** will still have a reference to the array.

Question 8

Which of the following statements about Java garbage collection are true?
[Check all correct answers]

❑ a. The following code will start the garbage collection mechanism:

```
Runtime.getRuntime().gc();
Thread.yield();
```

❑ b. The following code will start the garbage collection mechanism:

```
System.gc();
Thread.sleep(1000);
```

❑ c. The garbage collection **Thread** has a low priority.

❑ d. The method by which Java tracks unused objects is specified in the language definition.

❑ e. The method by which Java determines that a chunk of memory is garbage is up to the implementor of the JVM.

Answers c and e are correct. Answer c is correct because the JVM assigns a low priority to the garbage collection **Thread**. Answer e is correct because picking the best garbage collection method is left up to the individual JVM implementor. Answers a and b are incorrect because the key phrase here is *will* start: These code fragments *may* start the garbage collector, but there is no guarantee. Answer d is incorrect because the language specification does not prescribe a method.

Question 9

Which of the following statements about **finalize** methods is true?

○ a. The purpose of a **finalize** method is to recover system resources other than memory.

○ b. The purpose of a **finalize** method is to recover memory and other system resources.

○ c. You should always write a **finalize** method for every class.

○ d. The order in which objects are created controls the order in which their **finalize** methods are called.

Answer a is correct. A **finalize** method recovers system resources other than memory. Answer b is incorrect because memory is recovered by garbage collection; finalizers are for other resources. Answer c is incorrect because objects that do not use system resources other than memory do not need finalizers. Answer d is incorrect because there is no guarantee about the order of object finalization.

Question 10

The **GenericFruit** class declares the following method to return a **float** calculated from a serving size:

```
protected float calories( float serving )
```

In writing the **Apple** class that extends **GenericFruit**, you propose to declare an overriding method with the same parameter list and return type. Which access modifiers could you use with this overriding method? [Check all correct answers]

❏ a. **private**

❏ b. **protected**

❏ c. **public**

❏ d. "package"; that is, a blank access modifier

Answers b and c are correct. Answer b would work because the access does not change from the overridden method, and answer c would work because there is no problem with a more public access. Answer a is incorrect because the overriding method cannot be made more private than the method it is overriding. Answer d is incorrect because package access is more private than protected.

Need to Know More?

 Flanagan, David. *Java in a Nutshell, Third Edition*. O'Reilly & Associates, Inc., Sebastopol, CA, 1999. ISBN 1-56592-487-8. This is the most compact desktop reference book documenting the Java language. Chapter 3, "Object-Oriented Programming in Java," is pertinent to this chapter.

 Gamma, Erich, et al. *Design Patterns: Elements of Reusable Object-Oriented Software*. Addison-Wesley, Menlo Park, CA, 1994. ISBN 0-201-63361-2. Often humorously referred to as "Design Patterns by the Gang of Four," this book is a resource for inspiration when you are trying to figure out how to apply object-oriented design to a problem.

 Joy, Bill, et al. *The Java Language Specification, Second Edition*. Addison-Wesley, Reading, MA, 2000. ISBN 0-201-31008-2. This is the most authoritative source on the Java language. See Chapter 12 for details on garbage collection and finalization.

 Venners, Bill. *Inside the Java Virtual Machine, 2nd edition*. McGraw-Hill, New York, NY, December, 1999. ISBN 0-07-135093-4. If you want the bit-twiddling details of how the JVM interprets Java bytecodes, this is a good source. See Chapter 8 for details on Java garbage collection.

 www.mindview.net/Books/TIJ/ is where you can find the online version of the book *Thinking in Java, Second Edition*, by Bruce Eckel, which is highly recommended for object-oriented programming in Java. Hard-copy versions are also available at this site.

Java Threads

Terms you'll need to understand:

✓ **Thread**

✓ **Runnable**

✓ **InterruptedException**

✓ Deadlock

✓ Lock

✓ Monitor

✓ **Synchronized**

Techniques you'll need to master:

✓ Knowing all the states a **Thread** object can exist in and the transitions it can undergo

✓ Understanding the requirements of the **Runnable** interface

✓ Writing code that starts a new thread of execution

✓ Writing code that uses the **synchronized** keyword

✓ Writing code that uses **wait** and **notify** or **notifyAll** to coordinate access to objects by **Thread**s

Everything that happens in a Java program is the result of a thread executing a method associated with an object. Although Java provides many tools for manipulating threads, Java's portability has limitations because of variations in the underlying operating systems. It is essential for a Java programmer to understand both the power and limitations of Java threads.

Thread Background

One of the most striking features of Java is the ease with which a programmer can use multiple threads of execution. In C or C++, implementing multiple threads may involve you in a proprietary and platform-specific toolkit, using concepts that have been tacked on to the original language. Java, by contrast, was designed from the start to accommodate multiple threads.

Multithreading vs. Multitasking

In modern operating systems, such as Windows 2000, each program appears to run independently of all other programs. Although the CPU can do only one thing at a time, the operating system accomplishes *multitasking* by switching its attention so rapidly between the different applications that the applications appear to be running simultaneously. The operating system also prevents conflicts in the use of memory and other resources by the various programs.

In *multithreading*, multiple processes exist within a single program. If you use a modern Web browser, you have probably seen multithreading in action as the browser appears to load text and multiple images simultaneously. In the browser, each thread of execution tries to load a separate resource, so the overall loading process does not have to wait for a slow server response.

In the Java multithreaded environment, many separate threads can access the Java Virtual Machine (JVM) objects and resources. Each thread has its own path of execution but can potentially access any object in the program. It is up to the programmer to ensure that the threads do not interfere with each other. The Java language has built-in constructs that make this relatively easy, but you need to put some effort into becoming comfortable with multithreading.

The Java language specification does not say how the JVM should implement multithreading. Because there is so much variation among the various operating systems and hardware on which Java is expected to run, the language specification leaves the specific implementation up to JVM designers.

The Thread Class

The Java **Thread** class describes the required behavior of **Thread** objects. **Thread** objects are used to encapsulate and conceal the details of a particular operating system's approach to multithreading. The JVM creates and runs several **Thread**s to support even the simplest Java program. The **Thread**s are used to load class files, interpret operating system events, and start the execution of your program.

The Life of a **Thread**

Thread objects have a distinct life cycle with four basic states: new, runnable, blocked, and dead (see Figure 9.1). The transitions from new to runnable and from runnable to dead are simple and permanent; the transition between runnable and blocked occupies most of the Java programmer's attention.

A **Thread** in the runnable state can resume execution at the whim of the **Thread** scheduler in the JVM. Moving a **Thread** from the running to the ready state is also up to the **Thread** scheduler. Java also uses the term "Runnable" when referring to the **Runnable** interface. When referring to the interface, I will show the word in bold with the first letter capitalized. Running **Thread**s can be moved to and from the blocked state by various circumstances.

Creating a **Thread**

Thread objects are created by constructor methods, just like any other object. A **Thread** just created by **new** is essentially an empty object; it does not yet have any operating system resources and can only be started. When a **Thread** is started, it gets connected to the JVM scheduling mechanism and executes a method declared as follows:

```
public void run()
```

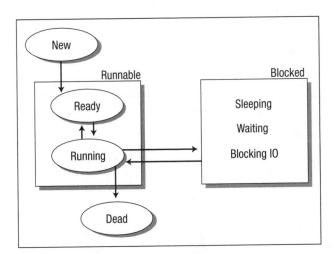

Figure 9.1   The possible states in the life of a **Thread**.

This method can be the **run** method of the **Thread** class, the overriding **run** method of a class that extends **Thread,** or the **run** method of a class that implements the **Runnable** interface.

A number of different **Thread** constructors exist, including some that let you create named **Thread**s and assign **Thread**s to **ThreadGroup** objects. However, the use of names and **ThreadGroup** objects is not one of the exam's objectives, so the interested student will have to investigate other sources. Here are the two types of constructors to consider:

```
1. Thread myT = new Thread();
2. Thread myT = new Thread( Runnable r );
```

Line 1 shows the construction of a plain **Thread.** Actually, plain **Thread**s are not useful for anything because the **run** method in the **Thread** class is empty, but classes extending **Thread** can be quite useful. Line 2 shows the creation of a **Thread** with a reference to an object that implements the **Runnable** interface. When started, this **Thread** executes the **run** method in the **Runnable** object.

The **Runnable** Interface

The **Runnable** interface is simple. A class that implements **Runnable** need only provide a method declared as:

```
public void run()
```

Any **Thread** attached to an object that implements **Runnable** executes the **run** method of that object. It is possible to attach more than one **Thread** to a **Runnable** object.

Starting a **Thread**

A **Thread** does not do anything until its **start** method is executed. When a **Thread** is started, the JVM sets up some resources and puts the **Thread** in the list of runnable **Thread**s. Exactly when a **Thread** gets to execute depends on its priority, the activity of other **Thread**s, and the characteristics of the particular JVM.

You can simultaneously create and start a **Thread** as in the following method:

```
public void startThread() {
  new Thread(this).start();
}
```

You might think that the new **Thread** in the preceding example would be garbage collected because no reference to it is being kept, but the JVM created a reference in its list of **Thread**s. After **Thread** A has called **Thread** B's **start** method, you have no way of knowing whether **Thread** A will continue to execute or whether

Thread B will start immediately. Make sure you have set up everything for **Thread** B before calling its **start** method.

Thread Priorities

Thread objects have an instance variable, **priority**, that has integer values from 1 through 10, with 10 being the most urgent. The JVM **Thread** scheduler always attempts to allow the highest priority available **Thread** to execute, but this is not guaranteed. The constants **MIN_PRIORITY**, **MAX_PRIORITY**, and **NORM_PRIORITY** are defined in the **Thread** class with the values 1, 10, and 5, respectively. It is considered good form to use these constants rather than integer literals when you are using the **setPriority** method.

 A newly created **Thread** inherits the priority of the **Thread** that creates it, not **NORM_PRIORITY**. If you want to have a particular priority, you should call **setPriority** before starting the **Thread**.

The JVM may adjust the priority downward to match the underlying operating system, so don't be surprised if the **getPriority** method returns a value different from the one you requested.

Death of a Thread

When a **Thread** exits the **run** method to which it is attached, it becomes a dead **Thread**. This may occur because of a normal return from the **run** method or from an exception that is not caught. A dead **Thread** cannot be restarted.

Killing a Thread

In the first version of the Java language, the instance method **stop** was used to cause a **Thread** to stop what it was doing and die. In Java Development Kit (JDK) 1.2, using **stop** is no longer recommended. (See the discussion in the "Some Deprecated Methods" section later in this chapter.)

Static Methods of the Thread Class

The **Thread** class has a number of methods affecting the operation of individual **Thread**s that are implemented as **static** (class) methods instead of instance methods. The methods of greatest interest are **sleep** and **yield**.

Sleeping for a While

The **Thread** that calls the **sleep** method is put to sleep for a number of milliseconds at least equal to the input parameter. This method has the following two forms:

```
1. Thread.sleep(long millisecs)
2. Thread.sleep(long millisecs, int nanosecs )
```

The inclusion of form 2 in the Java language specification is rather ambitious because no current computer provides software timers of that precision. Because **sleep** is a **static** method, you can also call it with a reference to a **Thread** object, as in the following example where **myT** is a **Thread** reference variable:

```
1. try {
2.   myT.sleep( 500 );
3. }catch (InterruptedException e ){ }
```

I don't recommend this approach because it misrepresents what is happening. It is the currently executing **Thread** that sleeps, not necessarily the one referred to.

Notice that in the preceding code fragment, I had to enclose the **sleep** call in a **try-catch** structure to catch an **InterruptedException**. A sleeping **Thread** can be rudely awakened before its time if another **Thread** calls the **interrupt** method of the particular **Thread** instance, which generates an **InterruptedException**.

 sleep is not a high-precision timing operation because it depends on the clock of the underlying operating system. In addition, there is no guarantee that the **Thread** will immediately begin to execute after the time delay is up; that is up to the JVM **Thread** scheduler. Be sure to keep this in mind.

Yielding to Other Threads

The **static** method **yield** simply suspends the operation of the current **Thread** and allows the **Thread** scheduler to choose another runnable **Thread** to execute, which may be the same **Thread** that yielded. If you have a **Thread** that is carrying out a complex computation, you should insert an occasional call to **yield** in the code to ensure that other **Thread**s get a chance to run.

The Java language specification does not require any particular method for **Thread** scheduling. A computationally intensive program that runs fine without using **yield** calls on systems using a time-slicing method of **Thread** scheduling may be delayed on systems that use a different scheduling method.

Blocking Input/Output

Java classes that deal with transferring data to and from the world outside the JVM are generally in the **java.io** package. Many of the methods in these classes are expected to read or write a certain amount of data before the **Thread** that executes them returns. Because there may be a considerable delay before the underlying operating system and hardware can accomplish this, these methods put the **Thread** in a blocked state until the operation is finished. This allows the **Thread** scheduler to choose another **Thread** to run.

Deadlocks

A moment's reflection will suggest many ways in which two or more **Threads** could be put into a condition where none of them can proceed until some locked object is released. For example, suppose **Thread** A locks object B in a method that must access object Z. However, **Thread** X has already locked object Z and is trying to access object B. This is called a *deadlock* condition, the bane of multithreaded programming. Although Java provides many tools for managing multiple **Threads**, the programmer is ultimately responsible for avoiding deadlocks.

Synchronizing Threads

The major problem in designing a multithreaded language is preventing collisions in which more than one **Thread** attempts to modify the same object at the same time. Naturally, the CPU cannot actually do two things at once, but one **Thread** might be halted in midcalculation and another allowed to use the same data, resulting in a disaster.

Java provides the foundation for solving this problem in the **Object** class, the ultimate parent of all Java objects. Each object has an associated *lock* variable that can be manipulated only by the JVM. This lock provides a *monitor* mechanism that can be used to allow only one **Thread** at a time to have access to an object.

In various Java books, "lock" and "monitor" are used interchangeably. Some language purists, however, feel that "monitor" has a specific formal definition. I will use "monitor" to mean the mechanism and "lock" in the context of a **Thread** that obtains the lock on an object.

Because it would take additional time for the JVM to check the lock condition of an object every time it is accessed, the lock is ignored by default. The keyword **synchronized** is used to indicate a method or block of code that needs to be guarded by the lock mechanism. Here is the syntax used with **synchronized** and a block of code, where **obj** must be an object reference:

```
synchronized( obj ) {
    balance += payment ;
    // any amount of code
}
```

When **synchronized** is used as a statement, it requires that a reference to the object be locked. For convenience, **synchronized** can be used as a method modifier, in which case the entire method is the block of code, and **this** is automatically the object reference.

Once obtained, a **Thread**'s lock on an object is not released until the **Thread** exits the **synchronized** code block or uses the special **wait** method in the **Object** class, which I will discuss shortly.

Overriding and **synchronized** Methods

If you have a **synchronized** method in a class, a subclass with an overriding method does not have to declare it as **synchronized**. The **synchronized** keyword affects only the code block in the original class.

A **synchronized** method consumes extra CPU cycles on entry and exit, so you should not synchronize without good cause. For example, the initial releases of the Java standard library made the access methods in the **java.util.Vector** class **synchronized**. Although this ensured that only one **Thread** at a time could modify a **Vector** object, it did not give the programmer any flexibility. Java 1.2 adds new collection types, including **ArrayList**, which can be used in place of **Vector** and does not use **synchronized** methods. With these new classes, programmers can use synchronization as needed.

How Not to Synchronize

Don't synchronize on a local variable, as shown in the following code fragment, which attempts to prevent interference with the addition of a new **String** to the **active** array:

```
1. String[] active ;
2. public int addActive( String name, int id ){
3.    String tmp = name + " ID= " + id ;
4.    synchronized( tmp ){
5.      for( int i = 0 ; i < active.length ; i++ ){
6.        if(active[i] == null ) { active[i] = tmp ;
7.          return i ;
8.        }
9.      }
10.     return -1 ;
11.   } // end synchronized block
12. }
```

The statement in line 4 accomplishes nothing because every **Thread** has its own copy of local variables, such as **tmp**. If you want to protect the **String** array from modification by multiple **Thread**s, line 4 should use the instance variable, **active**, as follows:

```
4.    synchronized( active ) {
```

 Remember that **synchronized** has to be used with an object reference because only objects can have locks. It does no good to synchronize on a local variable. Be sure that the object chosen really protects the data you want to protect.

How Many Locks? How Many Threads?

A single **Thread** can obtain locks on many objects and/or multiple locks on the same object. A new lock is obtained for each entry into a **synchronized** code block. The JVM ensures that the lock is removed when a **Thread** exits the code block, whether or not the exit is normal.

Any number of **Thread**s can be ready to execute a **synchronized** code block. The first one the **Thread** scheduler allows to run after the lock is released establishes a lock and prevents the rest from executing.

Coordinating **Threads** with **wait** and **notify**

Some applications require coordination of **Thread**s beyond that provided by **synchronized** code blocks. A classic example is that of an animated scene in which an object contains a collection of the parts of the scene. One **Thread** can generate an image of the current position of the changing scene. However, because of the way the JVM organizes operating system events, displaying the current image on the screen is best left to the system event thread that calls the **paint** method of a screen component. If both **Thread**s did not coordinate, the screen could show incomplete images.

What you want is a way for the **Thread** that is generating animation to wait after each animation step until the scene has been shown on the screen and for the painting **Thread** to wait until the animation **Thread** has completed a step before showing the image. In addition, you want the painting **Thread** to be able to tell the animation **Thread** that it can start work on the next step.

The following code fragment shows the **run** method executed by the animation **Thread**:

```
1. public synchronized void run(){
2.    while( true ){
3.       createNextScene() ;
```

```
4.       repaint();
5.       try{ wait() ;
6.       }catch( InterruptedException e){}
7.  }
8.  }
```

The entire method is **synchronized**, so the animation **Thread** has a lock on the object. The only time the lock is released is when the animation **Thread** calls **wait**. The **wait** method, which is defined in the **Object** class, puts the **Thread** that executes it into a special state. Any locks that the **Thread** has are released, and it is put in a "wait set" list of waiting **Threads** that is attached to the object.

After creating the next scene, the **repaint** method is called in line 4 of the previous code fragment just before the animation **Thread** calls **wait**. A call to **repaint** essentially is a request to the JVM to refresh the screen display for this component. When the JVM gets around to it, the **paint** method of the component is called by the **Thread** that the JVM devotes to handling screen events. As shown in the following code fragment, the **paint** method draws the image to the screen and calls **notify**:

```
1. public void paint(Graphics g ){
2.   if( sceneImage == null ) return ;
3.   synchronized( this ) {
4.     g.drawImage( sceneImage, 0, 0, null )
5.     notify();
6.   }
7. }
```

Before painting to the screen, the painting **Thread** has to enter the **synchronized** block starting at line 3. If the animation **Thread** has a lock on the object, the painting **Thread** is stopped at this point. When the painting **Thread** is allowed to proceed, the animation **Thread** must have called **wait**, so the **sceneImage** must be complete.

When **notify** is called, a **Thread** is removed from the wait set and returned to the list of runnable **Threads**. If more than one **Thread** is waiting, you cannot control or predict which one it will be. However, in this example, only the animation **Thread** is waiting. As soon as the painting **Thread** exits the **synchronized** code block, the animation **Thread** can lock the object and run again.

More about wait

There is a **wait** method with a timeout in milliseconds. After the time is exhausted, the **Thread** attempts to proceed but is allowed to do so only if no other **Thread** has a lock on the object. This method is handy when you are not sure that another **Thread** will be able to call **notify**, because it guarantees that the **Thread** will not be stuck in the **wait** state forever.

More about **notify** and **notifyAll**

If more than one **Thread** is waiting for an object lock, the programmer cannot control or predict which one will be returned to the runnable set when **notify** is called. If there is a chance that more than one **Thread** is waiting, you can use **notifyAll**.

The **notifyAll** call removes all waiting **Thread**s from the wait list. Only one of these actually gets a lock on the object and is allowed to execute the **synchronized** method; the others run and find that the object is still locked. If a **Thread** that has a lock on one or more objects dies, the JVM removes the locks and does the equivalent of **notifyAll** for each object locked.

IllegalMonitorStateException

If a **Thread** that does not have a lock on an object attempts to call the object's **wait** or **notify** method, an **IllegalMonitorStateException** is thrown—typically with the message "current thread not owner." To ensure that this never happens, your calls to **wait** or **notify** or **notifyAll** should be in **synchronized** code blocks.

Coordinating **Threads** with **join**

Another way to coordinate **Threads** is provided by the **join** method, an instance method of the **Thread** class. The **Thread** that calls the **join** method of another **Thread** waits for the other **Thread** to die before proceeding. In the following code fragment, the **Thread** that executes the **main** method joins the **Thread** created in the **jt** object:

```
1.  public static void main(String[] args){
2.    JoinTest jt = new JoinTest();
3.    try {
4.      jt.t.join();
5.      System.out.println( "after join");
6.    }catch(InterruptedException ex){
7.      System.out.println("main exception:" + ex);
8.    }
9.  }

10. Thread t ;
11. public JoinTest(){
12.   t = new Thread( this );
13.   t.setPriority( Thread.MIN_PRIORITY );
14.   t.start();
```

```
15. }
16. public void run(){ doSomeSlowThing(); }
```

The "after join" message is not printed until the **t Thread** exits the **run** method and dies.

Other versions of **join** specify a maximum number of milliseconds to wait for the joined **Thread** to die. When that time expires, an **InterruptedException** is generated. A practical example of this usage would be a program that uses the Internet to download a stock quote. If your main program **Thread** executed the download, it could hang for an uncontrollable amount of time. If you start another **Thread** to do the download and use **join** with a maximum delay, your main **Thread** is guaranteed to regain control despite network delays.

Some Deprecated Methods

The first version of Java used some **Thread** methods that are now considered unsafe and are *deprecated*. These methods are still in the Java standard library and may be used; however, programmers are advised to find substitutes because deprecated methods may not appear in future versions of the language. I discuss them here because they are used in sample programs from earlier versions of Java and because they illustrate some important points. The use of these methods should not appear on the test.

The suspend and resume Methods

The idea behind these methods was that you could temporarily halt a **Thread** by calling its **suspend** method and later allow it to proceed by calling **resume**. The problem with this is that if the **Thread** has a lock on an object, it retains the lock while suspended. If that locked object happens to be important for the progress of the rest of the program, a deadlock can result.

The stop Method

You would think that it ought to be possible to stop a **Thread** without causing any harm, but the designers now feel that arbitrarily stopping a **Thread** can leave an object in a damaged or inconsistent state that might then cause unpredictable program behavior. The suggested alternatives to using **stop** include using a flag variable in the **run** method. In a situation where a **Thread** is blocked while waiting for input, I suggest you use the **interrupt** method.

Keeping the Methods Straight

Let's review the classes and methods that you are likely to be using when working with **Thread**s. When I tested questions online for this chapter, many people made mistakes on this material.

Table 9.1	A summary of methods used with Threads.			
Class	**Method**	**Type**	**Needs**	**Timeout Form**
Thread	**yield()**	**static**	no	
Thread	**sleep(#)**	**static**	**try-catch**	always
Thread	**start()**	instance		no
Thread	**run()**	instance		no
Thread	**join()**	instance	**try-catch**	optional
Thread	**interrupt()**	instance		no
Object	**wait()**	instance	**synchronized, try-catch**	optional
Object	**notify()**	instance	**synchronized**	no
Object	**notifyAll()**	instance	**synchronized**	no

Table 9.1 summarizes the methods in the **Thread** and **Object** classes with which you need to be particularly familiar. Many more methods exist in the **Thread** class, but these are the ones you must be able to recognize and use correctly in programming. Naturally, because **Thread** descends from **Object**, it also has the **wait** and **notify** methods, but these are not used directly in **Thread** programming.

 Take particular note of which methods are static and which are instance methods, as shown in the "Type" column in Table 9.1. Also note which methods need to be enclosed in **synchronized** code blocks and/or **try-catch** structures to catch the **InterruptedException**, as shown in the "Needs" column. In the "Timeout Form" column, note that **sleep** is always used with a timeout and that **join** and **wait** have forms with and without timeouts.

Practice Questions

Question 1

You are creating a class that extends **Object** and implements **Runnable**. You have already written a **run** method for this class, and you need a way to create a **Thread** and have it execute the **run** method. Which of these **start** methods should you use?

○ a.
```
public void start(){
    new Thread( this ).start();
}
```

○ b.
```
public void start(){
    Thread myT = new Thread();
    myT.start();
}
```

○ c.
```
public void start(){
    Thread myT = new Thread(this);
    myT.run();
}
```

Answer a correctly creates a new **Thread** attached to the **Runnable** object and starts it. It does not matter that there is no reference to the **Thread** in the **start** method. Answer b is incorrect because the new **Thread** is not attached to the **Runnable** object, so it cannot find the **run** method. Instead, the default **run** in the **Thread** class is executed. Answer c is incorrect because the **Thread** that is executing the **start** method calls **run** in the **Thread** class. The **myT Thread** is not started.

Question 2

> Which of the following methods are **static** methods of the **Thread** class?
> [Check all correct answers]
>
> ❏ a. **sleep(long msec);**
>
> ❏ b. **yield();**
>
> ❏ c. **wait();**
>
> ❏ d. **notifyAll();**

Answers a and b are correct. As far as answer a, the **sleep** method is a static method of the **Thread** class. A typical call would be:

```
Thread.sleep( 1000 );
```

As far as answer b, the **yield** method is a static method of the **Thread** class. A typical call would be:

```
Thread.yield();
```

Answer c is incorrect because **wait** is an instance method of the **Object** class and thus an instance method of **Thread** by inheritance. Answer d is incorrect because **notifyAll** is also an instance method of the **Object** class.

Question 3

> You have an application that executes the following line:
>
> ```
> Thread myT = new Thread();
> ```
>
> Which of the following statements is true?
>
> ○ a. The **Thread myT** is now in a runnable state.
>
> ○ b. The **Thread myT** has the **NORM_PRIORITY** priority.
>
> ○ c. If **myT.start()** is called, the **run** method in the **Thread** class will be executed.
>
> ○ d. If **myT.start()** is called, the **run** method in the calling class will be executed.

Answer c is correct because **myT** is a **Thread** object created without a reference to a **Runnable** object, so the **run** method in the **Thread** class will be executed. Answer a is incorrect because the **Thread** is in the "new" state; **start()** must be called to put it in the runnable state. Answer b is incorrect because the priority will be that inherited from the **Thread** that called the constructor, which may or may not be **NORM_PRIORITY**. Answer d is incorrect because the **Thread** constructor method used did not connect the new **Thread** to a **Runnable** object.

Question 4

> You have written a class extending **Thread** that does time-consuming computations. In the first use of this class in an application, the system locked up for extended periods of time. Obviously, you need to provide a chance for other **Thread**s to run. The following is the **run** method that needs to be modified:
>
> ```
> 1. public void run(){
> 2.    boolean runFlg = true ;
> 3.    while( runFlg ){
> 4.       runFlg = doStuff();
> 5.
> 6.    }
> 7. }
> ```
>
> Which statements could be inserted at line 5 to allow other **Thread**s a chance to run? [Check all correct answers]
>
> ☐ a. **yield();**
>
> ☐ b. **try{ sleep(100); }catch(InterruptedException e){}**
>
> ☐ c. **suspend(100);**
>
> ☐ d. **wait(100);**

Answers a and b are correct. Answer a is correct because **yield** lets the thread-scheduling mechanism run another **Thread**. Answer b is correct because **sleep** allows time for other **Thread**s to run. Answer c is incorrect because there is no such method as **suspend** with a time delay. The **suspend()** method would permanently suspend your **Thread**, and, of course, **suspend** is a deprecated method. Answer d is incorrect because it would not compile as written; calls to **wait** must provide for catching an **InterruptedException**. Furthermore, the call to **wait** would have to be in a **synchronized** code block.

Question 5

The **Object** class has a **wait** method that is used to coordinate access to an object by multiple **Threads**. Which of the following statements about the **wait** method are true? [Check all correct answers]

❑ a. The **wait** method is an instance method of the **Object** class.

❑ b. The **wait** method is a static method of the **Object** class.

❑ c. To call **wait**, a **Thread** must have a lock on the object involved.

❑ d. An object can have only one **Thread** in a waiting state at a time.

Answers a and c are correct. Answer a is correct because **wait** is indeed an instance method. Answer c is correct because if a **Thread** that does not have a lock on an object attempts to **wait**, an **IllegalMonitorStateException** results. Answer b is incorrect because the idea of **wait** is to control access to each individual object; therefore, each object must have its own **wait** method. Answer d is incorrect because any number of **Threads** can be waiting for an object.

Question 6

Java **Thread** A is attached to an object, **B**, which is responsible for writing data to a file. After writing data, **Thread** A calls the following method in object **B**, where it waits until more data is available:

```
1. private void synchronized waitForData(){
2.     try{ wait();
3.     }catch(InterruptedException e) {}
4. }
```

Another **Thread**, executing a method in another object (**C**), needs to wake up **Thread** A. Assuming that object **C** has references to both **Thread** A and object **B**, what code fragments would cause **Thread** A to exit the **waitForData** method? [Check all correct answers]

❑ a. **A.interrupt();**

❑ b. **synchronized(A){ A.notifyAll() ; }**

❑ c. **synchronized(B){ B.notifyAll() ; }**

❑ d. **A.resume();**

Answers a and c are correct. Answer a is correct because this would generate an **InterruptedException**, bringing **Thread** A out of the **wait**. Because line 3 catches this exception, the **Thread** exits the **waitForData** method normally. Answer c is correct because it removes all **Thread**s waiting for object B from the **wait** list, including **Thread** A. Answer b is incorrect because it refers to **Thread** A, not to object B, for which the **Thread** is waiting. Answer d is incorrect because the **resume** method works only with suspended **Thread**s and is a deprecated method.

Question 7

Here is part of the code for a class that implements the **Runnable** interface:

```
1. public class Whiffler extends Object
      implements Runnable {
2.    Thread myT ;
3.    public void start(){
4.      myT = new Thread( this );
5.    }
6.    public void run(){
7.      while( true ){
8.        doStuff();
9.      }
10.     System.out.println("Exiting run");
11.   }
12. // more class code follows....
```

Assume that the rest of the class defines **doStuff**, and so on, and that the class compiles without error. Also assume that a Java application creates a **Whiffler** object and calls the **Whiffler start** method, that no other direct calls to **Whiffler** methods are made, and that the **Thread** in this object is the only one the application creates. Which of the following are correct statements? [Check all correct answers]

❏ a. The **doStuff** method will be called repeatedly.

❏ b. The **doStuff** method will never be executed.

❏ c. The **doStuff** method will execute at least one time.

❏ d. The statement in line 10 will never be reached.

Answers b and d are correct. Answer b is correct because **myT.start()** is never called; the **Thread** never runs. Answer d is correct because **myT.start()** is never called. Answers a and c are incorrect because the **Thread** is never started, so **run** is never executed.

Question 8

Which of the following methods are instance methods of the **Thread** class, excluding any methods deprecated in Java 1.2? [Check all correct answers]

❑ a. **start()**

❑ b. **stop()**

❑ c. **run()**

❑ d. **suspend()**

❑ e. **sleep(long msec)**

❑ f. **toString()**

Answers a, c, and f are correct. Answer a is correct because **start** is an instance method of **Thread** that makes a new **Thread** runnable. Answer c is correct because the **run** method is the key to **Thread** operation. Answer f is correct because all Java objects have a **toString** method. Answer b is incorrect because **stop** is a deprecated method. Answer d is incorrect because **suspend** is a deprecated method (because a suspended **Thread** may retain a lock on an important system object). Answer e is incorrect because **sleep** is a **static** (class) method, not an instance method.

Question 9

You have written an application that can accept orders from multiple sources, each one of which runs in a separate **Thread**. One object in the application is allowed to record orders in a file. This object uses the **recordOrder** method, which is **synchronized** to prevent conflict between **Thread**s.

While **Thread** A is executing **recordOrder**, **Thread**s B and C, in that order, attempt to execute the **recordOrder** method. What happens when **Thread** A exits the **synchronized** method?

○ a. **Thread** B, as the first waiting **Thread**, is allowed to execute the method.

○ b. **Thread** C, as the last waiting **Thread**, is allowed to execute the method.

○ c. One of the waiting **Thread**s will be allowed to execute the method, but you can't be sure which one it will be.

Answer c is correct. You cannot determine which **Thread** will be allowed to execute next. Answers a and b are incorrect because the JVM does not track the order in which **Thread**s attempt to access a locked object.

Question 10

You have created a **TimeOut** class as an extension of **Thread**, the purpose of which is to print a "Time's Up" message if the **Thread** is not interrupted within 10 seconds of being started.

Here is the **run** method that you have coded:

```
1. public void run(){
2.    System.out.println("Start!");
3.    try { Thread.sleep(10000 );
4.      System.out.println("Time's Up!");
5.    }catch(InterruptedException e){
6.      System.out.println("Interrupted!");
7.    }
8. }
```

Given that a program creates and starts a **TimeOut** object, which of the following statements is true?

○ a. Exactly 10 seconds after the **start** method is called, "Time's Up!" will be printed.

○ b. Exactly 10 seconds after "Start!" is printed, "Time's Up!" will be printed.

○ c. The delay between "Start!" being printed and "Time's Up!" will be 10 seconds plus or minus one tick of the system clock.

○ d. If "Time's Up!" is printed, you can be sure that at least 10 seconds have elapsed since "Start!" was printed.

Answer d is correct; it is the only statement that can be made with confidence. Answers a, b, and c are all incorrect because the expiration of a sleep timer does not guarantee that a **Thread** *will* run—only that it *can* run.

Need to Know More?

 Flanagan, David: *Java in a Nutshell, Third Edition.* O'Reilly & Associates, Inc., Sebastopol, CA, 1999. ISBN 1-56592-487-8. This is the most compact desktop reference book documenting the Java language. Documentation of the **Thread** class is in Chapter 12.

 Gamma, Erich, et al. *Design Patterns: Elements of Reusable Object-Oriented Software.* Addison-Wesley, Menlo Park, CA, 1994. ISBN 0-201-63361-2. Often humorously referred to as "Design Patterns by the Gang of Four," this entire book is a resource for inspiration when you are trying to figure out how to apply object orientation to a problem.

 Oaks, Scott, Henry Wong, and Mike Loukides. *Java Threads, Second Edition.* O'Reilly & Associates, Inc., Sebastopol, CA, 1999. ISBN 1-56592-418-5. This is a very useful overview of programming with **Thread**s.

 http://java.sun.com/docs/books/jls/second_edition/html/j.title.doc.html is where the definitive Java language specification document is maintained in HTML form. Parts of the document are also available in PDF form. This document has also been published as ISBN 0-201-31008-2, but most programmers find the online documentation to be sufficient. **Thread**s are covered in Chapter 17.

Standard Library Utility Classes

Terms you'll need to understand:

✓ Wrapper class

✓ **Enumeration**

✓ **Collection**

✓ **Set**

✓ **List**

✓ **Map**

✓ **Iterator**

Techniques you'll need to master:

✓ Using the arithmetic methods in the **Math** class

✓ Using the trigonometry methods in the **Math** class

✓ Converting numeric values to and from **String** objects

✓ Using the wrapper classes

✓ Understanding what the Reflection application programming interface (API) does

✓ Understanding the Collections APIs: **Collection**, **Set**, **List**, **Map**, **SortedSet**, and **SortedMap**

This chapter reviews some of the many utility classes that are in the Java standard library. Java has developed from version 1 to 1.2, so there has been an enormous increase in the number of classes and methods that are considered part of the standard programming library. I can't cover everything, but I will attempt to touch on those topics likely to be on the exam.

Utility Classes in the **java.lang** Package

The Java standard library places a large number of useful classes in the **java.lang** package. This package is automatically imported by the Java compiler for all programs. Because a working knowledge of these classes is essential for any Java programmer, you have probably used many of them already, so the purpose of this section is to review the most important aspects.

The Math Class

The **Math** class provides the usual mathematical functions and defines the commonly used constants, *e* and *pi*, as the **static double** variables **Math.E** and **Math.PI**. All elements of the **Math** class are **static**, so you never create an instance of **Math**. Here are some important points to remember about some of the more commonly used methods:

➤ *The trig functions*—The trigonometric functions take **double** primitive arguments and return **double** results. Angles are *always* expressed in radians.

➤ *The max, min, and abs functions*—These methods (for minimum, maximum, and absolute value) are overloaded, with separate versions for **int, long, float,** and **double** arguments. Remember that integer inputs that are smaller than 32 bits are automatically promoted to **int**.

➤ *The ceil (ceiling) and floor methods*—These take **double** inputs and return **double** values that represent the integers above and below the input, respectively.

➤ *The round method*—This is overloaded, with versions for **float** and **double** inputs that return the closest **int** and **long**, respectively.

➤ *The sqrt (square root) function*—This takes a **double** as an argument and returns a **double** value. Note that if the input is negative, the result is the special NaN (Not a Number) value.

➤ *The random function*—This method returns a **double** primitive randomly distributed between 0.0 and 1.0.

String and StringBuffer

The **String** class occupies a special position in the Java standard library in recognition of the fact that typical programs use text strings extensively. For example, as discussed in Chapter 3, the Java compiler allows the use of the operators + and += in connection with **String** objects. In terms of programming problems, you should always remember that once created, a **String** can't be changed.

You should use the **StringBuffer** class when you need to manipulate character strings efficiently. **StringBuffer** objects automatically expand as necessary, and the contents can be efficiently turned into a **String** when desired.

 Remember that **String** and **StringBuffer** objects deal with 16-bit Unicode characters to support international alphabets. Although you create **String** literals with 8-bit ASCII code, Java automatically converts them to 16-bit Unicode.

Wrapper Classes

Java uses "wrapper" classes to provide a variety of functions related to primitives. The **static** methods of these classes provide many convenient utility functions, such as conversion to and from **String** representation. The **static final** variables of these classes provide useful constants, such as the **MAX_VALUE** constant of the **Integer** class. Table 10.1 shows the Java wrapper classes along with their corresponding primitive variables.

 Because so many of these wrapper classes have only an uppercase initial letter to distinguish them from Java primitives, it is easy to make a mistake. Read the test questions carefully to ensure that you are not treating an object as a primitive or vice versa.

Table 10.1   Wrapper classes and their corresponding primitive variables.

Wrapper Class	Corresponding Java Primitive	Value
Byte	byte	8-bit signed integer
Short	short	16-bit signed integer
Character	char	16-bit unsigned Unicode integer
Integer	int	32-bit signed integer
Long	long	64-bit signed integer
Float	float	32-bit floating-point number
Double	double	64-bit floating-point number
Boolean	boolean	**true** or **false**

General Uses for Wrapper Objects

The wrapper classes let you use the many Java utility classes that manipulate objects for manipulating primitive values. For example, if you are creating a calculator application, you can store intermediate numeric results as **Double** objects on a **Stack**. The operation of Java **Stack** objects is considered later in this chapter.

The Integer Class

Frequently used methods include the following **static** methods that are typically used to turn user input **String**s into **int** primitive values, as shown in the following code:

```
public static int parseInt( String s )
public static int parseInt( String s, int radix )
```

Both of these methods throw a **NumberFormatException** if the input **String** contains any nonnumeric characters. It is easy to confuse these methods with the following, which returns **Integer** objects (when in doubt, check the documentation):

```
public static Integer valueOf( String s )
public static Integer valueOf( String s, int radix )
```

Handy constants for use with integers are provided as final static variables. **Integer.MAX_VALUE** is the largest (positive) value and **Integer.MIN_VALUE** the smallest (most negative) that an **int** primitive can contain.

Other Integer Wrapper Classes

Classes similar to **Integer** are provided to wrap **byte**, **short**, and **long** integer primitives. As you would expect, these classes are named **Byte**, **Short**, and **Long**. Each class provides constants for the largest and smallest value they can contain.

The Character Class

The **Character** class provides many handy character classification static methods, such as **isDigit, isLetter,** and **isJavaIdentifierStart,** which take a **char** primitive and return a **boolean** result depending on the type of character represented.

The float and double Classes

These classes provide wrapper objects for the **float** and **double** primitive values. They also define constants for the special **NEGATIVE_INFINITY, POSITIVE_INFINITY,** and NaN values that can be created by floating-point arithmetic, as discussed in Chapter 3. In the integer classes, **MIN_VALUE** was the most negative number that could be represented, whereas in the floating-point classes, it is the smallest (nonzero) value.

The **Boolean** Class

The **Boolean** class simply provides an object to wrap a **boolean true** or **false** primitive value. To find out the value contained in a **Boolean** object, use the **boolean Value** method.

The **System** and **Runtime** Classes

The intent of the designers of the Java language was to make Java as platform independent as possible. To that end, the **System** and **Runtime** classes were designed to encapsulate the necessary connections to the underlying operating system. All methods and variables in the **System** class are static—you can't create a **System** object. The methods described in the following sections are some of the more useful **System** and **Runtime** methods.

Input and Output with the **System** Class

The **System** class automatically creates a standard input, standard output, and standard error output stream, named **System.in**, **System.out**, and **System.err**, respectively. The **in** stream gets data from the keyboard in applications that do not use a graphical interface. The **out** and **err** streams normally go to the Java console in a Web browser or a DOS window for an application on a Windows system. These three streams can be redirected but only if the security settings allow it.

A Timing Utility

The **System.currentTimeMillis** method returns a **long** primitive that represents the number of milliseconds since 00:00:00 GMT January 1, 1970, a base time commonly used with Unix systems. This is the method to use if you want to time a particular routine, because the **java.util.Date** class is rather clumsy and slow to use.

The Fast **arraycopy** Method

Java operators for working with arrays are inherently slowed by the fact that each array access is checked against the known size of the array. Suppose you needed to make a copy of an array, **myX**, of **int** primitives, known to be **mxX** in size. Doing it this way

```
1. int[] aX = new int[ mxX ];
2. for(int i = 0 ; i < mxX ; i++){ aX[i] = myX[i] ; }
```

would perform array bounds checks in both **aX** and **myX** for every *i* value. Obviously, if a method could first check whether the highest index is legal, all of the other bounds checks would be unnecessary. The **System.arraycopy** method does exactly that and uses optimized native code to do the actual copying. Here is the way the **arraycopy** method would replace line 2 in the preceding example:

```
2. System.arraycopy( myX, 0, aX, 0, mxX ) ;
```

All of the Java classes, such as **StringBuffer** and **Vector**, which expand as needed to hold more elements, use **System.arraycopy** to copy their current contents into enlarged arrays.

Stopping an Application

The **System** class provides the **exit** method to stop the Java Virtual Machine (JVM). It is called with an **int** status code that is returned to the operating system. By convention, a nonzero status indicates that an error has occurred, as shown in the following code fragment:

```
System.exit( status );
```

The **exit** method should not be called in a Java applet. It is the Web browser's responsibility to halt the JVM as needed.

Getting a **Runtime** Reference

A single **Runtime** object is automatically created when a program starts. You can get a reference to it as follows:

```
Runtime rt = Runtime.getRuntime();
```

Many of the **Runtime** methods, such as the garbage collector request (**gc**) are frequently called through the **System** class. **System.gc** actually calls the **Runtime** object's **gc** method. Other handy methods in the **Runtime** class include **totalMemory** and **freeMemory,** which return the total number of bytes the JVM has access to and the amount that is available for new object construction, respectively.

The **java.math** Package

Java 2 includes a **java.math** package with the **BigDecimal** and **BigInteger** classes for arbitrary precision arithmetic. Objects created from these classes can represent numbers with any desired degree of precision, and the methods can conduct any of Java's normal arithmetic operations. The **BigDecimal** methods are used primarily for financial calculations in which the rounding method needs to be specified exactly. **BigInteger** is mostly of interest to programmers doing cryptography.

The Reflection Package

An important innovation that first appeared in Java 1.1 is the Reflection application programming interface (API). Classes in the **java.lang.reflect** package allow a program to discover the variables, methods, and constructors available in any class, and the interfaces implemented. This capability is essential to the JavaBeans concept and to the Serialization API.

Access to class information starts with getting a **Class** object using the static **forName** method in the **java.lang.Class** class, which takes a **String** input, as shown here:

```
1.   Class c = Class.forName( namestr );
```

This object is then used to get instances of the classes in the **java.lang.reflect** package that are specialized for providing information about the individual variables, methods, interfaces, and constructors, as shown in this code fragment:

```
2.   Field[] fields = c.getDeclaredFields();
3.   Method[] methods = c.getDeclaredMethods();
4.   Class[] interfaces = c.getInterfaces();
5.   Constructor[] constructors = c.getDeclaredConstructors();
```

In line 4, the interfaces that a class implements are represented as **Class** objects because interface specifications are compiled to class files. Most programmers do not have to work with the Reflection API directly. The important thing for you to know is that Reflection permits JavaBeans and object serialization.

JavaBeans

The JavaBeans API allows you to create reusable "software components" that can be manipulated in a visual development tool. The usefulness of the "plugging components together to make a program" model of software development is shown by the great success of Visual Basic. With JavaBeans, you can have a rapid development environment and the virtue of Java's true object orientation.

The Reflection API classes and methods permit a development tool to present the programmer with a list of the properties of a JavaBeans component without having access to the source code. This, in turn, makes it feasible for developers to create and sell toolkits of JavaBeans components.

Serialization

Object serialization refers to the ability to write out the complete state of an object to a file or over a network connection to another computer. To re-create the object, the receiving computer takes the class file for the class that the object belongs to and uses the Reflection API to understand how to rebuild the object. The classes **ObjectOutputStream** and **ObjectInputStream**, which perform serialization, are discussed in Chapter 14.

The Serializable Interface

Only objects that implement the **java.io.Serializable** interface can be serialized with the **ObjectOutputStream** and **ObjectInputStream** standard classes. This interface does not define any methods or constants. It just exists to tag an object as being serializable. For Java 2—Java Development Kit 1.2 (JDK 1.2)—a surprisingly large number of classes in the standard library have been made serializable.

Utility Classes in the **java.util** Package

The **java.util** package contains many useful classes. In this section, I will review the most commonly used interfaces and classes.

The **Arrays** Class

The **java.util.Arrays** class is similar in purpose to the **java.lang.Math** class. It contains many static methods for sorting and searching arrays of the Java primitives and arrays of objects. This class can also be used to create array objects and manipulate individual elements.

The **Arrays** class also provides a method for creating a **List** object from the data in an array of objects (but not an array of primitives). **List** is a new interface for collections of objects (which are discussed in "The New Collections" section later in this chapter). Here is an example of this transformation in action:

```
String[] days = { "Mon","Tue","Wed","Thu","Fri","Sat","Sun"};
List dayList = Arrays.asList ( days );
```

However, the **List** that is created simply provides methods for accessing the array as a **List**; it does not create a separate copy of the data.

The **Comparator** Interface

The **Comparator** interface in the **java.util** package allows the programmer to define principles for ordering and comparing custom objects. This means that your custom objects that implement **Comparator** can automatically use all of the sorting and searching methods in the **Arrays** class. All you have to provide is a method named **compare**, which takes two object references, **oA** and **oB**, and returns an integer that is negative, zero, or positive (if **oA** is less than, equal to, or greater than **oB**).

The **Original Collections**

The original classes in the **java.util** package were the only ones for dealing with collections of objects in the initial release of Java. Although simple, they are very powerful, and you will undoubtedly find them used in many code examples. The new Collections API will supplement rather than supplant these original collection classes.

Vector

The **Vector** class holds an array of **Object** references that can automatically grow in size as needed. Because all Java classes inherit from **Object**, you can add any reference to a **Vector**. All methods that retrieve an object are defined as returning **Object**; therefore, you must use a cast to any other reference type, as in the following:

```
int[] xx = ( int[] )myVector.firstElement() ;
```

Various methods provide for retrieving objects by index and for searching. The internal storage order retains the order in which objects are added. All of the **Vector** methods that alter the contents are **synchronized** to coordinate access by multiple threads.

For JDK 1.2 and subsequent releases of Java, several changes were made to the **Vector** class. These changes do not break existing code but add functions to make **Vector** compatible with the new Collections API. In particular, **Vector** now implements the **List** interface (discussed later in this chapter) and has an **AbstractList** parent class.

The Hashtable Object

A **Hashtable** object can store and retrieve "value" objects indexed by "key" objects. **Hashtable** extends **Dictionary**, but for Software Development Kit (SDK) 1.2, **Hashtable** implements the new **Map** interface. **Hashtable** objects are used extensively in Java to associate objects with names efficiently. Although the key objects are frequently **String**s, any non-**null** object can be a key.

For example, this code fragment creates a **Hashtable** and stores a Uniform Resource Locator (URL) **String** with a short **String** as a key:

```
1. Hashtable pageTable = new Hashtable();
2. String page = "http://www.coriolis.com" ;
3. String key = "coriolis";
4. pageTable.put( key, page );
```

As with **Vector**, the methods that retrieve objects from **Hashtable**s are defined as returning an **Object** reference. You have to provide a specific cast that would retrieve the **String** stored in the **Hashtable** under the "coriolis" key, as in the following line:

```
String val = (String)pageTable.get("coriolis");
```

A **Hashtable** can store only one "value" per "key"—if you add a new reference with a duplicate key, the old reference is dropped. The **contains** and **containsKey** methods let you discover whether a given object or key is present. Internally, **Hashtables** store object references according to hashcodes, so if you get an **Enumeration** of all of the stored "value" or "key" objects, the order is not predictable.

The Stack Class

This class, which extends **Vector**, lets you store objects in a last-in/first-out (LIFO) stack. In addition to the **Vector** methods, **push** and **pop** methods let you manipulate the objects on the top of the stack. The following code fragment illustrates the use of a **Stack** of numeric operands (**opStack**) with **Double** wrapper objects in a calculator application:

```
1. double addTopTwo(){
2.   double d1 = ((Double)opStack.pop()).doubleValue() ;
3.   double d2 = ((Double)opStack.pop()).doubleValue()  + d1 ;
4.   opStack.push( new Double( d2 ) );
5.   return d2 ;
6. }
```

The method puts the result back on the **Stack** and returns the value. In this case, we know that **opStack** has only **Double** objects and that at least two objects are on the **Stack**.

The Enumeration Interface

The **Enumeration** interface provides a way to iterate over all of the objects contained in a **Vector, Hashtable,** or **Stack**. For example, if **v** is a **Vector**, the following code would do a **println** for every object contained in the **Vector**:

```
1. for (Enumeration e = v.elements(); e.hasMoreElements(); ){
2.   System.out.println( e.nextElement() ) ;
3. }
```

While an **Enumeration** is in use, nothing can be allowed to modify the underlying **Vector** data because the **Enumeration** is still using it. If you need to continue using the **Vector**, create the **Enumeration** from a clone of the **Vector** as in the following code fragment:

```
1. Vector clonev = (Vector)v.clone();
2. for(Enumeration e = clonev.elements(); e.hasMoreElements();){
3.   System.out.println( e.nextElement() ) ;
4. }
```

The new Collections API provides the **Iterator** interface that is expected to supplant the **Enumeration** interface in most applications. The **Vector, Stack,** and

Hashtable classes have been modified for SDK 1.2 to support both the **Enumeration** and **Iterator** interfaces. This support is accomplished with a new method that creates and returns an **Iterator** object like this:

```
1. // where v is an instance of Vector
2. Iterator isL = v.iterator();
3. while ( isL.hasNext() ) System.out.println( isL.next() ) ;
4. }
```

The **iterator** method used in line 2 is required by the **Collection** interface implemented by **Vector**. The specialized **Iterator** that is returned is created from an inner class. This class is inside the **java.util.AbstractList** class, from which **Vector** inherits.

The New Collections

One of the biggest changes in the Java standard library with the SDK 1.2 release is the introduction of a totally new set of classes and interfaces for dealing with collections of objects. This new Collections API has many benefits for the programmer, primarily as a standard for communication between unrelated toolkits. For example, a database query that results in a **Collection** can cooperate seamlessly with an interface toolkit that expects a **Collection**.

The new classes also cooperate well with each other and with Java arrays. For example, **Collections** can be converted into arrays of objects.

Collections API Interfaces

The basis for the new Collections API is a set of six interfaces that define the basic types. These are supplemented by a set of classes, such as **AbstractCollection**, that implement the interfaces to provide root classes suitable for programmers to extend.

Although a huge number of classes implement these interfaces, the intent of the designers is that most programmers will use the interface methods as much as possible; therefore, you should concentrate on learning the interfaces first.

The Collection Interface

This interface is the root of the Collections API hierarchy and defines the basic functions that all **Collection** classes must provide. The **AbstractCollection** class provides a skeleton set of the interface methods to serve as a starting point for concrete classes. Among other things, the **Collection** interface requires methods for adding, removing, locating, and selecting objects. Classes that implement **Collection** may contain duplicates and **null** values.

The **Set** Interface

A class that implements this interface holds objects in an order that is fixed when the set is created. No duplicates are allowed, and one element, at most, can have the **null** value. The **Set** interface extends the **Collection** interface, so any class that implements **Set** also implements **Collection**.

The **List** Interface

A class that implements this interface holds an ordered collection of objects. The **Vector** class as revised for SDK 1.2 implements the **List** interface. The Abstract Windowing Toolkit (AWT) graphics package also contains a **List** class used for presenting a list of choices. This means you may have to specify the full name **java.awt.List** or **java.util.List** to avoid confusing the compiler. The **List** interface extends the **Collection** interface.

The **Map** Interface

A class that implements **Map** associates "key" objects with "value" objects. Each key must be unique. The **Hashtable** class as modified for SDK 1.2 implements the **Map** interface. The actual order of the keys and values is not specified.

The **SortedSet** Interface

This interface extends the **Set** interface by adding the requirement that the contents be ordered. Only a **SortedSet** can hold objects that implement the **Comparator** interface or that can be compared by an external **Comparator** object.

The **SortedMap** Interface

This interface extends the **Map** interface by adding the requirement that the collection be ordered according to key values.

The **Iterator** Interface

This interface replaces the **Enumeration** interface that was used in Java 1. An object that implements **Iterator** lets the programmer examine every object in a **Collection** in a fixed order. All classes that implement **Collection** must have an **iterator** method that returns an **Iterator** object. The main differences between **Iterator** and **Enumeration** are that **Iterator** has more compact names, and a method that allows the removal of an object from the underlying **Collection**. Table 10.2 summarizes the **Iterator** methods.

Table 10.2 Iterator interface methods.		
Iterator Method	Returns	Replaces Enumeration Method
hasNext	boolean	hasMoreElements
next	Object	nextElement
remove	void	(No equivalent)

Collections API Classes

The SDK 1.3 standard library has a large number of classes that implement the new Collections API interfaces. It is unlikely that you will need to have detailed knowledge of these classes for the exam. For details on these classes, consult the SDK documentation.

The Abstract Classes

These classes provide a barebones implementation of most of the methods required by the various interfaces. This makes it easier for the programmer to extend one of these classes in concrete implementations, as opposed to having to write a custom class implementing all of the required methods:

➤ *AbstractCollection*—This class implements all of the methods of the **Collection** interface except **iterator** and **size**. It is extended by **AbstractList** and **AbstractSet**.

➤ *AbstractList*—This class extends **AbstractCollection** and implements the **List** interface.

➤ *AbstractSet*—This class extends **AbstractCollection** and implements the **Set** interface.

➤ *AbstractMap*—This class implements the **Map** interface.

➤ *AbstractSequentialList*—This class extends the **AbstractList** class, and provides the basis for the **LinkedList** class.

Some Concrete Classes

Finally, it's time for some nonabstract classes. Here is a quick survey of the classes most likely to be useful to the programmer:

➤ *ArrayList*—This class, which extends **AbstractList**, is roughly equivalent to the **Vector** class in the original library. It can expand as needed just like **Vector**. However, it does not use **synchronized** methods, so it is somewhat faster than **Vector**.

➤ *HashMap*—This class extends **AbstractMap** and is similar to **Hashtable** in the original library.

➤ *LinkedList*—This is an implementation of the classic linked list data structure.

➤ *TreeMap*—Extending **AbstractMap** and implementing the **SortedMap** interface, a **TreeMap** object keeps entries in ascending key order.

The Collections Class

Now here is a source of potential confusion! The **java.util.Collections** class—not to be confused with the **java.util.Collection** interface—implements a number of utility methods that can be applied to objects that implement the various interfaces in the Collections API. For example, there are methods for sorting objects contained in a **List** and for searching for an object in an ordered collection.

Probably the most significant methods in the **Collections** class are used to wrap objects that implement the various Collections API interfaces in code that enforces **synchronized** access to the data. For example, if you have an object named **myMap** that implements **Map**, the following code will give you a reference to a new **Map** that accesses the existing data but with **synchronized** methods:

```
Map safeMap = Collections.synchronizedMap( myMap );
```

Performance Considerations

In Java 1.1 and earlier versions, most of the methods in the **Vector, Hashtable,** and **Stack** classes were **synchronized** to prevent simultaneous modification by more than one **Thread,** which would lead to unpredictable results. The disadvantage of synchronization is the extra overhead imposed by the process that obtains and releases object locks. The new **Collections** classes do not use synchronization; instead, they throw a **ConcurrentModificationException** if more than one **Thread** tries to modify a **Collection**.

Thus, it is up to the programmer to decide whether a risk exists and make provisions for preventing simultaneous modification. As previously described in "The New Collections" section earlier in this chapter, the **Collections** class provides a set of methods that wrap the unsynchronized collections in an object that synchronizes all of the access methods. There is one of each of these methods for each interface. However, an **Iterator** derived from the synchronized collection has to be protected separately by the programmer's code, as shown here:

```
/* In the following, List syncL is a local reference used to get
   an Iterator and L is a reference to an object that implements
   the List interface The reference that is returned is to a static
   nested class named SynchronizedList in the Collections class,
```

```
   but that class has only package visibility, so I have to refer
   to it by the List interface
*/
List syncL = Collections.synchronizedList( L )
// Now all normal list methods should use syncL to be safe;
// however, if you need an Iterator, it should be synchronized
// on the list separately as follows
 synchronized( syncL ) {
     Iterator isL = syncL.iterator();
     while( isL.hasNext() ) doSomething( isL.next() );
 } // end synchronized access
```

Practice Questions

Question 1

You need a method to take a **double** primitive value and return the square root, ignoring the sign. Which one of these options is correct?

○ a.

```
double mySqrt( double val ){
      return Math.sqrt( val );
   }
```

○ b.

```
double mySqrt( double val ){
      return Math.sqrt( Math.abs( val ) ) ;
   }
```

○ c.

```
double mySqrt( double val ){
      Math myM = new Math();
      return myM.sqrt( myM.abs( val )) ;
   }
```

Answer b correctly uses the **Math static** methods to take the absolute value of the input before passing it to the square root function. Answer a is incorrect because it does not take into account the possibility of a negative input. Answer c is incorrect because it attempts to create and use a **Math** object, which is not possible.

Question 2

Trying to compile the following method causes an error:

```
1. public void status( Boolean flag ){
2.   if( flag ) {
3.       System.out.println("TRUE!");
4.   }
5.   else System.out.println("FALSE!");
6. }
```

Which of the following suggested changes will allow the method to compile? [Check all correct answers]

❑ a. Change line 2 to read:

```
2.   if( flag.equals( true ) ){
```

❑ b. Change line 1 to read:

```
1. public void status( boolean flag ){
```

❑ c. Change line 2 to read:

```
2.   if( flag.booleanValue()){
```

Answers b and c are correct. Answer b is correct because it changes the input parameter to the primitive **boolean** type expected by the **if** statement. Answer c is correct because it gets the **boolean** value contained in the **Boolean** object. Answer a is incorrect because the **equals** method requires an object reference, and **true** is a **boolean** primitive value.

Question 3

> Which statement about the **java.lang.System** class is correct?
>
> ○ a. You must initialize **System** with a path and file name if you want to use the **System.err** output.
>
> ○ b. The **System.timer** method allows timing processes to the nearest microsecond.
>
> ○ c. The **System.arraycopy** method works only with arrays of primitives.
>
> ○ d. The **System.exit** method takes an **int** primitive parameter.

Answer d is correct. The **exit** method expects an **int** primitive, which by convention is 0 if no error has occurred. Answer a is incorrect because **System.err** is automatically created when your program starts. Answer b is incorrect because no such method exists. Answer c is incorrect because **arraycopy** can copy arrays of primitives or object references.

Question 4

> Which statement about the **java.lang.Runtime** class is incorrect?
>
> ○ a. A **Runtime** object is created by the following code:
>
> ```
> Runtime rt = Runtime.getRuntime();
> ```
>
> ○ b. There is a **Runtime** method to request that the JVM start garbage collection.
>
> ○ c. The following **Runtime** method call returns the approximate amount of free memory available to the JVM:
>
> ```
> long avail =
>         Runtime.getRuntime().freeMemory();
> ```

Answer a is correct because the statement is in error: A **Runtime** object is created when the program is started, and the **getRuntime** method simply returns a reference to it. Answer b is incorrect because the statement is correct. Answer c is incorrect because the statement shows the correct way to call the **Runtime** **freeMemory** method.

Question 5

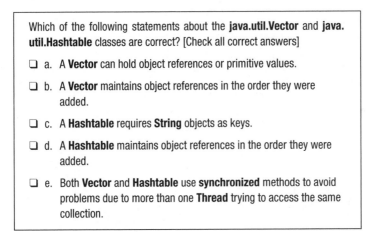

Which of the following statements about the **java.util.Vector** and **java. util.Hashtable** classes are correct? [Check all correct answers]

❑ a. A **Vector** can hold object references or primitive values.

❑ b. A **Vector** maintains object references in the order they were added.

❑ c. A **Hashtable** requires **String** objects as keys.

❑ d. A **Hashtable** maintains object references in the order they were added.

❑ e. Both **Vector** and **Hashtable** use **synchronized** methods to avoid problems due to more than one **Thread** trying to access the same collection.

Answers b and e are correct. Answer b is correct because **Vector** objects maintain the order in which objects are added. Answer e is correct because this is one of the major distinctions between the original and new Collections API classes. Answer a is incorrect because only object references can be held in a **Vector**. If you need to store primitive values, you have to use the wrapper classes to create objects. Answer c is incorrect because although keys are frequently **Strings**, they can be any object. Answer d is incorrect because the order of items in a **Hashtable** is not predictable.

Question 6

In a celestial navigation application, you need a method to take a sextant reading in degrees and return the tangent of the angle. Which of the following options will do the job?

○ a.
```
double calcTan( double angle ){
return Math.tan( angle * Math.PI /180.0 );
}
```

○ b.
```
double calcTan( double angle ){
return Math.tan( angle * PI /180.0 ) ;
}
```

○ c.
```
double calcTan( double angle ){
return Math.tan( angle );
}
```

○ d.
```
double calcTan( double angle ){
Math myM = new Math( );
return myM.tan( angle * (myM.PI /180.0));
}
```

Answer a is correct because it recognizes that all **Math** trig functions take angle inputs in radians and uses the **PI** constant to convert degrees to radians. Answer b is incorrect because it does not address the **PI** constant correctly. Answer c is incorrect because the question specified that the angle was in degrees and the trig functions require radians. Answer d is incorrect because it attempts to create a **Math** object, which is not possible.

Question 7

The new Collections API introduces a number of interfaces and classes to the Java standard library. Which of the following are interfaces? [Check all correct answers]

❑ a. **java.util.List**

❑ b. **java.util.TreeMap**

❑ c. **java.util.AbstractList**

❑ d. **java.util.SortedMap**

❑ e. **java.util.Iterator**

❑ f. **java.util.Collections**

Answers a, d, and e are correct. These are the names of interfaces. Answer b is incorrect because **TreeMap** is a class that implements the **SortedMap** interface. Answer c is incorrect because **AbstractList** is an abstract class that implements the **List** interface. Answer f is incorrect because **Collections** (with a final s) is a utility class that you must distinguish from the **Collection** (no final s) interface.

Question 8

The **java.lang.reflect.Method** class is used to obtain information on the methods available in a given class. How do you get a **Method** object?

○ a. From any instance of the class to be examined

○ b. From a **Class** object created using the name of the class to be examined

○ c. From a **Reflect** object created using the name of the class to be examined

Answer b is correct. You obtain an array of **Method** objects from the **Class** object that represents the class to be examined. Answer a is incorrect because there is no method in the **Object** class to obtain a **Method** object. Answer c is incorrect because there is no such thing as a **Reflect** object.

Question 9

> Which class in the new Collections API is most similar to the **Vector** class?
>
> ○ a. **LinkedList**
>
> ○ b. **TreeSet**
>
> ○ c. **AbstractCollection**
>
> ○ d. **ArrayList**
>
> ○ e. **Collections**

Answer d is correct. **ArrayList** is similar in function to the **Vector** class. Answer a is incorrect because **LinkedList** provides many functions in excess of those in **Vector**. Answer b is incorrect because a **TreeSet** has restrictions on duplicated items that do not occur in **Vector**. Answer c is incorrect because **AbstractCollection** is an abstract class. Answer e is incorrect because the **Collections** class is a utility class used, among other things, for sorting and transforming collections.

Question 10

> An object of the **Hashtable** class can store and retrieve object references based on associated "key" objects. Which interface does **Hashtable** implement?
>
> ○ a. **SortedMap**
>
> ○ b. **Map**
>
> ○ c. **List**
>
> ○ d. **SortedSet**

Answer b is correct. **Hashtable** implements the **Map** interface. Answer a is incorrect because **SortedMap** would require that **Hashtable** impose a sorting order on keys, which it does not. Answer c is incorrect because the **List** interface does not require keys to recover stored objects. Answer d is incorrect because a **SortedSet** is a completely different kind of collection than **Hashtable**.

Need to Know More?

 Flanagan, David. *Java in a Nutshell, Third Edition*. O'Reilly & Associates, Inc., Sebastopol, CA, 1999. ISBN 1-56592-487-8. This is the most compact desktop reference book documenting the Java language. Chapter 23 has a good summary of the Collections API classes.

 http://java.sun.com/docs/books/tutorial/collections/ contains an online Java tutorial that has a special section on the Collections API classes. You can also download the entire tutorial.

 http://java.sun.com/products/javabeans/ is where you can find the Bean Development Kit (BDK), which provides a testing environment for JavaBeans component development and a number of sample beans that you can use as a basis for your own bean development.

Java AWT Components

Terms you'll need to understand:

✓ **Component** class

✓ AWT component peer

✓ **Container** class

✓ **Frame** class

✓ **Panel** class

✓ **MenuItem** class

✓ **Color** class

✓ **Font** class

✓ **FontMetrics** class

✓ **Graphics** class

Techniques you'll need to master:

✓ Controlling user access to interface elements

✓ Understanding the Abstract Windowing Toolkit (AWT) class hierarchy

✓ Understanding how to control the appearance of text

✓ Understanding how to control the placement and appearance of user controls

The Abstract Windowing Toolkit (AWT) library is the essential basis for creating graphical user interfaces (GUIs) in Java. It will take several chapters to cover the topics you need to understand so that you can effectively build GUIs in Java. This chapter concentrates on the AWT component library. Chapter 12 covers layout managers and interface-building topics, and Chapter 13 covers handling user events.

Overview of the AWT Packages

The original release of Java used a relatively simple set of classes to create user interfaces. As people tried to develop more complex user interfaces, the deficiencies in these classes became apparent. The 1.1 release of Java fixed some of the problems, especially those stemming from the crude interface event handling of the 1 release. This improved event handling is used in the Java 1.2 and later Software Development Kit (SDK) releases.

The main additions to the AWT library for the Java SDK 1.2 are designed to provide much greater flexibility and power than available in previous versions, but they still rely on basic AWT concepts. There are now 12 related **java.awt** packages; the following list gives a short description of each:

➤ *java.awt*—The set of classes used to create user interfaces in the original release of Java. Although many simple concepts in the original AWT now have more advanced capabilities in additional packages, the original classes still work.

➤ *java.awt.color*—Advanced color-manipulation classes that allow you to represent and convert colors in a variety of standard forms.

➤ *java.awt.datatransfer*—Classes that facilitate cut-and-paste operations between Java components and with native applications. Note that Multipurpose Internet Mail Extensions (MIME) types play an important role.

➤ *java.awt.dnd*—Classes to support a drag-and-drop user interface.

➤ *java.awt.event*—Classes that encapsulate and process the huge variety of events that can occur in a program with a GUI.

➤ *java.awt.font*—Classes that provide advanced text layout and rendering with techniques much more powerful than those available with the original AWT. These techniques provide better support for international alphabets and symbol systems.

➤ *java.awt.geom*—Classes that support advanced 2D drawing capabilities.

➤ *java.awt.im*—Contains the **InputContext** class, which manages communication between user input events and text-editing components, and the **InputMethodHighlight** class, which handles text highlighting in a variety of languages.

➤ *java.awt.im.spi*—Interfaces for further extension of input methods.

➤ *java.awt.image*—This package, which was in the original Java release, has been greatly expanded with a variety of image-manipulation classes.

➤ *java.awt.image.renderable*—A group of classes to make image rendering more flexible.

➤ *java.awt.print*—A group of classes that supports flexible printing from Java applications.

The Basic AWT Classes

One of the reasons for the rise in popularity of object-oriented programming is the ease with which screen objects can have corresponding software objects. The AWT classes illustrate very clearly the virtues of object-oriented programming. By basing almost all of the display classes on the **Component** class, the designers greatly simplified the interface designer's task. All of the graphical objects that inherit from **Component** can use the same method calls for basic functions.

The **Component** Class

Objects derived from **Component** have a graphical representation on the screen and can interact with the user. **Component** is an **abstract** class, which is extended by a large number of classes in various packages.

To rapidly get Java 1 available on several different operating systems, the designers used the facilities of the underlying operating system as much as possible. Thus, to show a **Button** on the screen, Java has the operating system create a corresponding object. These native operating system objects that correspond to Java objects are called *peers*, and the resulting combination of a Java object and an operating system object is called a *heavyweight* component. As a Java programmer, you cannot directly manipulate the AWT peer objects.

There are many more methods in the **Component** class than I have room to discuss here. The methods discussed in the next few sections, arranged in functional groups, are those you are most likely to use. In general, if you need a way to control the appearance or behavior of a screen object in the **java.awt** package, start your search by looking at the methods in the **Component** class.

In the following discussion of **Component** methods, I'll show the method return type, name, and parameter list as they appear in the javadoc documentation. I use the word "component" to refer to any graphical object that has **Component** as an ancestor.

Controlling Position and Size

Component objects always occupy a rectangle on the screen. Position is always relative to the containing object, not to the overall screen. Note that if a layout manager (discussed in Chapter 12) is controlling a container, the methods discussed here may be ineffective. The following list shows the commonly used methods related to component position and size:

➤ *void setBounds(int x, int y, int width, int height)*—Sets the location of the upper-left corner of the component and its width and height in pixels

➤ *void setBounds(Rectangle rec)*—A version of **setBounds** that takes a **Rectangle** as input

➤ *void setLocation(int x, int y)*—Moves the component

➤ *void setLocation(Point pt)*—A version of **setLocation** that takes a **Point** as input

➤ *void setSize(int width, int height)*—Resizes the component

➤ *void setSize(Dimension dim)*—Resizes the **Component** using a **Dimension** object

➤ *Rectangle getBounds()*—Returns a **Rectangle** object with the component's location and size

➤ *boolean contains(int x, int y)*—Returns **true** if this point is inside the component

➤ *boolean contains(Point pt)*—A version that uses a **Point** object

 Screen positions are always measured in pixels from the upper-left corner of the container. The upper-left pixel is at x = 0 and y = 0, with x increasing to the right and y increasing downward. For an independent window, the measurement is from the upper-left corner of the screen.

Controlling Appearance

Each component has a set of defaults for background and foreground colors and for the font to be used. If you don't set these, the default values of the container this component is in will be used when a font or color is required. If you don't specify any appearance factors, the Java Virtual Machine (JVM) will provide defaults. Not all components will use the background color you set because the appearance of these heavyweight components depends on the operating system peer. The following list shows how to set appearance features:

➤ *void setBackground(Color c)*—The default background color when the component is repainted. The **Color** object is discussed later in this chapter.

➤ *void setForeground(Color c)*—Sets the default color to be used to draw lines or text in this component.

➤ *void setFont(Font f)*—Sets the default font to be used when you are drawing text.

➤ *void setCursor(Cursor cr)*—Establishes the cursor image that will be displayed when the cursor is over the component.

Controlling User Access and Visibility

In user interface design, you will frequently want to permit the use of **Button** objects and other controls according to the program state. For example, you might want to enable a Save button only when data has been modified. The following list shows methods that control access and visibility:

➤ *void setEnabled(boolean flag)*—By default, components are enabled when they are created, but you can use this method to disable and re-enable them. An enabled component can respond to user input and generate events. For components such as buttons, the enabled state is reflected in the way they are displayed.

➤ *void setVisible(boolean flag)*—If the flag is **true**, the component is shown; if it is **false**, it is not displayed. This replaces the **show** method used in Java 1.

Figure 11.1 shows **java.awt.Label** and **java.awt.Button** objects in their enabled and disabled states on a Windows NT system. On another operating system, the appearance might be different.

Generating Events

Component objects can generate a variety of events based on the user's actions with the mouse and keyboard. Event handling is discussed in detail in Chapter 13. The important thing to note here is that the programmer has control over which events a **Component** will generate. The **AWTEvent** class defines "event mask" constants for each of the various types of events that a **Component** can generate. You can combine these into a single **long** primitive that has a bit set for

Figure 11.1   The appearance of enabled and disabled **Label** and **Button** objects.

each type of event to be generated, as shown in the following code fragment:

```
long mask = AWTEvent.ACTION_EVENT_MASK |
                AWTEvent.FOCUS_EVENT_MASK;
```

The methods that use this mask are:

➤ *void disableEvents(long bitmask)*—Generation of the events specified in the bitmask is turned off.

➤ *void enableEvents(long bitmask)*—Generation of the events specified in the bitmask is turned on.

The Subclasses of Component

The following classes are those most commonly used in the **java.awt** package that extend **Component** (the Swing classes that are in other packages also extend **Component**, but they are not covered on the exam):

➤ *Button*—This class creates a labeled button in the style of the underlying operating system. Clicking on a **Button** creates an **ActionEvent**.

➤ *Canvas*—This class is typically extended to create a screen component with a custom **paint** method to generate a display.

➤ *Checkbox*—This class creates the typical checkbox, which displays an on or off state. **Checkbox** objects controlled by a **CheckboxGroup** appear as radio buttons.

➤ *Choice*—A **Choice** object presents a pop-up-style menu of choices.

➤ *Container*—This class is the parent of a range of AWT components that can hold a number of components and control their display. See "The **Container** Class" section later in this chapter for an extended discussion.

➤ *Label*—A **Label** object displays a single line of noneditable text.

➤ *List*—A **List** object presents a scrollable list of items that the user can select. The programmer can control whether multiple selections are allowed.

➤ *Scrollbar*—This class can be used to create a vertical or horizontal scrollbar in the style of the underlying operating system.

➤ *TextComponent*—This class is extended by **TextField** and **TextArea**, which are the classes actually used in interface design. A **TextField** object allows editing of a single line of text, whereas **TextArea** handles multiple line input. The "Text Entry Classes" section later in this chapter discusses these further.

Text Entry Classes

Two AWT components are designed for user text entry: **TextField** for a single line and **TextArea** for multiple lines. Both of these are extensions of the **TextComponent** class, which contains many of the methods you will need to control user text input. Some of the most useful are as follows:

➤ *void setEditable(boolean flag)*—Use this method to allow or prevent user editing of the displayed text.

➤ *void setText(String s)*—The current contents of the field are replaced with this **String**. To clear the field, set the text to "" (the empty **String**).

➤ *String getText()*—This method returns a **String** that represents the entire contents of the component. The size of the largest **String** a **TextComponent** can hold depends on the underlying operating system.

➤ *String getSelectedText()*—This method returns the text that the user has highlighted.

 Don't confuse the **setEditable** method with the **setEnabled** method in the **Component** class. A **TextComponent** can be *enabled* but not *editable*, in which case the user can select text and move the cursor around in the field but cannot change the text.

Figure 11.2 shows two **TextField** objects, both of which are enabled. The right field shows an editing cursor that can be moved through the text with the keyboard arrow keys, but the text can't be changed.

Interfaces Implemented by Component

The following interfaces are implemented by the **java.awt.Component** class and thus by all subclasses of **Component**:

➤ *ImageObserver*—This interface notifies a component about changes in **Image** information. This is necessary because Java can accomplish image loading as a background process that may not have a complete image ready when a component is ready to be painted. This interface requires the **imageUpdate** method, which is called by the process that loads an image to report status changes.

➤ *MenuContainer*—This interface provides methods used to coordinate with menu-related classes. You are not likely to have to deal with these methods directly.

Enabled and Editable	Enabled, not Editable

Figure 11.2 Two apparently identical text fields, only one of which is editable.

➤ *Serializable*—This interface tags objects that can be saved to a file or other output stream. The significance for programmers is that the entire collection of objects that make up a user interface can be written to a file with all of their state data intact and later read back in to reconstruct the interface.

The **Container** Class

The **Container** class adds to **Component** the capability of containing other AWT graphical components. The main function of a **Container** is to maintain and control a list of the components it contains. The order of components in the list is determined by the order of addition unless you use one of the **add** methods that specifies an absolute list position.

 Be sure you can distinguish between the functions provided by a **Container** and those provided by a **LayoutManager** object. **LayoutManager**s are covered in Chapter 12.

Container Methods

The methods that **Container** adds to **Component** generally have to do with adding, removing, positioning, and locating components. Here are some of the most frequently used:

➤ *void add(Component c)*—Adds this component to the internal list. Alternate forms of this method provide for specifying various constraints on the layout that affect this component.

➤ *void remove(Component c)*—Removes this component from the list.

➤ *void setLayout(LayoutManager m)*—Puts this **LayoutManager** object in charge of laying out the contained components. **LayoutManager** objects are discussed in Chapter 12.

➤ *void validate()*—Causes the **Container** to lay out all of the contained components. This is usually called after components have been added or removed.

➤ *int getComponentCount()*—Returns the number of components in this container.

➤ *Component getComponentAt(int x, int y)*—Returns a reference to the component located at this position relative to the container.

The Subclasses of **Container**

Container was an **abstract** class in Java 1 and 1.1, but for the Java SDK 1.2, it is no longer declared **abstract**. Nevertheless, you are more likely to be using one of the following classes in an actual program rather than **Component** (note that a *top-level* container is one that can create an independent window):

➤ *java.awt.Panel*—The **Panel** class provides the simplest AWT container.

➤ *java.awt.ScrollPane*—A **ScrollPane** object provides scrolling action for the display of a single component that is larger than the available display area.

➤ *java.applet.Applet*—The **Applet** class is an extension of **Panel** with a provision for interacting with a Web browser so that it can be a top-level container.

➤ *java.awt.Window*—A **Window** object is a top-level window with no borders and no menu bar or window controls.

➤ *java.awt.Dialog*—This is a top-level window with a title bar typically used to get user input. Although a **Dialog** forms an independent window, it must have a **Frame** as its owner.

➤ *java.awt.Frame*—This extension of **Window** adds a title bar, menu bar, and window control widgets. A **Frame** must be the top-level container for applications. Being able to contain a menu bar is a special property of a **Frame**; this property is not related to its ability to contain **Component**s.

The **Container**-Contents Relationship

The relationship of a **Container** to its contents forms a sort of hierarchy of relationships that may lead to some confusion. For example, if you have a **Button** object in a **Panel**, the following code

```
Container c = myButton.getParent() ;
```

returns a reference to the **Panel**, not the parent class of **myButton**. You may also see this relationship referred to as the **Panel** *that owns* **myButton**. This terminology of *owner* extends to independent windows, such as **Dialog** objects. If an application based on **Frame** creates a **Dialog**, it is said that the owner of the **Dialog** is the **Frame**, although they are two separate windows.

By default, **Component** objects inherit the colors and **Font** properties of the container they are in. This means that you don't have to set the font style for every component in an application—just set it for the primary container and the rest of the interface will use that font.

The **Window**-Related Classes

The **Window** class extends **Container** and creates top-level window objects that do not have a title bar, a menu bar, or window controls. The classes in the **java.awt** package that extend **Window** are **Frame** and **Dialog**. Although a **Window** is an independent top-level window, to properly interface with the operating system, it must be constructed from a **Frame** or another **Window**. The constructors for a **Window** are:

➤ *Window(Frame owner)*—Creates a new **Window** "owned" by the **Frame**. The new **Window** is not initially visible. When you are ready for the **Window** to be displayed, call the **show** method.

➤ *Window(Window owner)*—Creates a new **Window** "owned" by another **Window**.

Window objects can be sized and moved with the basic **Component** methods, but note that the positioning will be relative to the upper-left corner of the screen.

Creating a Frame

The **java.awt.Frame** class is the starting point for creating a graphical application using the AWT components. A Frame creates a window that has a title bar and a border, and may optionally host a menu bar. Listing 11.1 shows the minimum code for creating a **Frame**, and Figure 11.3 shows the resulting window.

Listing 11.1   Source code for a simple **Frame**.

```
1. import java.awt.* ;
2. import java.awt.event.* ;
3. class FrameDemo extends Frame {
4.   public static void main(String[] args ){
5.     new FrameDemo().show();
6.   }
7.   // constructor for FrameDemo
8.   FrameDemo(){
9.     super("Example Frame");
10.    setBounds( 10, 10, 200, 150 );
11.    addWindowListener( new WindowAdapter(){
12.      public void  windowClosing( WindowEvent e ){
13.          setVisible( false );
14.          dispose();
15.          System.exit(0);
16.      }
17.    } ); // end statement starting on line 11
18.  } // end constructor
19. } // end class
```

Here are the important points to note about the **FrameDemo** code:

➤ The constructor in line 9 sets the title for the **Frame**. There is also a constructor without a title, in which case the title bar is empty.

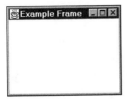

Figure 11.3   The appearance of a **FrameDemo** application on a Windows NT system.

➤ The call to **setBounds** in line 10 establishes the size and position of the **Frame** relative to the upper-left corner of the screen. Without this call, a **Frame** barely large enough to show the window controls would show at the upper-left corner of the screen.

➤ The statement that starts in line 11 and continues to line 17 creates an anonymous inner class extending **WindowAdapter** and installing it as a **WindowListener**. Event listeners are discussed in Chapter 13; for now, note that this listener is what allows the window to be closed when the user clicks on the close control. The **windowClosing** method is the last chance for the programmer to warn the user to save modified data, close open databases, and generally ensure correct termination of the program.

Creating a Dialog

The **java.awt** package provides only one standard dialog box, the **FileDialog** class. This class creates a file selection dialog in the style of the underlying operating system. A **FileDialog** is always *modal*—while it is being shown, the remainder of the application cannot receive user events.

The **java.awt.Dialog** class can be used to create either a modal or nonmodal dialog. The main limitation on uses of a **Dialog** is that all constructors must have a **Frame** or another **Dialog**, so an application cannot be based on the **Dialog** class. You might think that this restriction prevents you from using a **Dialog** from a Java **Applet** because an **Applet** is not a descendent of **Frame**, but for **Applet**s, the Web browser constitutes a **Frame**. You can use code similar to the following to locate that **Frame** and use it to construct a **Dialog**:

```
public void showDlg(){
  Container c = getParent();
  while( c != null ){
    if( c instanceof Frame ){
      myDlg = new TestDialog((Frame) c );
      myDlg.show(); return ;
    }
    c = c.getParent(); // try next parent
  }
}
```

The Menu-Related Classes

Adding menus to an application requires a class that implements the **MenuContainer** interface. The classes in the **java.awt** package that implement **MenuContainer** are **Component, Frame, Menu,** and **MenuBar,** so practically anything on the screen can host a menu.

The classes that create menus are the only screen display classes that do not extend **java.awt.Component.** Here is the hierarchy of the menu-related classes:

```
java.lang.Object
  |
  +— java.awt.MenuShortcut
  |
  +— java.awt.MenuComponent
       |
       +— java.awt.MenuBar
       |
       +— java.awt.MenuItem
            |
            +— java.awt.CheckboxMenuItem
            |
            +— java.awt.Menu
                 |
                 +— java.awt.PopupMenu
```

To create a traditional pull-down menu attached to a frame, you create a **MenuBar** object and add **Menu** objects that contain **MenuItem** objects. It is the **MenuItem** object that registers a mouse click and creates an **ActionEvent.** The following code fragment, when inserted in the **FrameDemo** constructor after line 10 in Listing 11.1, creates a pull-down menu system, as shown in Figure 11.4 (note that I have indented the statements to indicate how the objects created are related to the menu structure).

```
MenuBar mb = new MenuBar();
  Menu fileMenu = new Menu("File");
    fileMenu.add( new MenuItem("New") );
    fileMenu.addSeparator();
    fileMenu.add( new MenuItem("Exit") );
mb.add( fileMenu );
  Menu helpMenu = new Menu("Help");
    helpMenu.add( new MenuItem("About") );
mb.add( helpMenu );
setMenuBar( mb );
```

Here is a quick summary of the menu-related classes in the **java.awt** package:

➤ *MenuBar*—A **MenuBar** organizes **Menu** objects to create the familiar drop-down menu interface. Only a **Frame** can host a **MenuBar**.

➤ *PopUpMenu*—A **PopUpMenu** can be attached to any screen component.

➤ *Menu*—A **Menu** object creates a single drop-down menu such as the File menu in Figure 11.4. Everything in a **Menu** must be a **MenuItem** or **CheckboxMenuItem**.

➤ *MenuItem*—This object represents the thing that is selected in a **Menu**. **MenuItem**s are also used to create separators.

➤ *CheckboxMenuItem*—This descendent of **MenuItem** has a checked or unchecked state.

➤ *MenuShortcut*—**MenuShortcut** objects represent keyboard alternatives to activate a **MenuItem**.

Geometric Utility Classes

The **java.awt** package provides several utility classes that encapsulate geometric data related to screen displays. In earlier versions of Java, all of these classes used only 32-bit integers. With the expanded graphics capabilities of Java 1.2, some methods that set or get floating-point dimensions were added. However, the constructors expect **int** values. The following list shows the geometric data classes:

➤ *Dimension*—**Dimension** objects are typically used to encapsulate the width and height of components. These measurements are always in pixels.

➤ *Point*—**Point** objects encapsulate the x and y axis positions of a point in 2D space.

➤ *Rectangle*—A **Rectangle** object has an x and y position for the upper-left corner plus a width and height.

Figure 11.4   A **Frame** with an added **MenuBar** that contains two drop-down menus.

➤ *Polygon*—A **Polygon** object represents a closed two-dimensional region composed of an arbitrary number of lines that connect points in a list of coordinates. The first and final points in the list are joined to complete the polygon. **Polygon** objects can be constructed from arrays of x and y point coordinates or by adding individual points to an existing object. **Polygon** objects are used to define arbitrary regions in display space.

AWT Classes Related to Graphics

The **java.awt** package has a large number of classes related to creating a graphical display. Here is a quick tour of the classes you will most likely use:

➤ *java.awt.Color*—A **Color** object represents a screen color with red, green, and blue intensity values plus an opacity, or alpha, component. The **Color** class also provides common colors as constants.

➤ *java.awt.Cursor*—This class can be used to create either a custom or standard cursor bitmap object. You can define an image source and active point, but only in the format used by the underlying operating system. Any **Component** can have a **Cursor** assigned for use when the cursor is over the **Component**.

➤ *java.awt.Font*—A **Font** object encapsulates a single font face and size. A **Font** is attached to a **Graphics** object to draw text in a particular style and size.

➤ *java.awt.FontMetrics*—This class is used to generate information about how a particular **Font** will appear on the screen; for example, it determines the number of pixels a given **String** will consume.

➤ *java.awt.Graphics*—This is the base class for all graphics contexts that allow a program to draw on the screen. A subclass of the **abstract Graphics** class will be provided by the JVM for a particular operating system.

➤ *java.awt.Graphics2D*—This extension of the **Graphics** class adds a number of drawing methods that are a substantial advance over the original Java capabilities. Various methods provide for rendering two-dimensional shapes and greater control over display of text and images.

➤ *java.awt.GraphicsEnvironment*—This contains information on the fonts and graphics devices available to a Java program in a particular operating system environment.

The Font Class

Fonts are characterized by a font family name, such as Helvetica or Times Roman; a style, such as bold or italic; and a point size. In earlier releases of Java, font selection was restricted to a few standard fonts, but in the SDK 1.2 release, the programmer has access to all of the fonts on the host operating system. Although it's beyond the scope of this book to discuss how to take full advantage of these new capabilities, I do cover some general points here. You create a new **Font** object with a constructor that takes a font name, a style constant, and a point size, as in the following example:

```
Font myFont = new Font( "Serif", Font.BOLD, 50 ) ;
```

In Java 1, the font names used included "TimesRoman," "Helvetica," and "Courier," but to avoid copyright problems, Java 1.1 preferred to use "Serif," "SansSerif," and "Monospaced," respectively.

To control the drawing of text on the screen, it is necessary to get a **FontMetrics** object for the **Font** in use. Use of a **FontMetrics** object is illustrated in the next section.

The Graphics Class

To help you understand how the **Graphics** class is used, I'll look at the sequence of events that occurs when for some reason a screen object derived from the **Component** class must be redrawn. First, the JVM generates a **Graphics** object that contains the following information:

➤ The **Component** to draw on and its screen location.

➤ A "clipping" **Rectangle,** which limits the area to be drawn in. This is never larger than the **Component,** so a **Component** can never draw out of its own screen area. If part of the **Component** is covered by another window, the clipping rectangle reflects that.

➤ The current drawing **Color,** set to the default foreground color of the **Component.** A **Graphics** object knows about only one **Color** at a time.

➤ The current **Font** attached to the **Component.** If you have not specified a **Font** for a **Component,** the **Font** attached to its container is used, so there is never a situation in which a **Graphics** object does not have a **Font.**

Next, the JVM calls the **update** method of the **Component** to be redrawn. The default functionality of this method is to clear the rectangle occupied by the **Component** using the **Component's** background **Color,** and then to call the **paint** method, as shown here:

```
public void update(Graphics g) {
  g.clearRect(0, 0, width, height);
  paint(g);
}
```

The **paint** method is responsible for drawing the rest of the **Component** using the **Graphics** object. Some of the methods provided by the **Graphics** class are shown in Listing 11.2.

Listing 11.2   A sample paint method that demonstrates text drawing.

```
public void paint(Graphics g ){
  String str = "Joy of Java!" ;
  FontMetrics fm = g.getFontMetrics() ;
  int ascent = fm.getAscent();
  int descent = fm.getDescent();
  int length = fm.stringWidth( str );
  int X = 30, Y = 120 ;
  g.setColor( Color.darkGray );
  g.drawString( str , X, Y );
  g.setColor( Color.black );
  g.drawLine( X, Y, X + length, Y ); // baseline
  g.drawLine( X, Y - ascent, X + length, Y - ascent ); // top
  g.drawLine( X, Y - ascent, X, Y + descent );
  g.drawLine( X, Y + descent, X + length, Y + descent );
}
```

This **paint** method was used in a class derived from **Frame** to create the display shown in Figure 11.5. The lines and text on the left side were drawn by the **paint** method, whereas the annotation on the right indicates the various **FontMetrics** parameters. The **X** and **Y** positions used in the **drawString** method call refer to a point at the left end of the baseline. Note how a portion of the "y" character descends below the baseline.

The programmer can request that the JVM execute the **update-paint** sequence on a component by calling the **repaint** method in the **Component** class. This is a request, not a command—the JVM repaints the **Component** when it gets around to it. Therefore, you must be sure that your program **Thread** does not hog all the CPU time. Here is an example of a **run** method used to create an animated display on a **Canvas**-derived object named **animCanvas**:

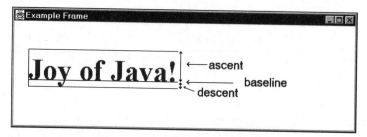

Figure 11.5   The result of the **paint** method used in Listing 11.2 (with annotations added).

```
public void run(){
  while( true ){
    doAnimationMoves();
    animCanvas.repaint();
    try {
      Thread.sleep( 50 );
    }catch(InterruptedException ex){
    }
  }
}
```

Note that because the **animCanvas repaint** method is called, the JVM calls the **update** method that belongs to the **animCanvas** object. The **sleep** method makes the **Thread** sleep for a fixed amount of time; this would make the animation run at a nearly constant rate on different systems.

More about Drawing

The logical coordinates for drawing on the screen are considered to lie between the pixels of the output device. When drawing a real pixel, the "pen" fills in the pixel below and to the right of the logical pixel coordinates. Here are some of the line-drawing methods in the **Graphics** class:

➤ *drawLine(int x1, int y1, int x2, int y2)*—This draws a line one pixel wide from point (x1, y1) to point (x2, y2).

➤ *drawRect(int x, int y, int wide, int high)*—This draws a rectangle based on the upper-left corner at point (x, y) with the prescribed width and height.

➤ *fillRect(int x, int y, int wide, int high)*—This draws a filled-in rectangle using the current **Color**.

➤ *drawOval(int x, int y, int wide, int high)*—This draws a line one pixel wide to create an oval that just fits the rectangle that the parameters describe.

➤ *fillOval(int x, int y, int wide, int high)*—This draws a filled-in oval.

➤ *drawArc(int x, int y, int wide, int high, int startAngle, int arcExtent)*—This draws the outline of an arc that just fits the rectangle described by the first four parameters. The start angle and arc extent are in degrees measured counterclockwise from the 3 o'clock position.

➤ *fillArc(int x, int y, int wide, int high, int startAngle, int arcExtent)*—This is similar to **drawArc** except that the entire figure is filled. This is an ideal routine for drawing pie charts.

➤ *drawPolygon(Polygon p)*—This outlines the polygon with a line one pixel wide. If the first and last points are not identical, they are automatically connected with a line.

➤ *fillPolygon(Polygon p)*—This is similar to **drawPolygon** but it draws a polygon that is filled in with the current **Color**. This is an ideal routine for drawing special controls.

Listing 11.3 shows some of these methods as they were used to create Figure 11.6. Note how the **fillArc** method starts at 0 degrees in the 3 o'clock position with the end point at 45 degrees measured counterclockwise.

Listing 11.3   The paint method used to create Figure 11.6.

```
public void paint(Graphics g ){
    g.drawRect( 30,40,200, 160);
    g.setColor( Color.cyan );
    g.fillOval( 30,40,200, 160);
    g.setColor( Color.black );
    g.fillArc( 40, 50, 180, 140, 0, 45 );
    g.setColor( Color.black );
    g.fillPolygon( arrow );
}
```

Displaying Images Onscreen

Java has extensive image-manipulation features. The **java.awt.Image** class creates objects that represent images, and the **java.awt.image** package has a number of classes that can be used to manipulate images. Here are some of the methods in the **Graphics** class that can be used to draw an **Image**:

```
1. boolean drawImage( Image img, int x, int y,
      ImageObserver obs )
2. boolean drawImage( Image img, int x, int y, int wide,
      int high, Color bkg, ImageObserver obs )
```

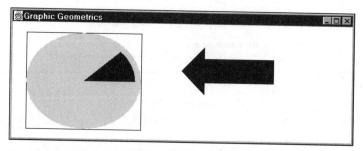

Figure 11.6   A demonstration of drawing geometric figures with the code in Listing 11.3.

The method in line 2 scales the **Image** to fit in the rectangle defined by the parameters. The **ImageObserver** reference may be **null** or a reference to an object (such as a **Component**) that implements the **ImageObserver** interface. The **bkg Color** is used wherever a transparent pixel appears in the **Image**. There are a large number of variations of **drawImage** in the **Graphics** and **Graphics2D** classes, but these are beyond the scope of this book.

Off-Screen Images

You can create off-screen or memory images that can be used to create complex images that are then drawn to the screen. The technique of working with an off-screen image that can be rapidly drawn to the screen is often referred to as *double buffering*. This technique is used to avoid the flicker that can result when an **update** method clears the component and the **paint** method does a lot of time-consuming drawing.

An off-screen **Image** can supply a **Graphics** object so you can use all of the **Graphics** methods to modify the **Image**. The following code fragment, from a custom **Component**, creates an off-screen image and gets the associated **Graphics** object:

```
Image imgA = createImage( 200, 150 ); // method in Component
Graphic gr = imgA.getGraphics();
// gr can now be used to draw in the off-screen image
```

The **Component** getGraphics Method

So far, I have talked about drawing on the screen with the **paint** method, which is called by the JVM with a **Graphics** object. You can also use the following **Component** method to get a **Graphics** object for any **Component** currently displayed on the screen:

```
public Graphics getGraphics()
```

One danger of this approach is that the operating system may have limits on the number of graphics context objects that can exist simultaneously. So, if you use **getGraphics**, be sure to use the

```
public void dispose()
```

method of the **Graphics** class to properly dispose of any system resources. You don't need to dispose of the **Graphics** object provided in the JVM calls to **update** and **paint** methods because that is handled by the JVM.

*Note: Do not try to get a **Graphics** reference in a method that runs before something is shown on the screen. The JVM does not determine the characteristics of the display until the first window is shown. Any call to **getGraphics** before then will return **null** and cause you endless trouble.*

Practice Questions

Question 1

> You want to use a particular color for text in an **Applet**, but you have forgotten the syntax for the method that sets the color for drawing. Which class do you look in first?
>
> ○ a. **java.awt.Applet**
>
> ○ b. **java.awt.Panel**
>
> ○ c. **java.applet.Applet**
>
> ○ d. **java.awt.Component**
>
> ○ e. **java.lang.Object**

Answer d is correct. **Component** should always be your first stop when you are looking for AWT methods that affect appearance. Answer a cites the wrong package for the Applet class. Although **Applet** (answer c) inherits from **Panel** (answer b), which inherits container methods from **Container**, the common appearance-changing methods and event-related methods are all in **Component**. Because Object, answer e, is the root of all Java classes, both graphic and nongraphic, you would certainly not expect to find appearance related methods there.

Question 2

> Which of the following AWT components can have a menu, either as a menu bar or pop-up menu, attached to it? [Check all correct answers]
>
> ❑ a. **java.awt.Frame**
>
> ❑ b. **java.awt.Window**
>
> ❑ c. **java.awt.Applet**
>
> ❑ d. **java.awt.Panel**

Answers a, b, c, and d are correct. All of these components may have an attached menu because the **Component** class implements the **MenuContainer** interface, and all of these classes have **Component** in their ancestry. However, only the **Frame** can have a **MenuBar**.

Question 3

The **Component** methods for setting the position and size of a screen object use which Java primitive?

- ○ a. **byte**
- ○ b. **short**
- ○ c. **char**
- ○ d. **int**
- ○ e. **long**
- ○ f. **float**

Answer d is correct. All of the **Component** methods expect an **int** primitive for screen position and dimension values; therefore, the other answers are incorrect.

Question 4

Which of the following describes how the angle parameters in the **Graphics** class **drawArc** method are used?

- ○ a. Angles are interpreted as radians, with 0 at the 12 o'clock position and positive angles in a clockwise direction.
- ○ b. Angles are interpreted as degrees, with 0 at the 3 o'clock position and positive angles in a counterclockwise direction.
- ○ c. Angles are interpreted as radians, with 0 at the 3 o'clock position and positive angles in a counterclockwise direction.
- ○ d. Angles are interpreted as degrees, with 0 at the 12 o'clock position and positive angles in a clockwise direction.

Answer b is correct and the others incorrect. Note that measuring angles in integer degrees obviously limits the method to crude screen graphics. The **Graphics2D** class has much more flexible drawing methods than the **Graphics** class.

Question 5

A Java application based on the **Frame** class contains a **Panel**, which in turn contains a **Label**. The only statements in the entire application that have to do with color or font settings are:

```
// in the Frame
setFont( new Font("Serif", Font.ITALIC, 18 );
setBackground( Color.cyan );

// in the Panel
setBackground( Color.white );
setForeground( Color.magenta );
```

What colors and font will the **Label** display?

○ a. Background = white; foreground = magenta; font = Serif Italic style, 18 point

○ b. Background = cyan; foreground = black; font = Serif Italic style, 18 point

○ c. Background = cyan; foreground = black; font = system default style for labels

○ d. Background = white; foreground = magenta; font = system default style for labels

Answer a is correct and the others incorrect. The **Font** is inherited from the **Frame** and the colors from the **Panel**. Note that there is a JVM default for colors and a **Font** that is characteristic of the JVM, not the operating system.

Question 6

Which of the following statements about the ancestry of the class **java.applet.Applet** is incorrect?

- ○ a. An **Applet** is a kind of **Container**.
- ○ b. An **Applet** is a kind of **Window**.
- ○ c. An **Applet** is a kind of **Component**.
- ○ d. An **Applet** is a kind of **Panel**.

Answer b is an incorrect statement and thus the correct answer. **Window** extends **Container** directly, whereas **Applet** extends **Panel**, which extends **Container**, which extends **Component**. Therefore a, c, and d are correct statements and thus not the correct answer. When you take the actual exam, watch out for questions that ask you to spot the incorrect statements.

Question 7

In which category does **java.awt.Container** belong?

- ○ a. Interface
- ○ b. **abstract** class
- ○ c. Normal class
- ○ d. None of the above

Answer c is correct. **Container** is now a regular class. **Container** is not an interface, but it does inherit implementation of several interfaces from **Component**. Therefore, answer a is incorrect. **Container** was an **abstract** class in SDK 1.1 but is not now. Therefore, answer b is incorrect. Answer d is incorrect because a correct answer is given.

Question 8

Which of the following do not inherit from **java.awt.MenuItem**? [Check all correct answers]

❑ a. **java.awt.MenuComponent**

❑ b. **java.awt.Menu**

❑ c. **java.awt.CheckboxMenuItem**

❑ d. **java.awt.MenuSeparator**

Answers a and d are correct. **MenuItem** inherits from **MenuComponent**, not the other way around. There is no such class as **MenuSeparator**; separators are added to menus with the **addSeparator** method. **Menu** and **CheckboxMenuItem** are direct descendents of **MenuItem**. Therefore, answers b and c are incorrect.

Question 9

Of the three classes **TextField**, **TextArea**, and **TextComponent**, which is the parent of the other two?

○ a. **TextField**

○ b. **TextArea**

○ c. **TextComponent**

Answer c is correct. Both **TextField** (for single lines) and **TextArea** (for multiple lines) are extensions of **TextComponent**.

Question 10

> You want to show a single line of text in a component that the user can select but not edit. Which of the following would be the way to create this component?
>
> ○ a.
> ```
> msgTx = new TextField( 60 );
>     msgTx.setEditable( false );
> ```
> ○ b.
> ```
> msgTx = new TextArea( 60 );
>     msgTx.setEnabled( false );
>     msgTx.setEditable( false );
> ```
> ○ c.
> ```
> msgTx = new TextField( 60 );
>     msgTx.setEnabled( true )
> ```

Answer a is correct. The **setEditable** method controls whether or not a text field can be edited. Answer b is incorrect because **setEnabled(false)** prevents the user from selecting the field. Answer c is incorrect because the default for **TextField** components is to be editable.

Need to Know More?

 Geary, David M. *Graphic Java 2, Mastering the JFC: AWT, Volume 1.* Prentice Hall PTR/Sun Microsystems Press, Upper Saddle River, NJ, 1998. ISBN 0-13079-666-2. This is a well-regarded book on AWT usage. The other volume in this series treats the Swing classes.

 Zukowski, John. *Java AWT Reference.* O'Reilly & Associates, Inc, Sebastopol, CA, 1997. ISBN 1-56592-240-9. This volume contains over 1,000 pages of details on the AWT classes. This version for SDK 1.1 is out of print. However, if you can find a copy, almost all of the material is applicable to Java 2.

 http://java.sun.com/docs/books/tutorial/collections/ is where you can find an online Java tutorial that has a special section on the AWT classes. You can also download the entire tutorial.

Building Graphical Interfaces with the AWT Components

. . . .

Terms you'll need to understand:

✓ LayoutManager

✓ LayoutManager2

✓ **Constraints**

✓ **Insets**

✓ minimumLayoutSize

✓ preferredLayoutSize

✓ maximumLayoutSize

Techniques you'll need to master:

✓ Choosing the right layout manager for a particular design problem

✓ Predicting the result of resizing containers with different layout managers

Creating a graphical user interface (GUI) using the Java Abstract Windowing Toolkit (AWT) library is a matter of choosing the right components and placing them on the screen under the control of layout managers. Layout managers are essential in creating GUIs that have similar behavior on all hardware. The capabilities of a layout manager are specified in two interfaces. **java.awt.LayoutManager** and **java.awt.LayoutManager2. java.awt.LayoutManager** is part of the original Java 1 language release. The 1.1 release of Java includes the **java.awt.LayoutManager2** interface, which adds some refinements to **LayoutManager**.

The **LayoutManager** Interface

All Java AWT containers can have an attached **LayoutManager** object added with the following method:

```
public void set setLayout(LayoutManager m )
```

The object controls the size and position of all components in the container. You should add the **LayoutManager** to the container before you add any components. Some layout managers let you get away with adding the manager after the components, but others produce very odd results if you do so.

Some containers have a constructor that takes a **LayoutManager** so you can combine creation of the container with setting the **LayoutManager**, as in the following:

```
Panel p2 = new Panel( new BorderLayout() );
```

In general, you do not need to deal with the **LayoutManager** directly after it has been created. However, if you do, the **java.awt.Container** class has the following method:

```
LayoutManager getLayout();
```

The **LayoutManager** interface calls for the following methods:

➤ *void addLayoutComponent(String name, Component c)*—This method is called when a component is added to the container. Some layout managers ignore the name.

➤ *void layoutContainer(Container parent)*—This method performs the actual positioning and sizing of all of the contained **Component** objects.

➤ *Dimension minimumLayoutSize(Container parent)*—This is the method that a **Container** uses to calculate its minimum size requirements.

➤ *Dimension preferredLayoutSize(Container parent)*—This method calculates a preferred size based on the preferred size of the components and the layout rules.

➤ *void removeLayoutComponent(Component c)*—This removes the component from the list of components controlled by the **LayoutManager**.

 Generally speaking, a programmer never needs to call these methods directly. The **Container** to which the **LayoutManager** is attached calls them as needed.

The **LayoutManager2** Interface

The release of Java 1.1 brought an extension to the **LayoutManager** interface named **LayoutManager2**. This interface adds a general method for attaching constraints to a component in a more general form:

```
void addLayoutComponent( Component c, Object constraints )
```

The **BorderLayout**, **CardLayout**, and **GridBagLayout** classes implement **LayoutManager2** because they all can use constraints. The other new methods in **LayoutManager2** are as follows:

➤ *float getLayoutAlignmentX(Container parent)*—These methods related to alignment are apparently used only in Swing classes and are not covered on the exam.

➤ *float getLayoutAlignmentY(Container parent)*— These methods related to alignment are apparently used only in Swing classes and are not covered on the exam.

➤ *void invalidateLayout(Container parent)*—This method forces the layout manager to completely recalculate the layout, discarding any intermediate results it may have cached.

➤ *Dimension maximumLayoutSize(Container target)*—This returns a **Dimension** based on the maximum sizes of the contained components, similar to the **getPreferredSize** method of **LayoutManager**.

Review of the AWT Containers

Before looking at specific layout managers, I'll review some facts about AWT container classes; additionally, you can go back and study Chapter 11 for more detail on the AWT. The size of a container as returned in a **Dimension** object by the **getSize** method reflects the amount of space the container occupies, *not* the space available inside the container. This distinction is not noticeable unless the container has a significant border, as in the case of **Frame** and **Dialog** containers.

A **java.awt.Container** maintains an internal list of **Component** references. Five methods are used to add a component to a container. The following lists the method signatures (note that the last two **add** methods were introduced with Java 1.1):

➤ *Component add(Component c)*—The component is added to the end of the list and the **c** reference is returned.

➤ *Component add(String name, Component c)*—The component is added to the end of the list and the **name** is associated with it in case the layout manager uses the **name** as a constraint. Although this method is not deprecated, Sun suggests that you not use it because it puts the component in the second position of the method call. Use the more general **add** with a constraint, making the name **String** the constraint.

➤ *Component add(Component c, int index)*—This adds the component at the index position in the internal list, bumping up any existing components at this position or higher.

➤ *void add(Component c, Object constraints)*—This adds the component with this **constraints** object. Whether or not the constraint is used depends on the layout manager.

➤ *void add(Component c, Object constraints, int index)*—This adds the component with this **constraints** object at the specified index.

The methods that specify an index can throw an **IllegalArgumentException** if the index is out of range. All methods throw an **IllegalArgumentException** if you try to add a container to itself or if you try to add a **Window** object to the container.

Here are some of the important characteristics of various AWT containers:

➤ *Panel*—This is the basic utility container. **Panel** and its subclass, **java.applet. Applet**, have a **FlowLayout**, discussed in more detail later in this chapter, by default.

➤ *Window*—This is the simplest container that can exist as an independent window. **Window** and its descendents have a **BorderLayout**, discussed in more detail later in this chapter, by default. A **Window** has no borders and no menu bar.

➤ *Frame*—This extension of **java.awt.Window** has a border and can host a **MenuBar**. If you replace the default **BorderLayout** with a **null** layout, be sure to take into account the **Insets** when you are positioning components. Unfortunately, because the border and **MenuBar** size are platform dependent, you can't evaluate the **Insets** until the **Frame** has been shown.

➤ *Dialog*—**Dialog** is also an extension of **Window** and thus has a default **BorderLayout**. You must also take **Insets** into account with a **Dialog**.

Working with **BorderLayout**

A **BorderLayout** can manage up to five components that are placed in named positions: North, South, East, West, and Center. Only one component can be in each position. The **BorderLayout** class has these five **String** objects as constants named **NORTH, SOUTH, EAST, WEST,** and **CENTER**. Here is an example of the code to add some elements to a **java.awt.Frame**, which, as you will no doubt recall, has a **BorderLayout** by default:

```
add( new Button( "North" ), BorderLayout.NORTH );
add( new Button( "South" ), BorderLayout.SOUTH );
add( new Button( "East" ),  BorderLayout.EAST );
add( new Button( "West" ),  BorderLayout.WEST );
add( new Button( "Center" ), BorderLayout.CENTER );
```

This code results in the display shown in Figure 12.1. On the left is the **Frame**, sized so all **Button**s are visible, whereas the right image shows how the layout manager compensates for a smaller window by compressing the center component.

BorderLayout Defaults

Here are some important facts to remember about the default behavior of AWT components with respect to **BorderLayout**:

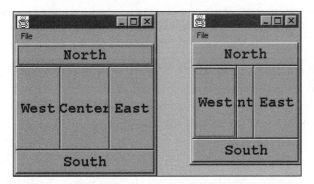

Figure 12.1   A **Frame** that contains five **Button** objects at two different sizes.

➤ BorderLayout is the default layout manager for the **java.awt.Frame,** **java.awt.Window,** and **java.awt.Dialog** containers.

➤ If you don't specify a constraint when you add a component to a container with a **BorderLayout,** a constraint of **CENTER** is assumed. If you add more than one component without a constraint, only the last one is kept and the others are not shown in any position.

➤ None of the border positions in a **BorderLayout** shows up at all if no component has been added. If nothing is added to the center position, it is painted in the container's background color.

 A **BorderLayout** tries to preserve the preferred width of the **EAST** and **WEST** components and the preferred height of the **NORTH** and **SOUTH** components. The **CENTER** component gets the leftovers.

Working with FlowLayout

The most important characteristics of a **FlowLayout** are as follows:

➤ **FlowLayout** gives every component its preferred size and does not resize components.

➤ **FlowLayout** adds components from left to right and starts a new row when the first one is filled.

➤ Components that don't fit are simply not shown.

Using one of the constants in the **FlowLayout** class, you can specify how the components will be aligned within rows when you create a **FlowLayout.** These constants are **LEFT, CENTER,** and **RIGHT.** The following statements illustrate the three constructors for **FlowLayout:**

```
1. FlowLayout f1 = new FlowLayout( );
2. FlowLayout f2 = new FlowLayout( FlowLayout.LEFT );
3. FlowLayout f3 = new FlowLayout( FlowLayout.RIGHT, 10, 2 );
```

The code in line 1 will result in **f1** having a center alignment and the default gap of five pixels between components horizontally and vertically. The **f2** layout will have the default gap and will align the components on the left, whereas **f3** will align the components on the right with a horizontal gap of 10 pixels and a vertical gap of 2.

Figure 12.2 shows a **Frame** that contains six **Button** objects, using a layout constructed as in the **f3** layout in line 3 of the preceding code. Note that the left-to-right order of the buttons is preserved when buttons 5 and 6 overflow the first row and are aligned on the next.

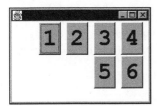

Figure 12.2   A set of six **Button** objects managed by a **FlowLayout**.

Working with **GridLayout**

GridLayout follows very simple rules. The available space is divided into a rectangular grid of equal-sized cells and the components are forced to fit. The order of addition defines where each component goes, with rows being filled from left to right starting at the top left. The following code illustrates the three constructors for a **GridLayout**:

```
1. GridLayout g1 = new GridLayout();
2. GridLayout g2 = new GridLayout( int rows, int cols );
3. GridLayout g3 = new GridLayout( int rows, int cols, int hgap,
     int vgap );
```

The constructor in line 1 results in a grid with only one row that will be divided equally among all components and will have the default gap of zero pixels between components. The constructor in line 2 creates an initial grid with the specified rows and columns and the default gap of zero pixels between components. The constructor in line 3 lets you specify the horizontal and vertical gap between components.

Figure 12.3 illustrates the result of placing six **Button** objects in a **GridLayout** created with the following code:

```
new Gridlayout( 2, 3, 10, 15 )
```

Figure 12.3   A **Frame** that holds six **Button** objects in a **GridLayout**.

Note that the specified gap is inserted only between components, not between components and the container border. To control this gap, you have to create a custom container that has an implementation of **getInsets**, as in the following example:

```
class XPanel extends Panel {
  public Insets getInsets(){return new Insets( 25, 15, 10, 5) ;}
}
```

 When a container with a **GridLayout** has fewer components than the number of grid positions, the unoccupied grid areas are painted in the container's background color. When a container with a full **GridLayout** has another component added, the **GridLayout** automatically adds an additional column and recomputes the layout.

Working with **CardLayout**

CardLayout is an extremely handy way to organize a potentially complex display into understandable pieces. A **CardLayout** can manage a large number of components (cards), but only one is shown at a time. The program switches the view between components either by addressing it by name or by methods that "flip" through the cards in the order they were added.

To control a **CardLayout**, your program must keep a reference to it. This is in contrast with the other layout managers, which a program never calls directly. Here are the **CardLayout** constructors:

```
1. CardLayout card1 = new CardLayout();
2. CardLayout card2 = new CardLayout( int hborder, int vborder );
```

The constructor in line 1 creates a **CardLayout** that does not show a border around the contained components. The constructor in line 2 shows a gap painted in the container background color with **hborder** pixels on the left and right and **vborder** pixels on the top and bottom around the displayed component.

When adding a component to a container that uses a **CardLayout**, you can use a **String** name as a constraint. For example:

```
panel1.add( msgTextArea, "messages" );
```

Now, if you want to have **panel1** display the **msgTextArea** component, the following code will switch to that card (note that the **show** method requires a reference to the container as well as the card name):

```
CardLayout cd = (CardLayout)panel1.getLayout();
cd.show( panel1, "messages" );
```

The following other methods for switching between cards use the order in which the components were added; they also must have a reference to the container:

➤ *public void next(Container parent)*—Displays the next component, going back to the first when the last one is reached.

➤ *public void previous(Container parent)*—Displays the previous component, going to the last when the starting one is reached.

Working with GridBagLayout

Think of **GridBagLayout** as an extremely flexible version of **GridLayout**. Whereas in **GridLayout** each grid row and column is the same size and each component exactly fills a grid location, in **GridBagLayout**, these restrictions are relaxed. Rows and columns can be of different sizes and a component can use more than one grid location. The extent to which a component fills an area is under the programmer's control.

Unfortunately, this flexibility can be obtained only with a very complex programming interface. Basically, each component that goes into a **GridBagLayout** has to be tagged with a **GridBagConstraints** object that carries a number of parameters. The **GridBagLayout** object looks at the constraints of all the components it manages and tries to come up with a layout that satisfies all of them.

Even experienced Java programmers have trouble getting a **GridBagLayout** to do exactly what they want because of the parameters' interaction. For our purposes here, you need to be familiar only with the basic parameters as they affect the positioning of a single component.

The GridBagConstraints Class

Each component in a container controlled by a **GridBagLayout** gets an associated **GridBagConstraints** object. **GridBagLayout** uses the parameters that this object carries to decide on a position and size for each component. The class also defines a number of constants related to various defaults, including the following:

➤ *Positioning*—The **gridx** and **gridy** parameters are indexes to the grid position in which the component originates, with 0,0 being the upper-left corner. If the constant **RELATIVE** is used, the component is placed relative to the previous addition. Within the cell(s) that the component occupies, the **anchor** parameter can be used to place the component in the **CENTER** or one of eight "compass" directions, such as **NORTHEAST**, but only if the component is smaller than the space available.

➤ *Sizing*—The **gridwidth** and **gridheight** parameters indicate the number of cells allotted to the component horizontally and vertically. The constant **REMAIN-DER** can be used to indicate that the component takes up the remainder of the row or column. The amount of space the component actually occupies depends on several other parameters. The **fill** parameter can be set to **NONE, HORI-ZONTAL, VERTICAL,** or **BOTH.** You can set the **ipadx** and **ipady** parameters, which specify the number of pixels to be added to the component's minimum size, as an alternative to stretching the component with the **fill** parameter.

➤ *Padding*—The **insets** parameter takes an **Insets** object that defines the amount of space to leave clear on each side of the component.

➤ *Distributing extra space*—The **weightx** and **weighty** parameters control how extra space is distributed among rows and columns. If you leave these parameters at the default value of zero, all extra space gets distributed around the edges of the whole layout so the components do not expand when the total area is enlarged. The **GridBagLayout** looks at a row or column of components and finds the largest weight for each row (**weighty**) and each column (**weightx**). Extra space is distributed to rows and columns in proportion to the weight.

These parameters interact with each other, so getting the effect you want can involve a lot of experimentation. Java development environments such as Symantec's Visual Café and IBM's Visual Age provide a dynamic display that allows you to experiment to find satisfactory settings for **GridBagConstraints** parameters. Table 12.1 summarizes the constraint parameters; you should take a quick glance at this table before you go into the exam!

A **GridBagLayout** Example

Fully exploring the possibilities of **GridBagLayout** would take a large chapter. For *Exam Cram* purposes, I show a single example. In this example, three **Button** objects are placed in a **GridBagLayout** using the code in Listing 12.1, which results in the display shown in Figure 12.4.

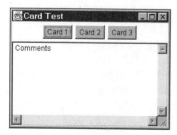

Figure 12.4 Three **Button** objects in a **GridBagLayout.** The **anchor** for A is **SOUTH**, whereas the **anchor** for B is **CENTER**.

Table 12.1   Summary of the GridBagConstraints variables.

Variable Constant(s)	Typical Values	Influence	Related
gridx	0 through n	The column location for the left edge of the component	**RELATIVE**
gridy	0 through n	The row location for the upper edge of the component	**RELATIVE**
gridwidth	1 through n	The number of columns used by the component	**REMAINDER, RELATIVE**
gridheight	1 through n	The number of rows used by the component	**REMAINDER, RELATIVE**
fill	One of the constants	Defines if/how to expand the component to fill the available space	**NONE, HORIZONTAL, VERTICAL, BOTH**
ipadx	0 through n	The number of pixels of extra horizontal size to give the component over the minimum size	-
ipady	0 through n	The number of pixels of extra vertical size to give the component over the minimum size	-
insets	An **Insets** object with four **int** values	The pixels of extra space around the component on each side	-
anchor	One of the constants	The placement within a grid if the component is smaller than the available space	**CENTER, NORTH, NORTHEAST, EAST, SOUTHEAST, SOUTH, SOUTHWEST, WEST, NORTHWEST**
weightx	0.0 through 1.0	Influences the distribution of extra horizontal space between columns	-
weighty	0.0 through 1.0	Influences the distribution of extra vertical space between rows	-

Listing 12.1   The constructor used to create the Frame shown in Figure 12.4.

```
public GridBagDemo() {
  super( "GridBagLayout" ); // Frame with title
  setFont( new Font("Helvetica", Font.BOLD, 18 ));
  addWindowListener( new WindowAdapter( ){
```

```
      public void windowClosing(WindowEvent evt){System.exit(0);}
} );
setSize( 220, 200 );
Button button;
GridBagLayout gridbag = new GridBagLayout();
GridBagConstraints c = new GridBagConstraints();
setLayout(gridbag);
button = new Button( "Button A" );
c.insets = new Insets( 5,5,5,5 );
c.fill = GridBagConstraints.HORIZONTAL;
c.gridx = 0;
c.gridy = 0;
c.gridwidth = 2; // occupy 2 columns
c.gridheight = 2; // and 2 rows
c.weightx = 0.5;
c.weighty = 0.5;
c.anchor = GridBagConstraints.SOUTH;
gridbag.setConstraints(button, c);
// that call clones the constraints object so you can continue
// to use it, making minor modifications for subsequent uses.
add(button);
 //
button = new Button( "B" );
c.fill  = GridBagConstraints.NONE;
c.gridx = 2; // because A occupies 2 columns
c.gridy = 1;
c.gridwidth = 1;
c.gridheight =1;
c.anchor = GridBagConstraints.CENTER;
gridbag.setConstraints(button, c);
add(button);
 //
button = new Button("Button C");
c.gridx = 0;
c.gridy = 2; // because A occupies 2 rows
c.gridwidth =1;
c.gridheight =1;
gridbag.setConstraints(button, c);
add( button );
}
```

It is important to note that the **setConstraints** call clones the **GridBagConstraints** object and keeps the clone. This means that you don't have to create a new **GridBagConstraints** and set all the parameters for each component. Instead, after the basic **GridBagConstraints** object has been set up, you only need to modify a few parameters for each new component. The **getConstraints** method of **GridBagLayout** returns a clone of the current **GridBagConstraints** object.

This simplifies the process of setting constraints based on those already set for another component.

Changing the **anchor** parameter for the A button results in the change shown in Figure 12.5.

Working without a Layout Manager

For many simple applications, some programmers prefer to lay out components in absolute pixel terms using the general **Component** positioning methods. To do this, you simply set the layout manager to **null**, as shown in the following code:

```
setLayout( null )
```

Many of the methods used for layout purposes in Java 1 were renamed in Java 1.1 for consistency. The original methods are still in the library but are deprecated. The following list reviews these methods:

➤ *void setLocation(int x, int y)*—This sets the location of the upper-left corner of the **Component** relative to the upper-left corner of the container. This method replaces the deprecated **move** method.

➤ *void setLocation(Point p)*—This sets the location using an object of the **Point** class.

➤ *void setBounds(int x, int y, int width, int height)*—This sets both location and size. This method replaces the deprecated **reshape** method.

➤ *void setBounds(Rectangle r)*—This method uses an object of the geometric utility **Rectangle** class.

➤ *void setSize(int width, int height)*—This sets the size without changing the location. It replaces the deprecated **resize** method.

➤ *void setSize(Dimension d)*—This sets the size using an object of the geometric utility **Dimension** class. There is also a deprecated **resize** method that takes a **Dimension**.

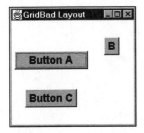

Figure 12.5   The same components as in Figure 12.4 with the **anchor** for A now **NORTH**.

Practice Questions

Question 1

> Which of the following layout managers can be used to display nine **Button** objects at one time? [Check all correct answers]
>
> ❏ a. **BorderLayout**
>
> ❏ b. **GridLayout**
>
> ❏ c. **CardLayout**
>
> ❏ d. **GridBagLayout**

Answers b and d are correct. A **GridLayout** or **GridBagLayout** can show nine objects at once. A **BorderLayout** can manage only five objects. Therefore, answer a is incorrect. A **CardLayout** shows only one object at a time, although it can manage more than one. Therefore, answer c is incorrect.

Question 2

> Which of the following is the correct way to create a **Panel** with a **BorderLayout**? Note: The **Panel** is to be used for a central **Canvas** and two **Scrollbar** objects.
>
> ○ a. Panel p = new Panel();
>
> ```
>     p.setLayout( new BorderLayout() );
> ```
>
> ○ b. Panel p = new Panel();
>
> ```
>     p.addLayoutManager( new BorderLayout() );
> ```
>
> ○ c. Panel p = new Panel();
>
> ```
>     p.setLayout( new BorderLayout( 3 ) );
> ```
>
> ○ d. Panel p = new Panel();
>
> ```
>     p.addLayoutManager( new BorderLayout( 3 ) );
> ```

Answer a is correct. The code listed is the correct way to create a **Panel** with a **BorderLayout**. The **addLayoutManager** method does not exist. Therefore, answer b is incorrect. There is no **BorderLayout** constructor that takes a single numeric parameter. Therefore, answer c is incorrect. Answer d combines the errors of answers b and c.

Question 3

You need a container to hold six equal-sized buttons in three columns of two. This arrangement must persist when the container is resized. Which of the following will create that container?

- ○ a. Canvas c = new Canvas(new GridLayout(2, 3)) ;
- ○ b. Panel p = new Panel(new GridLayout(2, 3));
- ○ c. Window w = new Window(new GridLayout(2, 3));
- ○ d. Panel p = new Panel(new GridLayout(3, 2));

Answer b correctly constructs a **Panel** container with a **LayoutManager** for two rows and three columns. **Canvas** is not a container. Therefore, answer a is incorrect. Although **Window** is a container, it does not have a constructor that takes a **LayoutManager**. Therefore, answer c is incorrect. The **LayoutManager** constructed here has three rows and two columns, not two rows of three columns. Therefore, answer d is incorrect.

Question 4

You have constructed a **Panel** with a **GridLayout** and added **Button** objects to it as follows:

```
Panel p = new Panel();
p.setLayout( new GridLayout() );
for( int i = 1 ; i <= 6 ; i++ ){
   p.add( new Button(Integer.toString( i )));
}
```

What is the result when the **Panel** is resized to 200x200 and is shown?

- ○ a. Only the **Button** "6" will be showing, filling the **Panel**.
- ○ b. Six narrow buttons in a row will be shown in the **Panel**.
- ○ c. Six thin buttons in a column will be shown in the **Panel**.
- ○ d. The number showing will depend on the font size.

Answer b is correct and answers a, c, and d are incorrect because without a specified number of rows and columns, **GridLayout** arranges components in a row with equal space for each.

Question 5

Assume you have created a **Panel** named **cnt** with a **CardLayout** named **card** using the following code:

```
card = new CardLayout();
cnt = new Panel( card );
```

How do you cause a specific component to be shown in the container?

○ a. **card.show(cnt, name);**

where **cnt** is the container and **name** is the **String** used as a constraint for that component when it was added

○ b. **card.show(cnt, n);**

where **cnt** is the container and **n** is an integer that reflects the order in which the component was added to the container

○ c. **card.show(name);**

where **name** is the **String** used as a constraint for that component when it was added

○ d. **card.show(n);**

where **n** is an integer that reflects the order in which the component was added to the container

Answer a is correct. You have to call the **CardLayout show** method with a **Container** reference and a **String** name. **CardLayout** uses a **String**, not an integer to select a component. Therefore, answers b and d are incorrect. The **CardLayout** show method also requires a reference to the container. Therefore, answer c is incorrect.

Question 6

Which of the following are valid alignment parameters for a **FlowLayout**? [Check all correct answers]

❑ a. **FlowLayout.TOP**

❑ b. **FlowLayout.LEFT**

❑ c. **FlowLayout.BOTTOM**

❑ d. **FlowLayout.CENTER**

❑ e. **FlowLayout.RIGHT**

Answers b, d, and e are correct. **FlowLayout** uses a left-to-right flow and always starts at the top of a container. TOP and BOTTOM are not constants in the **FlowLayout** class. Therefore, answers a and c are incorrect.

Question 7

Which of the following layout managers does not alter the height of a component?

○ a. **BorderLayout**

○ b. **GridBagLayout**

○ c. **CardLayout**

○ d. **FlowLayout**

Answer d is correct. A **FlowLayout** attempts to fit in components without changing their height. The **EAST, WEST,** and **CENTER** components of a **BorderLayout** have their height changed. Therefore, answer a is incorrect. A **GridBagLayout** typically alters both the height and width of components. Therefore, answer b is incorrect. Components in a **CardLayout** are resized to fit the container exactly. Therefore, answer c is incorrect.

Question 8

The component in the East position of a **BorderLayout** cannot be wider than a **Scrollbar**.

○ a. True

○ b. False

Answer b is correct. This statement is false. **BorderLayout** attempts to use the preferred width of the component. Although the East position is typically used for a **Scrollbar**, it can contain any component.

Question 9

Suppose you have a working program that has a **Panel**, **p1**, with a **BorderLayout** that already has components in the North, South, East, West, and Center positions. You then add the following statement to the end of the method that creates the **Panel**:

```
p1.add( new Button("Help") );
```

What happens when you try to compile and run the program?

○ a. The compiler objects to the statement because **p1** is already full.

○ b. The **Button** labeled "Help" is shown in the Center position of the **Panel**.

○ c. The original **CENTER** component is shown in the Center position of the **Panel**.

○ d. The first component added to the container is discarded and all components move up one position. The "Help" button ends up in the **CENTER** position.

Answer b is correct because a component added to a **BorderLayout** without a constraint is assigned the center position by default. The compiler does not have any way to track the eventual contents of containers. Therefore, answer a is incorrect. Only the original **CENTER** component is displaced. Therefore, answers c and d are incorrect.

Question 10

You create a calculator application that has a **Panel** with a **GridLayout** to hold 16 **Button** objects for numerals and operators, using the following constructor for the **Panel**:

```
Panel p = new Panel(
          new GridLayout( 4, 4, 5, 8 ) );
```

Which of the following statements about the resulting display are true? [Check all correct answers]

- ❏ a. The horizontal space between the buttons will be five pixels.
- ❏ b. The gap between the buttons and the edge of the **Panel** will be five pixels on the sides and eight on the top and the bottom.
- ❏ c. The order in which the **Button** objects are added controls their position, filling a row first, from left to right.
- ❏ d. The order in which the **Button** objects are added controls their position, filling a column first, from top to bottom.

Answers a and c are correct. The **GridLayout** is constructed with a **hgap** = 5. The **hgap** and **vgap** parameters control only spacing between components. Container insets control the gap between components and the edge of the container. Therefore, answer b is incorrect. The normal filling order for a **GridLayout** is to fill a row first, from left to right. Therefore, answer d is incorrect.

Question 11

Which variable in the **GridBagConstraints** class can use the constant named **CENTER**?

- ○ a. **gridx**
- ○ b. **fill**
- ○ c. **insets**
- ○ d. **anchor**
- ○ e. **weightx**

Answer d is correct. The **gridx** variable can use CENTER. The **CENTER** constant is a value for the **anchor** variable. It causes a component that is smaller than the available space to be centered in that space. The variables corresponding to answers a, b, c, and e use different sets of constants.

Question 12

The **ipadx** and **ipady** variables in the **GridBagConstraints** class influence which of the following characteristics of a component in a **GridBagLayout**?

○ a. The position relative to the upper-left corner of the container

○ b. Additional pixels of width and height occupied by the component

○ c. Additional pixels of extra space around the component

○ d. The amount the component is allowed to overlap its neighbors

---

Answer b is correct. These parameters give internal padding in the **x** and **y** directions, hence **ipadx** and **ipady**. Answer a is incorrect because it applies to the **gridx** and **gridy** variables. Answer c is incorrect because it applies to the **insets** variable. There is no variable that corresponds to answer d; therefore, it is incorrect.

Need to Know More?

http://java.sun.com/docs/books/tutorial/uiswing/layout/gridbag.html has an extensive discussion of all the layouts. The components used in the examples are Swing components, but the principles are exactly the same for AWT components.

http://members.tripod.com/pateldn/layout.htm has dynamic applets that let you play around with all the different layouts and parameters and see the results. This is very useful when you are trying to understand **GridBagLayout** especially.

The Java Event Model

Terms you'll need to understand:

✓ Listener
✓ **ActionEvent**
✓ **AdjustmentEvent**
✓ **TextEvent**
✓ **ItemEvent**
✓ **MouseEvent**
✓ **KeyEvent**
✓ Adapter

Techniques you'll need to master:

✓ Attaching the appropriate listener to a component
✓ Interpreting mouse events
✓ Enabling events
✓ Processing key events
✓ Implementing listener interface methods
✓ Extending event adapters

Communication between the user and your program occurs entirely in the form of events. The Java Virtual Machine (JVM) gets raw event data from the operating system and creates event objects for your program to process. In this chapter, I'll look at the content of these objects and how they are processed in Java 2. I'll start with a quick survey of how events were handled in Java 1 to give you a historical perspective.

The Java 1 Event Model

In the original event model, all operating system events are turned into **java.awt.Event** objects. The JVM then searches the containment hierarchy and graphical component hierarchy trying to locate a method that can handle the event. The first method to get a chance at the event is the **handleEvent** method in the container of the component that generated the event. If this method returns a **true** value, the JVM assumes the event is taken care of; otherwise, it continues searching.

One of the more notable problems with this model is that the JVM spends a lot of time looking for a method to handle events that are not of interest to anything in the program. For example, just moving the mouse across the display area of a window can generate dozens of events. Each event object must be created with mouse position information and a timestamp, which is a total waste of processing power if no part of the program is interested. The more complex the user interface, the more processing power is wasted.

Another problem is that the Java 1 JVM looks for an event handler only in the containment and **java.awt** hierarchy. This forces the programmer to do event processing in a custom version of one of the **java.awt** components even if that is not the most logical place for it. Furthermore, if more than one object is interested in an event, the programmer must add specific code to distribute it. All of these problems were addressed in the major redesign that resulted in Java 1.1 and is continued in Java 2.

Events in Java 2

The redesigned event model is often referred to as the *delegation* model. Java 2 handles events that are generated in a graphical component by delegating to objects that have registered an interest in that type of event. This is an example of the *observer-observable* design pattern, in which the observer is the object that has registered to receive events, and the observable is the component that generates events. In Java 2, event observer objects are called *listeners* and implement listener interfaces.

Instead of the single all-purpose **Event** class of Java 1, there is now a hierarchy of classes with specialized variables and methods to suit various purposes. In Java 2, event handling is more flexible and efficient than in Java 1, by far. However, nothing in programming is free; such flexibility and efficiency come at the cost of a large number of new classes and interfaces.

All event handling is performed by a single **Thread**, one event at a time. If your program undertakes a time-consuming operation as part of event handling, your interface will appear to be completely unresponsive during this time and your users will be very annoyed. Time-consuming calculations should be started in a separate **Thread**, allowing your program to remain responsive to user input.

Features of the Event Hierarchy

The root of the Java 2 event hierarchy is the **EventObject** class in the **java.util** package. An **EventObject** has only one variable, a reference to the object that generated it, which you can get with the following method:

```
public Object getSource()
```

Normally, this reference is to a graphical interface component such as a **Button**, but any object can be the source of an event.

A number of classes are derived from **EventObject**, but I am going to discuss only the **AWTEvent** branch of this hierarchy. The **java.awt.AWTEvent** class is the base class for all events that deal with user interface components, both in the **java.awt** package and in the Swing classes. **AWTEvent** adds the **int** variable **id** and the **boolean** variable **consumed**, plus the following method that returns the **id** of an **AWTEvent**:

```
public int getID()
```

AWTEvent is an **abstract** class that has subclasses, as shown in the following diagram:

```
java.util.EventObject
   |
   +— java.awt.AWTEvent
         |
         +— java.awt.event.ActionEvent
         |
         +— java.awt.event.AdjustmentEvent
         |
         +— java.awt.event.AncestorEvent
```

```
        |
        +— java.awt.event.ComponentEvent
        |
        +— java.awt.event.HierarchyEvent (new in Java 1.3)
        |
        +— java.awt.event.InputMethodEvent
        |
        +— java.awt.event.InternalFrameEvent
        |
        +— java.awt.event.InvocationEvent
        |
        +— java.awt.event.ItemEvent
        |
        +— java.awt.event.TextEvent
```

Each one of these event classes adds only the variables and methods needed to carry out a particular task. For instance, **Scrollbar** objects generate **AdjustmentEvent** events, so they carry the current **Scrollbar** value setting. Each class also provides constants for various types of a particular event. For example, six constants for different kinds of **AdjustmentEvent** are defined in the **AdjustmentEvent** class. The **getAdjustmentType** method returns these values.

For typical programming of graphical interfaces, you will probably be working with only a few of the events in this group, along with some events that descend from **ComponentEvent**, as follows:

```
java.awt.event.ComponentEvent
   |
   +— java.awt.event.ContainerEvent
   |
   +— java.awt.event.FocusEvent
   |
   +— java.awt.event.PaintEvent
   |
   +— java.awt.event.WindowEvent
   |
   +— java.awt.event.InputEvent
          |
          +— java.awt.event.MouseEvent
          |
          +— java.awt.event.KeyEvent
```

Here is a quick summary of how some common events are generated:

➤ *ActionEvent*—A button has been selected or a menu item has been double-clicked on. This is considered a "high-level" or "semantic" event because additional processing logic was applied to mouse or keyboard primitive events.

➤ *AdjustmentEvent*—The setting of a scrollbar has changed.

➤ *ItemEvent*—The status of an item in a list, checkbox, or checkable menu item has changed. This is also considered a high-level event because of the additional processing logic.

➤ *FocusEvent*—A component has gained or lost focus.

➤ *WindowEvent*—The status of a window has changed. Not all changes to a window generate this event.

➤ *MouseEvent*—The user has moved, clicked on, or dragged the mouse within the area of a Java component.

➤ *KeyEvent*—Depressing or releasing any key creates a **KeyEvent**. A separate **KeyEvent** is created for any key sequence that generates a character.

➤ *TextEvent*—The text in an object such as a **TextField** or **TextArea** has changed. This is considered a high-level event because it can result from a combination of mouse movements and keypress events.

Enabling Events

Events are generated by a Java component only if they have been specifically enabled. Every graphical component carries an event mask variable that is a 64-bit **long** primitive. Each bit enables a particular kind of event. The JVM checks this event mask when processing an operating system event and continues to process event objects only for events that have been enabled.

Enabling events is done with constants defined in the **java.awt.AWTEvent** class. There are only 16 constants at present, so using a 64-bit **long** leaves plenty of room for expansion. The **java.awt.Component** class defines **enableEvents** and **disableEvents** methods that take a **long** primitive input that can combine several event mask constants. For example, if you want **object1** to generate keyboard and focus events, you execute this statement in which two constants are ORed together:

```
object1.enableEvents( AWTEvent.KEY_EVENT_MASK |
                      AWTEvent.FOCUS_EVENT_MASK );
```

Processing Events

The first method for getting a newly created event is the **processEvent** method in the originating component. This method, shown here, is defined in **java.awt.Component**, but it is frequently overridden to provide custom event processing:

```
public void processEvent( AWTEvent e )
```

The default behavior of **processEvent** is to determine the event type and call one of the following:

```
public void processFocusEvent( FocusEvent e)
public void processMouseEvent( MouseEvent e)
public void processMouseMotionEvent( MouseEvent e)
public void processKeyEvent( KeyEvent e )
public void processComponentEvent( ComponentEvent e )
public void processInputMethodEvent( InputMethodEvent e )
public void processHierarchyEvent( HierarchyEvent e )
public void processHierarchyBoundsEvent( HierarchyEvent e )
```

The normal behavior of these methods is to send the event to the correct method of any listener that has registered with the component. If you build a custom component class that overrides one of these methods, you should also call the method in the parent class to ensure that listeners are notified, as shown here:

```
public void processMouseEvent( MouseEvent evt ){
  if( evt.getID() == MouseEvent.MOUSE_PRESSED ){
     doMousePressStuff( evt ) ;
  }
  super.processMouseEvent( evt );
}
```

If the call to the parent class is not used, listeners will not get the event.

Listeners and Adapters

The **java.awt.event** package defines a number of listener interfaces that are named according to the events they process. For programmer convenience, **java.awt.event** also includes classes called *adapters* that provide empty methods for the more complex interfaces. Table 13.1 summarizes the relationship between some common events and the interfaces and adapter classes in the **java.awt.event** package.

 You must be familiar with the listener interfaces and adapter classes that are associated with these events.

The keen-eyed student will observe that this table has two lines for **MouseEvent** events. Events that are generated by the mouse being moved over a component are generated in great profusion but frequently are not of interest to the programmer. For greater efficiency, the distinction between mouse movement and all other mouse events is made as early as possible in event processing. Processing mouse events is discussed in detail in "The **MouseEvent** Class" section later in this chapter.

Table 13.1 Events, listener interfaces, and adapter classes.		
Event Class	**Interface**	**Adapter Class**
ActionEvent	ActionListener	(None)
AdjustmentEvent	AdjustmentListener	(None)
AWTEvent	AWTEventListener	(None)
ComponentEvent	ComponentListener	ComponentAdapter
ContainerEvent	ContainerListener	ContainerAdapter
FocusEvent	FocusListener	FocusAdapter
HierarchyEvent	HierarchyBoundsListener	HierarchyBoundsAdapter
HierarchyEvent	HierarchyListener	(None)
InputMethodEvent	InputMethodListener	(None)
ItemEvent	ItemListener	(None)
KeyEvent	KeyListener	KeyAdapter
MouseEvent	MouseListener	MouseAdapter
MouseEvent	MouseMotionListener	MouseMotionAdapter
TextEvent	TextListener	(None)
WindowEvent	WindowListener	WindowAdapter

Each class that can generate one of these events has a method to add a listener for that event. This method is always named by combining "add" with the name of a listener, so the **Button** class has an **addActionListener** method, as follows:

```
public void addActionListener( ActionListener a )
```

The **Component** class has a system for keeping an unlimited number of listeners for every event descended from **AWTEvent**. The order in which listeners get called is *not* guaranteed.

Controls and **ActionEvent** Events

Controls that can generate **ActionEvent** events include (but are not limited to) **java.awt.Button**, **java.awt.MenuItem**, **java.awt.TextField**, and their Swing equivalents. A **TextField** object generates an **ActionEvent** when the user presses the Enter key.

The **ActionListener** interface has only one method, shown here:

```
public void actionPerformed( ActionEvent e )
```

To demonstrate how to work with **ActionEvent** events, I'll suppose you have an application with two **Button** objects and a **TextField**. One way to handle the **ActionEvent** events generated by these components is to make the basic application implement the interface. The class declaration could be:

```
public class MyApp extends Frame implements ActionListener
```

Skipping over the creation and placement of the components, the following code fragment shows how to add the application as an **ActionListener** to the components, most likely in the **MyApp** constructor:

```
button1.addActionListener( this );
button2.addActionListener( this );
textField1.addActionListener( this );
```

Your **MyApp** class has to have an **actionPerformed** method to satisfy the **ActionListener** interface. In that method, you can find out which component generated the event with code such as the following:

```
public void actionPerformed( ActionEvent evt ){
  Object source = evt.getSource() ;
  if( source == button1 ) doButton1();
  if( source == button2 ) doButton2();
  if( source == textField1 ){
     processEntry( textField1.getText() );
  }
}
```

It is essential that you know how to get information from an event and process it in the various listener interface methods.

An alternative to making your application the **ActionListener** is to use an anonymous inner class. Inner classes are ideally suited to implement listener interfaces because they have access to all of the containing class variables. Using the previous sample application, the code to create and add an **ActionListener** looks like this:

```
ActionListener al = new ActionListener(){
  public void actionPerformed( ActionEvent evt ){
    Object source = evt.getSource() ;
    if( source == button1 ) doButton1();
    ...// etc as before
  }
}
```

```
} ; // end inner class creation
button1.addActionListener( al );
button2.addActionListener( al );
textField1.addActionListener( al );
```

Item Selection and Item Events

The **java.awt.ItemSelectable** interface specifies methods of interface objects that have one or more items that can be selected. Typical AWT controls that implement **ItemSelectable** include **List, Choice,** and **Checkbox.** When the selection status of an item changes, these controls generate an **ItemEvent** that is communicated to **ItemListener** objects.

An **ItemListener** has the following single method:

```
public void itemStateChanged( ItemEvent evt )
```

When processing an **ItemEvent,** you can find out which control had a changed item with **getSource** and then compare the result of the **getID** method with the constants **ItemEvent.SELECTED** and **ItemEvent.DESELECTED.** The actual list item whose state changed can be obtained with the **ItemEvent** method, as follows:

```
public Object getItem()
```

If you have a **List** that presently has a selected item and you click on another item, any **ItemListener** first gets an **ItemEvent** with an **id** of DESELECTED, followed by an event for the newly selected item with an **id** of SELECTED.

Controls and AdjustmentEvent Events

The **java.awt.Scrollbar** and **javax.swing.JScrollBar** class objects generate **AdjustmentEvent** events. Classes that create **AdjustmentEvent** events are expected to implement the **java.awt.Adjustable** interface. The **AdjustmentListener** interface defines one method, as follows:

```
public void adjustmentValueChanged( AdjustmentEvent e )
```

Methods of interest in the **AdjustmentEvent** class are:

➤ *getAdjustable*—This returns the object that generated the event.

➤ *getAdjustmentType*—This returns an **int** value that can be compared with constants in the **AdjustmentEvent** class to determine the user action that caused the value to change.

➤ *getValue*—This method returns an **int** primitive value for the control setting.

You might expect that the **javax.swing.JSlider** control generates **AdjustmentEvent** events, but the designers chose to have it generate **ChangeEvent** events. This class is derived directly from **EventObject** and is not part of the **AWTEvent** hierarchy, so you don't have to worry about it for the exam.

Component Events

In addition to being generated when certain changes affect **Component** objects, the **ComponentEvent** class is the parent of several event classes. The **ComponentEvent** class defines the method as follows:

```
public Component getComponent()
```

The **ComponentListener** interface defines the methods **componentHidden**, **componentMoved**, **componentResized**, and **componentShown**. For convenience, there is also a **ComponentAdapter** class. Here is an example of code using an inner class derived from **ComponentAdapter** to detect when a window has been resized:

```
addComponentListener( new ComponentAdapter() {
  public void componentResized(ComponentEvent e ){
      System.out.println("Resized");
  }
  } ) ;
```

The FocusEvent Class

FocusEvent events are generated whenever an interface component gains or loses the user input focus. The component with the focus is the one that receives a key event if the user types something. This component is indicated with different conventions, depending on the operating system for Abstract Windowing Toolkit (AWT) components or on the installed look and feel for Swing components. To determine whether focus has been gained or lost, compare the result of the **getID** method with the constants **FocusEvent.FOCUS_GAINED** and **FocusEvent. FOCUS_LOST**.

The **FocusEvent** class also defines the following method:

```
public boolean isTemporary()
```

This method returns **true** if the loss of focus is temporary. A temporary loss of focus can occur when a second window comes to the top. The component regains focus when the first window comes to the top again. The **FocusListener** interface defines **focusGained** and **focusLost** methods. There is also a **FocusAdapter** that has empty versions of these two methods.

When the user is filling in text fields, the loss of focus event is frequently used as a signal to start parsing or otherwise processing the input. Obviously, the programmer should check to see if the loss of focus is only temporary before starting this process.

The **HierarchyEvent** Class

A new addition in the 1.3 release of Java, a **HierarchyEvent** is generated when the containment hierarchy that a component lives in is changed. This information is used mainly by development environments; under normal programming circumstances, you will not have to work with events of this type.

The **WindowEvent** Class

Changes in certain aspects of the status of a window generate **WindowEvent** events. The **WindowListener** interface defines the following methods to handle these events:

➤ *windowActivated*—Is called when the window has been brought to the front of the user's desktop and has the focus.

➤ *windowOpened*—Is called the first time a window is displayed.

➤ *windowClosed*—Is called when the window has been closed and cannot be reopened.

➤ *windowClosing*—Is called when the user has tried to close the window. This is the programmer's last chance to save data. If the method does not specifically exit the program, nothing will happen.

➤ *windowIconified*—Is called when the window has been put in the minimized state. Exactly how a minimized window behaves depends on the operating system.

➤ *windowDeiconified*—Is called when the window is restored after being iconified.

➤ *windowDeactivated*—Is called when the window loses the focus through being closed, being minimized, or through another window gaining the focus.

Note: No WindowEvent is generated when a window is resized. You can attach a ComponentListener to catch the ComponentEvent events caused by resizing.

Here is typical code used to create an inner class derived from **WindowAdapter** to provide for closing an application derived from **java.awt.Frame**:

```
addWindowListener( new WindowAdapter() {
   public void windowClosing( WindowEvent evt ){
      setVisible( false ) ;
      System.exit( 0 );
   }
} ) ;
```

Note: If an application is closed in the windowClosing method by using System.exit, no more events of any kind will be processed.

The **MouseEvent** and **KeyEvent** Classes

The abstract **InputEvent** class has two subclasses you will use a lot: **MouseEvent** and **KeyEvent**. The following reviews the hierarchy that leads to these classes:

```
java.util.EventObject
   |
   +— java.awt.AWTEvent
         |
         +— java.awt.event.ComponentEvent
               |
               +— java.awt.event.InputEvent
                     |
                     +— java.awt.event.KeyEvent
                     |
                     +— java.awt.event.MouseEvent
```

Because of the variety of keyboards that Java programs must work with, provision has been made for signalling the use of special keys, which are referred to as Alt, Graph, and Meta. Naturally, no single computer can generate every possible keyboard modifier. The **InputEvent** class adds the following methods to those it inherits:

➤ *consume()*—Sets a **boolean** variable named **consumed** in the event, which subsequent listeners can examine.

➤ *getModifiers()*—Returns an **int** that encodes various keyboard and mouse button modifier flags. Constants for these flags are defined in the **InputEvent** class.

➤ *getWhen()*—Returns a **long** primitive value of the system timestamp for the creation of the event. This is the same time as returned by the **System. currentTimeMillis** method.

➤ *isAltDown()*—Returns the state of the Alt key that existed when the event was created. Note that not all operating systems support all of these special flags.

➤ *isAltGraphDown()*—Returns the state of the Alt+Graph key that existed when the event was created.

➤ *isConsumed()*—Returns true if this event's **consume** method has been called.

➤ *isControlDown()*—Returns the state of the Ctrl key that existed when the event was created.

➤ *isMetaDown()*—Returns the state of the Meta key that existed when the event was created.

➤ *isShiftDown()*—Returns the state of the Shift key that existed when the event was created.

The constants defined in the **InputEvent** class that you can use to interpret the value returned by **getModifiers** are related to the keyboard or mouse. The keyboard-related constants are **SHIFT_MASK, ALT_MASK, CTRL_MASK, META_MASK,** and **ALT_GRAPH_MASK.** The mouse-related constants are **BUTTON1_MASK, BUTTON2_MASK,** and **BUTTON3_MASK.** Obviously, the underlying operating system and hardware determine which of these constants is useful. With a typical Windows mouse, the left button is **BUTTON1** and the right is **BUTTON3.**

Each bit in the 32-bit **int** returned by **getModifiers** is set independently, so you perform a bitwise AND with a constant to determine whether the condition exists. For example, the following operation results in a boolean value of **true** if the Shift key was depressed when the event **evt** was generated:

```
( evt.getModifiers() & InputEvent.SHIFT_MASK ) != 0
```

The MouseEvent Class

In addition to the timestamp and modifiers added in the **InputEvent** class, **MouseEvent** objects carry x and y coordinates as **int** primitive values. Here are the methods provided in the **MouseEvent** class for accessing these coordinates and other properties:

➤ *getX()*—Returns the horizontal position of the event as an **int** measured in pixels from the left edge of the source component. If the event is a mouse drag outside the component, position values may be negative.

➤ *getY()*—Returns the vertical position of the event as an **int** measured in pixels from the top edge of the source component.

➤ *getPoint()*—Returns the x and y coordinates as a **Point** object.

➤ *getClickCount()*—Returns an **int** number of clicks associated with the event. This number is determined by operating system conventions, not Java.

➤ *isPopupTrigger()*—Returns **true** if the event is a trigger for a pop-up menu under operating system conventions.

➤ *translatePoint(int x, int y)*—Modifies the stored location by adding these values. This method is used to translate the event to the coordinate system of another component.

➤ *paramString()*—This routine returns a **String** that describes the event.

Mouse events are confusing because there are two types of listener interface, the **MouseMotionListener** and the **MouseListener** interfaces, and two types of adapter class, **MouseMotionAdapter** and **MouseAdapter**. The methods in **MouseMotionListener** are:

➤ *mouseDragged(MouseEvent evt)*—This handles events produced when the mouse is moved with a button pressed. You can determine which button is pressed by looking at the value returned by the **getModifiers** method. Note that mouse-dragged events are sent to a component *only* if the drag was started in the component. Furthermore, events continue to be sent to the component long after the drag has exited the component.

While the drag is in operation, *no* other **MouseMotionListener** attached to another component gets **MouseEvent** events. **MouseListener**s attached to other components do get the other type of mouse events. When the mouse button is finally released, the component where the mouse drag started gets a mouse-released event.

➤ *mouseMoved(MouseEvent evt)*—This handles events produced when the mouse is moved without any button pressed. Note that a tremendous number of these events can be produced, so your handling of them should be as fast as possible.

The **MouseListener** interface handles mouse events that are more likely to be of interest to a programmer. The **MouseListener** interface defines the following methods:

➤ *mouseClicked(MouseEvent evt)*—This handles the event created when a mouse button is depressed. The value returned by **getModifiers** can be used to determine which button was pressed by comparison with constants in the **InputEvent** class.

➤ *mouseEntered(MouseEvent evt)*—This event goes to a component when the mouse first enters the component, whether or not a mouse drag is in progress.

➤ *mouseExited(MouseEvent evt)*—This event goes to a component when the mouse leaves the component, whether or not a mouse drag is in progress.

➤ *mousePressed(MouseEvent evt)*—Any press of a mouse button causes an event going to this method.

➤ *mouseReleased(MouseEvent evt)*—When a mouse button is released, an event goes to this method. Note that the event modifiers reflect the state of the mouse buttons after the release, so you can tell which button was released only if you have stored information from previous events.

The KeyEvent Class

The three kinds of key events are processed by three methods in the **KeyListener** interface:

➤ *keyPressed(KeyEvent evt)*—Every press of a key causes an event to be sent to this method.

➤ *keyReleased(KeyEvent evt)*—Every release of a key causes an event to be sent to this method.

➤ *keyTyped(KeyEvent evt)*—The event processed by this method is created only when one or more key events has generated a character.

Each **KeyEvent** carries a key code that can be obtained with the following method:

```
public int getKeyCode();
```

The **KeyEvent** class defines a huge number of key codes for both normal characters and special keys, such as the function key, cursor control keys, and modifiers. Although some of these codes coincide with ASCII codes for characters, you should use the method

```
public char getKeyChar()
```

to determine the Unicode character from a **KeyEvent** in the **keyTyped** method. Some other methods of interest in the **KeyEvent** class are as follows:

```
public void setKeyChar( char ch )
public void setModifiers( int mod )
```

These methods allow you to completely change a **KeyEvent** before it goes to a **TextComponent** such as a **TextField**. For instance, if you want to ensure that all alphabetic characters added to **textField1** are in uppercase, you could create an anonymous inner class that extends **KeyAdapter**, as follows:

```
textField1.addKeyListener( new KeyAdapter(){
    public void keyTyped( KeyEvent e ){
      e.setKeyChar( Character.toUpperCase( e.getKeyChar() ));
    }
} ) ;
```

KeyListener objects are typically used to monitor user input in a **TextField** or similar component. All **KeyListener** objects registered with a **TextField** see a new **KeyEvent** before a character is added to the text. If a **KeyListener** calls the **KeyEvent** **consume** method, the character is not added to the text field. For example, the following statement creates an anonymous inner class that extends **KeyAdapter**, which ensures that only numeric characters can be entered in **textField1**:

```
textField1.addKeyListener( new KeyAdapter(){
    public void keyTyped( KeyEvent e ){
      if( !Character.isDigit( e.getKeyChar()) )e.consume();
    }
} ) ;
```

The TextEvent Class

Rather than monitor individual **KeyEvent** events, you can simply use a **TextEventListener**. This interface has a single method:

```
public void textValueChanged( TextEvent evt )
```

This event is generated only when the text contained in the control is actually changed. One use of a **TextEventListener** is to look up a keyword while a user has the word only partially entered.

Event Processing Review

Event handling in Java can get pretty complicated. The following reviews the steps involved in event processing:

1. The operating system decides that certain events belong to a Java application and communicates them to the JVM. Exactly how much processing is done by the operating system depends on the type of component. Components

created by operating system peers have much of their low-level event processing done by the operating system, but Swing components have low-level events processed by Java.

2. The JVM creates event objects and directs them to a specific component according to various rules. For instance, the component that has the current focus gets key events, but the screen location is used to direct mouse events.

3. If a particular kind of event is enabled, **processEvent** in **java.awt.Component** (or in a class that overrides **processEvent**) is called. The default behavior of **processEvent** is to call a more specific event processing method according to the type of the event object.

4. If any listeners for this type of event are registered with the component, the appropriate method in each listener is called with the reference to the event object. Each registered listener gets called, but the order in which they are called is not guaranteed.

As a programmer, you have an opportunity to process an event at several points in this chain. You can override **processEvent** or one of the other process methods in **Component,** you can write a class that implements one of the listener interfaces, or you can create a custom version of one of the adapter classes.

Practice Questions

Question 1

> Which of the following statements about adapter classes are true? [Check all correct answers]
>
> ❑ a. Adapter classes may provide default processing of an event.
>
> ❑ b. Every listener interface has a corresponding adapter class.
>
> ❑ c. All methods in adapter classes are empty.
>
> ❑ d. Adapter classes are named according to the event they process.

Answers c and d are correct. All methods in adapter classes are empty and the classes are named according to the event they process. Adapters provide empty method implementations for all methods in a particular interface. Therefore, answer a is incorrect. Adapters are not provided for interfaces with only one method. Therefore, answer b is incorrect.

Question 2

> If you want to prevent the character represented by a **KeyEvent** from being added to a **TextField**, what should you do in the **keyTyped** method of a listener that gets the event?
>
> ○ a. Execute the **KeyEvent** object's **consume** method.
>
> ○ b. Return **true** from the **keyTyped** method.
>
> ○ c. Call the **KeyEvent** object's **setKeyChar** method with a zero value.
>
> ○ d. Get the current text from the **TextField**, remove the last character from the **String**, and reset the text.

Answer a is correct. The purpose of the **consume** method is to prevent further processing of the input event. All listener interface methods have a void return type. Therefore, answer b is incorrect. Answer c is incorrect because it would change the character but would not prevent it from being added. When a **KeyListener** gets the event, the **TextField** has not yet processed it. Therefore, answer d is incorrect.

Question 3

When you add a **KeyListener** to a **Button** component, which of the following statements are true? [Check all correct answers]

- ❏ a. You must also call the **Button**'s **enableEvents** method with the correct constants to enable key and mouse click events.

- ❏ b. You must also call the **Button**'s **enableEvents** method with the constant **AWTEvent.KEY_EVENT_MASK**.

- ❏ c. The **KeyListener** must provide the **keyPressed, keyReleased**, and **keyTyped** methods.

- ❏ d. The act of adding the listener ensures that key events are enabled for the **Button**.

Answers c and d are correct. The listed methods are required in a KeyListener, and the **addKeyListener** method in the **Button** object turns action events on. Note that the **addKeyListener** method is in the **Component** class, so all AWT components can have **KeyListeners**. Therefore, answers a and b are incorrect.

Question 4

Which statement about **ActionEvent** events is *wrong*?

- ○ a. Only one method in **ActionListener** takes an **ActionEvent**.

- ○ b. When you are entering text into a **TextField**, pressing the Enter key causes an **ActionEvent**.

- ○ c. When you are in an application, clicking on the window close control causes an **ActionEvent**.

- ○ d. **Scrollbar** objects do not generate **ActionEvent** events.

Answer c is the only incorrect statement and is thus the correct answer. Window controls are a special case and generate **WindowEvent** events.

Question 5

Seven kinds of **MouseEvent** events and two kinds of listeners handle mouse events. From the following list of method signatures, select the methods found in the **MouseListener** interface. [Check all correct answers]

❑ a. **public void mouseEntered(MouseEvent e)**

❑ b. **public void mouseDragged(MouseEvent e)**

❑ c. **public void mouseReleased(MouseEvent e)**

❑ d. **public void mousePressed(MouseEvent e)**

Answers a, c, and d are correct. These are all methods found in the **MouseListener** interface. **mouseDragged** is in the **MouseMotionListener** interface. Therefore, answer b is incorrect.

Question 6

What value is returned by the **MouseEvent** method **getX()**?

○ a. An **int** primitive value that represents the horizontal position of the mouse event relative to the left edge of the **Component** that generates the event

○ b. A **long** primitive value that represents the horizontal position of the mouse event relative to the left edge of the **Component** that generates the event

○ c. An **int** primitive value that represents the horizontal position of the mouse event relative to the left edge of the application window

○ d. An **int** primitive value that represents the horizontal position of the mouse event relative to the left edge of the container that holds the **Component** generating the event

Answer a is correct. The position information in a **MouseEvent** is relative to the upper-left corner of the object that generates the event. Like all screen position calculations, the x position is an **int** value. Therefore, answer b is incorrect. The **MouseEvent** position information is generated at the component level; no attempt is made to convert to other coordinate systems. Therefore, answers c and d are incorrect.

Question 7

> When an **AdjustmentListener** gets an **AdjustmentEvent** event from a **Scrollbar**, which **AdjustmentEvent** instance method is used to retrieve the current setting of the **Scrollbar**?
>
> ○ a. **public int getPosition()**
>
> ○ b. **public int getValue()**
>
> ○ c. **public float getPosition()**
>
> ○ d. **public float getValue()**

Answer b is correct. **public int getValue()** is used to retrieve the current setting of the **Scrollbar**. The method **public int getPosition()** does not exist. Therefore, answer a is incorrect. A **Scrollbar** value is an **int**. Therefore, answers c and d are incorrect.

Question 8

> Your user interface has a **java.awt.Choice** component that displays a list of colors the user can select to set the application foreground color. Which kind of listener should you attach to this component so that you can be notified of a new color selection?
>
> ○ a. **ItemListener**
>
> ○ b. **ActionListener**
>
> ○ c. **SelectionListener**
>
> ○ d. **MouseEventListener**

Answer a is correct. Selecting or deselecting an item in a **Choice, List,** or menu creates an **ItemEvent** that is sent to an **ItemListener**. **ActionEvent** events are not generated in a **Choice**. Therefore, answer b is incorrect. There is no such thing as a **SelectionEvent**. Therefore, answer c is incorrect. It would be very difficult to interpret mouse events in terms of item selection in the **Choice**. Therefore, answer d is incorrect.

Question 9

The following code illustrates how to test the modifiers of a **MouseEvent** to detect the left mouse button being depressed:

```
public void mouseClicked( MouseEvent evt ){
  if( (evt.getModifiers() &
      XXXXXX.BUTTON1_MASK) != 0 ) {
    System.out.println("Left button" );
  }
}
```

However, **XXXXXX** has been substituted for the class name for the **BUTTON1_MASK** constant. Which of the following classes could be used to replace **XXXXXX** and result in working code? [Check all correct answers]

❑ a. **AWTEvent**

❑ b. **ComponentEvent**

❑ c. **InputEvent**

❑ d. **MouseEvent**

Answers c and d are correct. The modifier constants are defined in **InputEvent** and inherited by **MouseEvent**. Answers a and b are incorrect because they are ancestors of **InputEvent** and thus do not have access to these constants.

Question 10

A **TextEvent** is generated when a user changes the position of the editing cursor in a **TextField**.

○ a. True

○ b. False

Answer b is correct. This is a false statement. A **TextEvent** is generated only when the text content is changed, no matter what the sequence of low-level events.

Need to Know More?

 Geary, David M. *Graphic Java 2, Mastering the JFC: AWT, Volume 1.* Prentice Hall PTR/Sun Microsystems Press, Upper Saddle River, NJ, 1998. ISBN 0-13079-666-2. This is a well-regarded book on AWT usage. The other volume in this series treats the Swing classes.

 Zukowski, John. *Java AWT Reference.* O'Reilly & Associates, Inc, Sebastopol, CA, 1997. ISBN 1-56592-240-9. This volume contains over 1,000 pages of details on the AWT classes. This version for Software Development Kit (SDK) 1.1 is out of print. However, if you can find a copy, almost all of the material is applicable to Java 2.

 http://java.sun.com/docs/books/tutorial/uiswing/overview/event.html is an online tutorial that is directed mostly at Swing graphical user interface (GUI) components, but the information on event handling is useful.

Java IO

Terms you'll need to understand:

✓ The **File** class

✓ **InputStream**

✓ **OutputStream**

✓ **Filter**

✓ Unicode Transformation Format (UTF) encoding

✓ **Reader**

✓ **Writer**

Techniques you'll need to master:

✓ Using Java **File** objects to get information on files and directories

✓ Constructing objects to read and write bytes

✓ Constructing objects to read and write characters with specific encodings

✓ Reading and writing Java objects

For access to local files, Java provides classes for both random and sequential access of text and data files. Special methods are provided to support internationalization of programs by reading a variety of character formats into Java's standard Unicode format. In addition to reading and writing primitive values, the serialization mechanism lets you store the complete state of an object in a file and rebuild the object on demand.

From the beginning, Java has been aware of networks. The extensive library of network-related classes makes it easy for even the beginning programmer to write programs that communicate over networks.

How Java Handles Files

The **java.io.File** class is the central organizing principle for manipulating file systems independently of the operating system. The primary use of a **File** object is to manipulate directory and file names. The **File** class knows about the conventions of the particular operating system on which the Java Virtual Machine (JVM) is running and, in fact, has constants for the file separator character that are set by the JVM. Here are the constructors for **File** objects:

```
1. File( File parent, String path )
2. File( String path )
3. File( String parent, String path )
```

Note that in the preceding code, **path** may contain a directory name, a file name, or a combination. A **File** contains an *abstract pathname* that can represent either a directory or a path plus a file name. Paths can be either relative to the current user directory or absolute.

The static variables in the **File** class that represent system conventions are:

➤ *File.pathSeparator*—The character used to separate paths in path lists as a **String**. In Windows, this is ";".

➤ *File.pathSeparatorChar*—The character used to separate paths in path lists as a **char**.

➤ *File.separator*—The character used to separate parts of a path as a **String**. In Windows, this is "\".

➤ *File.separatorChar*—The character used to separate parts of a path as a **char**.

These variables may be used to work with directory and file names completely independent of the operating system.

File Methods for Directories

If you have a **File** object that represents a directory, you can use it to get a list of files and subdirectories as either an array of **File** objects or an array of **String** objects. Note that all methods that get file system information check with the security manager and may throw a **SecurityException** if the program does not have clearance to access the file system. That is how applets are prevented from accessing a user's file system. Getting directory information is illustrated in this code fragment, where **filter** is an object that implements the **FileNameFilter** interface:

```
1. File start = new File( "C:\\java" ); // the java directory
2. File[] grp = start.listFiles() ;
3. File[] selgrp = start.listFiles( filter ) ;
4. String[] names = start.list() ;
5. String[] selnames = start.list( filter );
```

To implement the **FileNameFilter** interface, a class simply has to have an **accept** method that is handed a **File** object representing a directory and a **String** file name, and returns **true** if the file belongs in the list. In the following code fragment, which illustrates creating a **FileNameFilter** as an anonymous inner class, **f** is a **File** object:

```
1. String[] ss = f.list( new FilenameFilter(){
2.   public boolean accept( File dir, String name ){
3.     return( name.endsWith( ".java" ) ) ;
4.   }
5. }
6. );
```

There is also a **FileFilter** interface in which the **accept** method is handed only a **File** object that represents a candidate file. To remember the difference, note that **FileNameFilter** takes a **File** and a name, whereas **FileFilter** takes only a **File**.

Here are some of the methods you can use with a **File** object, such as those returned by lines 2 and 3 in the preceding code:

➤ *boolean exists()*—Returns **true** if the directory or file exists

➤ *boolean isDirectory()*—Returns **true** if the **File** represents a directory

➤ *boolean isFile()*—Returns **true** if the **File** represents a normal file

You can also get an array of **File** objects that represent the file system roots with the **listRoots** method. On a Windows system, the roots are the individual drives, such as "A:\", "C:\", and so on.

Although **File** objects can deal with absolute paths or paths relative to the "current" directory, there is no method in **File** to change the current directory. It is best to determine the current directory from the system properties, as follows:

```
String currentDir = System.getProperty("user.dir") ;
```

Using that information, you can then create absolute paths.

File Methods for Files

Here are some of the most useful instance methods related to files in the **java. io.File** class:

➤ *boolean canRead()*—Returns **true** if the current program is allowed to read the file.

➤ *boolean canWrite()*—Returns **true** if the current program is allowed to write to the file.

➤ *long length()*—Returns the length of the file as a **long** primitive.

➤ *long lastModified()*—Returns a **long** primitive that represents the date the file was last modified. The value is milliseconds since the beginning of January 1, 1970, compatible with the **currentTimeMillis** method in the **java.lang.System** class.

➤ *boolean delete()*—Attempts to delete a file or directory and returns **true** if it succeeds.

➤ *boolean createNewFile()*—Creates a new empty file with this name unless a file with this name already exists. This operation is done atomically, meaning that it is not possible for separate **Thread**s to succeed with the same file name. It returns **true** if a new file was created.

Each one of these may throw a **SecurityException** if the current program does not have clearance to access file system data.

 Remember that simply creating a **File** object with the path and file name of a file does not do anything to the file system itself. To create or open the file, you must use the **createNewFile** method or pass the **File** object to a constructor for one of the other classes in the **java.io** package.

InputStream and OutputStream

InputStream and **OutputStream** are the **abstract** classes at the base of the hierarchy of Java classes that represent streams of 8-bit bytes. The basic requirement of a class extending **InputStream** is that it can read the next **byte** of data from a source. Likewise, an extension of **OutputStream** must be able to write a single **byte** of data. From this simple base, Java constructs a wide variety of classes. Here are some of the commonly used extensions:

➤ *FileInputStream*—The constructor takes a file name or **File** object and opens the file for reading.

➤ *FileOutputStream*—The constructor opens an existing file or creates a new one. One of the constructors lets you append data to the end of an existing file, but generally any existing data is written over.

➤ *ByteArrayInputStream*—This class lets you read a **byte** array as if it were a file.

➤ *ByteArrayOutputStream*—With one of these, you can write an arbitrary sequence of data to a memory buffer that automatically expands as needed.

Stream Filters

Unless your program requires only reading and writing bytes, you will be using a stream filter. A filter connects to an **InputStream** or **OutputStream** and performs some transformation on the data or provides some additional functionality. For example, in the following code fragment, a **DataInputStream** object interprets a stream of bytes from the **FileInputStream** as **double** primitive values:

```
double d[] = new double[100] ;
try {
FileInputStream fis = new FileInputStream( "mydata.bin" );
DataInputStream dis = new DataInputStream( fis ) ;
for int i = 0 ; i < 100 ; i++ ){
  d[i] = dis.readDouble();
}
}catch(IOException e ) {}
```

Note how the **DataInputStream** is constructed from the **FileInputStream**, a technique sometimes called *chaining*.

The following code fragment constructs a chain of output stream objects in which the **DataOutputStream** provides the methods to output primitive values, and the **BufferedOutputStream** stores the bytes in a buffer and writes buffer loads to the file via the **FileOutputStream** object:

```
try {
FileOutputStream fos = new FileOutputStream( "moredata.bin" );
BufferedOutputStream bos = new BufferedOutputStream( fos, 4096 );
DataOutputStream dos = new DataOutputStream( bos );
  // assume lots of data writing goes on here
dos.flush() ; // also flushes the buffered stream
dos.close() ;
```

 For programming advanced input/output (IO) methods in Java, it is essential to understand this approach of chaining together stream-handling classes.

By extending the **InputStream** or **OutputStream** classes, you can turn just about anything into a stream of bytes that will fit right into the powerful classes in the **java.io** package. Alternately, you can extend **FilterInputStream** or **FilterOutputStream** to create classes that modify a stream of bytes and are compatible with the basic Java IO (input/output) classes.

Here are the classes in the **java.io** package that can be built on an **InputStream** and extend **FilterInputStream**:

➤ *BufferedInputStream*—As discussed later in this chapter, buffered streams provide for efficient reading of bytes and a limited ability to back up the point of reading.

➤ *DataInputStream*—This class implements the **DataInput** interface and provides for reading all of the Java primitive types from a stream of bytes.

➤ *LineNumberInputStream*—Originally intended for reading lines of text while tracking the line number, this class is deprecated in favor of the **Reader** equivalent because it cannot correctly handle Unicode.

➤ *PushbackInputStream*—This class can "unread" a single character.

Next are the classes in the **java.io** package that can be built on an **OutputStream** and extend **FilterOutputStream**:

➤ *BufferedOutputStream*—As discussed later in this chapter, this class provides for efficient writing of bytes.

➤ *DataOutputStream*—This class implements the **DataOutput** interface and provides for writing all of the Java primitive types to a stream of bytes.

➤ *PrintStream*—This class provides many convenient methods for printing various data types.

Buffered Streams

A basic **InputStream** can read the next byte in a file, but it can't back up the point of reading. Furthermore, reading a file one byte at a time can be very inefficient if each read has to call routines in the underlying operating system. The **BufferedInputStream** class tackles the efficiency problem by reading blocks of bytes into a buffer and then supplying the sequence of bytes without having to go to the operating system.

Input streams that store some of the stream data, such as **BufferedInputStream**, support the **mark** and **reset** methods. These methods allow a limited ability to back up in an **InputStream**. Here are the **InputStream** methods involved in this capability:

➤ *boolean markSupported()*—Returns **true** if this stream supports **mark** and **reset**.

➤ *void mark(int byteCt)*—Marks the current position in this stream and tells the stream to be prepared to be able to back up **byteCt** bytes.

➤ *void reset()*—Attempts to reset the reading point of the stream back to the marked location. If this is impossible, an **IOException** is thrown.

As you can see, the **mark** and **reset** capability is very limited and does not provide much flexibility. The programmer must carefully plan to ensure that resetting beyond the capability of the stream is not required. The **mark** and **reset** methods exist in all classes derived from **InputStream**, but unless **markSupported** returns **true**, they are do-nothing methods.

Here are the classes in the **java.io** package that support some degree of buffering:

➤ *PushbackInputStream*—This class supports the capability of *unreading* a single byte but does not support **mark** and **reset**.

➤ *BufferedInputStream*—This class attempts to fill a buffer every time it reads from a source. It supports **mark** and **reset**.

➤ *BufferedOutputStream*—Bytes written to this stream are stored in a buffer until the buffer is full or the **flush** method is called. Closing the stream calls **flush** automatically. The default buffer size is 512 bytes, but you can specify another size in the constructor. There is no equivalent of **mark** and **reset** in output streams, so if you want a class that *unwrites* bytes, you must code it yourself.

The PrintStream Class

You have probably already used this class extensively because the default **System.out** stream is a **PrintStream**. This class knows how to output text representations of various primitive values correctly. All output is in the form of 8-bit bytes in the default encoding of the operating system. A **PrintStream** traps all **IOExceptions** and sets an internal flag when one occurs.

This class does not correctly handle Unicode characters that use the high byte of a 16-bit character. To discourage the continued use of **PrintStream**, the constructors for the class were deprecated in Java 1.1, but Sun removed the deprecation tag for Java 2. The other methods are not deprecated because you need to be able to use them with the **System.out** stream. Programmers are encouraged to use the **PrintWriter** class instead of **PrintStream**.

Streams and Characters

As you will recall, Java uses 16-bit Unicode characters in **String** objects and the **char** primitive to support internationalization. However, all of the Java source code files in the standard library and those written by typical development environments are in 8-bit bytes, and they typically use the 7-bit ASCII code. When an object such as a **DataInputStream** interprets ASCII text into 16-bit characters, it simply adds an all-zero high byte, and when a **PrintStream** writes 16-bit characters, it simply drops the high byte.

The UTF-8 encoding system neatly bridges between the world of 7-bit ASCII and 16-bit Unicode. A UTF-8 encoded text file consists of bytes that are interpreted according to some simple rules. If the high bit of a byte is zero, it is considered an ASCII character, but if the high byte is one, it must be interpreted as part of a multibyte sequence that creates a 16-bit character. The Unicode characters between "\u0020" and "\u007F" are equivalent to ASCII and the ISO8859-1 (Latin-1) encoding.

A single character may end up encoded in 1, 2, or 3 bytes. Because there is no direct equivalence between the number of characters encoded with UTF-8 in a file and the number of bytes, the reading and writing methods use a special format as follows:

➤ *void writeUTF(String s)*—This method, specified in the **DataOutput** interface, writes the length of the **String** as a 2-byte unsigned integer and then writes the bytes that encode the characters.

➤ *String readUTF()*—This method, specified in the **DataInput** interface, first reads 2 bytes to get the count of the number of characters to follow and then reads and interprets the stream until that many characters have been decoded and placed in the **String**.

There are also a variety of other character encoding systems that got started long before the Unicode standard was created. Java provides for reading and writing streams of these characters via classes that extend the **abstract java.io.Reader** and **java.io.Writer** classes.

The **Reader** and **Writer** Classes

Classes derived from **Reader** and **Writer** can take into account the locale information that the operating system provides, or they can use a specified locale when converting between Unicode and other character systems. The following code fragment indicates how a Java program could write a file using ISO8859-8 (Hebrew) encoding:

```
try {
  FileOutputStream fos = new FileOutputStream( "sometext.txt" );
  OutputStreamWriter osw = new OutputStreamWriter( fos,
    "ISO8859-8" );
  // various write operations go here
  osw.close();
}catch( UnsupportedEncodingException ee ){
  System.out.println("Encoding ISO8859-8 not supported");
}catch( IOException ie ){
  System.out.println( ie );
}
```

Here are some of the **Reader**- and **Writer**-related classes you are likely to encounter:

➤ *BufferedReader*—This object reads ahead in a character input stream to improve efficiency. This is the preferred class for reading lines of text into **String** objects using the **readLine** method. It automatically handles the various end-of-line control codes.

➤ *BufferedWriter*—This object stores characters in a buffer and writes the entire buffer when it is full or when the **flush** method is called.

➤ *CharArrayReader*—With this class, an array of **char** can be turned into a character stream.

➤ *StringReader*—With this class, a **String** can be turned into a character stream.

➤ *CharArrayWriter*—This class writes to an array of **char** that is automatically expanded as needed.

➤ **StringWriter**—Characters output to this class go into a **StringBuffer** that expands as necessary.

➤ *FileReader*—This class is provided for convenience in reading character files. It is effectively an **InputStreamReader** combined with a **FileInputStream**. The default character encoding is assumed.

➤ *FileWriter*—This class is effectively an **OutputStreamWriter** combined with a **FileOutputStream**. It assumes the default character encoding.

➤ *InputStreamReader*—This is the bridge between byte streams and character streams. It can use the default encoding or one specified by name.

➤ *OutputStreamWriter*—This writes characters to an **OutputStream** of bytes, using a specified encoding or the default.

➤ *PrintWriter*—This is the **Writer**-derived analog to the **PrintStream** class.

➤ *LineNumberReader*—This object provides a buffer and counts lines as it reads a stream; in addition, it can provide the line number of the present position in the stream.

DataInput and **DataOutput** Interfaces

Classes that implement the **DataInput** or **DataOutput** interfaces must provide methods for reading or writing all of the Java primitive types. Note that the standard Java format for writing integer primitives is "big-endian"—that is, the most significant byte is written first. This is the opposite of the usual approach in the Intel/DOS/Windows environment, so if your Java method must read native files, you may have to provide special methods for interpreting the byte stream in a different order.

In addition to writing individual primitive values, these interfaces provide for reading and writing arrays of bytes, **String** objects, and the special UTF-8 en-coded character stream format.

Streams and URLs

From the beginning, Java has had many classes designed for communicating on the World Wide Web using the Hypertext Transport Protocol (HTTP) recognized by Web servers and browsers. A **URL** object represents the address of a resource on the World Wide Web; it includes information on the host computer, the protocol to be used, and the resource name. A **URL** may address a simple Web page, or it may include data being submitted to a process on the Web server.

In the environment of a Java applet, you can use the following methods to get specific **URL** objects:

➤ *getDocumentBase()*—Returns the **URL** for the Web page in which the applet is embedded.

➤ *getCodeBase()*—Returns the **URL** for the directory on the server that the applet class file came from. This may be different from the document base if the <APPLET> tag used a CODEBASE parameter to point to the applet source.

The following code fragment illustrates getting an **InputStream** for data provided by a request to a Web server by an applet:

```
URL theUrl = new URL( getDocumentBase(), "mydata.bin" );
InputStream ins = theUrl.openStream();
```

Calling the **openStream** method attempts to open a connection to the Web server with a **URL** for a specific file. If all goes well, the Web server sends that file using the HTTP protocol, and the programmer can read data from the resulting **InputStream**. Note that this code would have to be enclosed in a **try-catch** structure because **openStream** may throw an **IOException**. Because it may take some time for the server to respond, code like this should always be in a **Thread** that is separate from the JVM event-processing **Thread**.

The **RandomAccessFile** Class

One of the major divisions in the **java.io** package is between this class and all other classes. A **RandomAccessFile** object can both read and write data to any part of a file. All other file-reading and file-writing classes view files as streams of bytes that must be read from the beginning of the file. **RandomAccessFile** objects are created with a *mode* **String**, which can either be "r" for read-only or "rw" for read and write. The following constructors attempt to create a file if the mode is "rw" and the file does not already exist:

```
RandomAccessFile( File f, String mode )
RandomAccessFile( String filename, String mode )
```

These constructors can throw a **FileNotFoundException** or a **SecurityException**.

A **RandomAccessFile** has a file pointer that determines where in the file the next read or write operation will occur. When the file is initially opened, this pointer is at 0 (the beginning of the file). After that, it is positioned where the last read or write ended. You can position this pointer with the **seek** method, as illustrated in the following method for reading a selected fixed-length record:

```
public byte[] readRecord( int rn ) throws IOException {
  long fpos = rn * RECORD_SIZE ;
  ranf.seek( fpos );
  byte[] rec = new byte[ RECORD_SIZE ];
  ranf.read( rec );
  return rec ;
}
```

Here, **ranf** is a **RandomAccessFile** that is already open, and **RECORD_SIZE** is a constant.

In addition to methods for reading an arbitrary number of bytes into a buffer, the **RandomAccessFile** class implements all of the methods called for by the **DataInput** and **DataOutput** interfaces. This means that there are methods for reading and writing all Java primitives plus **String** objects.

Object Serialization

Using object serialization, you can permanently store a Java object in a file or transmit it over a network to another Java program. Although object serialization is not part of the exam, the techniques are an excellent illustration of Java IO flexibility.

Classes indicate that they make objects that can be serialized by implementing the **java.io.Serializable** interface. Serialization is at the core of all sorts of interesting Java applications. Writing an object is as simple as this example:

```
try {
  FileOutputStream fos = new FileOutputStream( "currentObject" );
  ObjectOutputStream oos = new ObjectOutputStream( fos );
  oos.writeObject( theObj );
  oos.close();
} catch(Exception e){}
```

Any system that has a copy of the class file for the class that **theObj** belongs to could now read the "currentObject" file with the **readObject** method of an **ObjectInputStream** and reconstitute the object. The object that is serialized may be quite complex, with many references to other objects. The serialization process takes care of writing all of the linked objects and keeps track of all objects that have been written so that no duplication occurs.

You do not have to accept Java's method of serialization. If you have a more efficient method, just make your custom class implement the **java.io. Externalizable** interface. The **writeObject** method will then call your **writeExternal** method, and the **readObject** method will call your **readExternal** method to serialize the object.

Java Archive (JAR) Files and Zip Files

JAR files provide a compact way to store a number of classes or other data resources. The format used in a JAR file is that of the familiar zip utility. Classes in the **java.util.zip** and **java.util.jar** packages provide methods for reading and writing data with stream methods that decompress or compress files. In addition to file names, a JAR or zip file may contain path information, essentially creating a directory system within a single file.

The JAR file format adds a *manifest* file to the zip format. This file gives extra information about each of the data items in the file. Extra information may include digital signatures to positively identify applications as coming from a known source.

Client/Server Programming

It is surprisingly easy to program communication between computers using Java's network classes. A **java.net.Socket** object represents one end of a Transmission Control Protocol/Internet Protocol (TCP/IP)-based communication link between two programs. The programmer does not have to worry about the details of the TCP/IP protocol. Once a **Socket** has established a connection, it can be used to create input streams and output streams that receive and transmit streams of bytes.

The draft objectives for the exam actually included a section on socket programming, but this got dropped in the final release. I am leaving this material in the book because it illustrates significant points about using streams and handling exceptions.

Here is some code from a simple client class in which the constructor creates a socket connection to a given port on a given host and opens streams for communication:

```
1.    // instance variables
2.    Socket sok ;
3.    OutputStreamWriter oswri ;
4.    InputStream ins ;
5.    BufferedReader bread ;
6.
7.    SimpleConnect( String host, int port ) throws IOException {
8.      sok = new Socket( host, port );
9.      oswri = new OutputStreamWriter( sok.getOutputStream() );
10.   InputStreamReader isr = new InputStreamReader(
11.           ins = sok.getInputStream() );
12.   bread = new BufferedReader( isr );
13.   System.out.println("Streams created" );
14. }
```

Note that because the streams are connected to **Reader** and **Writer** objects, this connection could be used only for character streams, not binary data. The constructor blocks at line 8 until a connection is established or an exception occurs. For this reason, applications involving network connections usually create separate **Thread**s to establish a connection and do the actual data transmission and reception. If you used the system **Thread** that handles user events and screen painting to execute the **SimpleConnect** constructor, your application could be unresponsive for a long time.

On the Server Side

For the preceding code to establish a connection, there must be a server application on the host computer that is listening for a connection on that port. In Java, this can be done with a **java.net.ServerSocket** object. The following code fragment shows the constructor for a simple server class that listens at a given port:

```
// instance variables
ServerSocket listenSok ;
Socket clientSok ;
boolean working ;

SimpleServer( ) throws IOException {
   listenSok = new ServerSocket( portn );
   working = true ;
}
```

After the **ServerSocket** is constructed, the server application executes the following method, which blocks at line 5 until a client application tries to establish a connection:

```
1.  void listen() {
2.    System.out.println("Listening");
3.    while( working ){
4.     try {
5.      clientSok = listenSok.accept();
6.      System.out.println("Client connect port:" +
7.          clientSok.getPort() );
8.      handleClient();
9.     }catch(IOException ex ){
10.      System.out.println("listen: " + ex );
11.    }
12.   } // end while
13. }
```

When a **ServerSocket** accepts a connection, it creates a **Socket** to be used for the actual communication. In the preceding code, the **handleClient** method is executed by the same **Thread** that created the **clientSok Socket**. This means that only one client could be handled at a time. In servers that need to handle multiple clients, a new **Thread** would be created for each client.

Datagram Sockets

The TCP/IP protocol used by **java.net.Socket** is actually two protocols that work at different levels. TCP performs error checking, requests retransmission of damaged or missing packets, and acknowledges packet receipt; IP is responsible for trying to get packets to their destination. The extra processing involved in error checking and packet acknowledgement consumes network bandwidth and processing power.

For applications that don't mind losing an occasional packet, such as audio transmissions, User Datagram Protocol (UDP) is much more efficient. This protocol is sometimes referred to as the *Unreliable* Datagram Protocol because it simply sends and receives packets of bytes without worrying about lost data or missing packets. It's up to the programmer to interpret the packets.

A **DatagramPacket** object encapsulates all details of a single packet transmission, including the network addresses of the source and destination, the port on the destination machine, and the actual data bytes. A new object should be created for every packet sent.

Packets are both sent and received on a **DatagramSocket** object, which listens on an assigned port number. When sending, you must supply the socket with a **DatagramPacket** that has been addressed and filled with data bytes. When receiving, you must supply a new **DatagramPacket** object, which the **DatagramSocket** will fill. It is up to the programmer to ensure that the byte array supplied for receiving a packet is large enough, or data will be lost.

Listing 15.1 shows an example of processing a **DatagramPacket** in an application. This method performs the trivial task of receiving a packet (line 13), interpreting the byte array as a **String** (line 16), converting it to uppercase, and retransmitting it (line 19). Note how the source information in the received packet (lines 14 and 15) is used to set the address in the transmitted packet (line 20).

Listing 15.1   An example of sending and receiving UDP datagrams.

```
1. // bufsz is a int giving the buffer size
2. // listenSoc is a DatagramSocket listening at a specified port
3. void listen() {
4.   byte[] buf = new byte[ bufsz ] ;
5.   DatagramPacket recDG ;
6.   DatagramPacket sendDG ;
7.   InetAddress fromaddr ;
8.   int fromport ;
9.   String tmp ;
10.  while( working ){
11.    try {
```

```
12.        recDG = new DatagramPacket( buf, bufsz );
13.        listenSok.receive( recDG );
14.        fromport = recDG.getPort();
15.        fromaddr = recDG.getAddress();
16.        tmp = new String( buf, 0, recDG.getLength() );
17.        tmp = tmp.toUpperCase();
18.        byte[] sendbuf = tmp.getBytes();
19.        sendDG = new DatagramPacket( sendbuf, sendbuf.length,
20.              fromaddr, fromport );
21.        listenSok.send( sendDG );
22.     }catch(IOException ex ){
23.         System.out.println("listen: " + ex );
24.     }
25.   }
26. }
```

Exceptions Thrown by IO Classes

Security-related exceptions may be thrown if a program does not have clearance to perform certain operations. In addition, a large number of possible exceptions descended from the **IOException** class can be thrown by input/output methods. Here are some of the ones you are most likely to encounter:

➤ *EOFException*—Is thrown when an input method hits an unexpected end of file. Some classes return a special value rather than throwing the exception.

➤ *FileNotFoundException*—Is thrown when a file specified by a **String** or **File** could not be opened.

➤ *InterruptedIOException*—Is thrown when a **Thread** performing an IO operation is interrupted. The exception object has a field that indicates how many bytes had been transferred before the interruption.

➤ *MalformedURLException*—Is thrown when an attempt to create a stream from a **URL** cannot interpret the data as a valid address.

➤ *ObjectStreamException*—Is the abstract class that is the base for all exceptions specific to serializing objects.

IO Class Overview

I have been able to skim only the high points of working with Java IO classes. Here are some of the most important points to remember:

➤ *File*—Remember that creating **File** objects doesn't change the file system.

➤ *InputStream and OutputStream*—The majority of Java IO classes are related to processing streams of bytes. Sources for objects derived from the **abstract**

InputStream and **Outputstream** classes include local files, HTTP connections, and **Sockets**.

➤ *Filters and chaining*—Classes that transform and interpret streams are called filters. Stream processing objects can be chained to provide a variety of functions.

➤ *Reader and Writer*—These classes read and write Unicode characters and support locale-dependent interpretation of text files. They are not used for reading and writing binary data.

➤ *RandomAccessFile*—This class is completely separate from the world of streams, but it does provide the methods of both the **DataInput** and **DataOutput** interfaces.

➤ *Socket and ServerSocket*—With these classes, you can implement TCP/IP communication between client and server applications. A **Socket** object provides an **InputStream** and an **OutputStream**.

➤ *DatagramSocket*—This class can send and receive blocks of bytes in UDP format over networks.

Practice Questions

Question 1

What happens to the file system when the following code is run and the **myFile** object is created (assume that **name** represents a valid path and file name for a file that does not presently exist)? [Check all correct answers]

```
File createFile( String name ){
  File myFile = new File( name ) ;
  return myFile ;
}
```

❑ a. A new empty file with that name is created but not opened.

❑ b. The current directory changes to that specified in **name**.

❑ c. A new empty file with that name is created and opened.

❑ d. None of the above.

Answer d is the only correct answer. Creating a **File** object does not do anything to the file system; therefore a, b, and c are incorrect.

Question 2

A Java programmer proposes to accomplish random access to a file that
exists on a Web server with the following code in an applet:

```
1. URL newU = new URL( getDocumentBase(),
   "thedata.txt" ) ;
2. RandomAccessFile raf = new
   RandomAccessFile( newU );
```

What is the result of trying to compile and run this code?

○ a. The compiler objects to the constructor in line 2.

○ b. The compiler objects to the constructor in line 1.

○ c. The code compiles but gets a security exception when it runs.

○ d. The code compiles and the **RandomAccessFile** is created when it
runs.

Answer a is correct. Line 1 shows correct creation of a URL, so answer b does
not occur. But there is no way to create a **RandomAccessFile** from a URL, so
the compiler rejects this line. The basic reason is that there is no protocol for
random access to files via HTTP. Because the code does not compile, c and d
cannot be correct.

Question 3

Which of the following statements about the default **System.out** stream
are correct? [Check all correct answers]

❏ a. **System.out** is a **PrintStream**.

❏ b. **System.out** is an **OutputStream**.

❏ c. **System.out** is a **FilterOutputStream**.

❏ d. **System.out** throws **IOException** exceptions if it encounters an
error.

Answers a, b, and c are correct because **System.out** is a **PrintStream** and
PrintStream inherits from **FilterOutputStream**, which inherits from
OutputStream. **PrintStream** objects never throw **IOExceptions**. Therefore, an-
swer d is incorrect.

Question 4

Which approach would you use to create an **InputStream** for data being transmitted through a **DatagramSocket**?

○ a. Call the **DatagramSocket getInputStream** method.

○ b. Custom programming would be required to do error checking and create the stream of bytes required by an **InputStream**.

○ c. It is impossible to create an **InputStream** to work with a **DatagramSocket**.

Answer b is correct because the Java library does not supply methods to do additional processing of any kind on UDP packets. Answer a is incorrect because **DatagramSocket** does not have a **getInputStream** method. **DatagramSocket** just sends and receives packets. Answer c is incorrect because the **InputStream** methods could be accomplished by custom programming.

Question 5

Which of the following objects can't be used in the constructor of a **DataInputStream** object?

○ a. **FileInputStream**

○ b. **RandomAccessFile**

○ c. **BufferedInputStream**

○ d. **ByteArrayInputStream**

Answer b is correct. The **RandomAccessFile** class already implements the **DataInput** interface methods and cannot be used as an **InputStream**. The classes in answers a, c, and d can be used in a DataInputStream constructor and thus cannot be the answer to the question. On the real test, questions asking you to identify what will not work, as opposed to asking what will work, are likely to occur.

Question 6

Which statement about encoding a character stream using UTF-8 is correct?

- ○ a. A single Java character may end up as 1, 2, or 3 bytes when encoded.
- ○ b. A single Java character will always occupy 2 bytes when encoded.
- ○ c. A single Java character will always occupy either 2 or 3 bytes when encoded.
- ○ d. A single Java character may end up as 1, 2, 3, or 4 bytes when encoded.

Answer a is correct. Normal ASCII characters are encoded as a single byte, whereas others occupy 2 or 3 bytes but never more. Therefore, the other answers are incorrect.

Question 7

Here is the complete code for a class to list the contents of a text file to the console, except that the name of one of the classes has been replaced by **XXXX** in two places:

```java
import java.io.* ;
class LineRead {
  public static void main(String args[] ){
   String s1 = args[0] ;
   try {
    LineRead x = new LineRead(new File(s1));
    x.list( System.out );
   }catch(Exception e){}
  }

  XXXX lr ;
  public LineRead(File f)throws IOException {
    lr = new XXXX( new FileReader( f ) ) ;
  }

  public void list(PrintStream out)
       throws IOException {
   String tmp = lr.readLine();
   while( tmp != null ){
     out.println( tmp );
     tmp = lr.readLine();
   }
  }
}
}
```

Which class, substituted for XXXX in the code, will make this a functional program?

O a. **InputStream**

O b. **BufferedInputStream**

O c. **DataInputStream**

O d. **Reader**

O e. **BufferedReader**

The correct answer is e. A **BufferedReader** is constructed from a **Reader** and provides the **readLine** method. Answer a is incorrect because the **InputStream** class is **abstract**. **BufferedInputStream** does not provide a **readLine** method and is constructed from an **InputStream**, not a **Reader**. Therefore, answer b is incorrect. **DataInputStream** does provide a **readLine** method but it is deprecated; it also must be constructed from an **InputStream**. Therefore, answer c is incorrect. Answer d is incorrect because the **Reader** class is the abstract parent of all readers and can't be instantiated.

Question 8

In the following method for listing all files with a ".java" type in a directory, the name of the class or interface extended or implemented starting in line 2 has been replaced with **XXXX**:

```
1.  public void listJavaFiles( File f,
        PrintStream out ){
2.    String[] ss = f.list( new XXXX(){
3.      public boolean accept( File ff,
          String name ){
4.        return( name.endsWith( ".java" ));
5.      }
6.    }
7.    );
8.    out.println("Found " + ss.length + " Java
      files");
9.    for( int i = 0 ; i < ss.length ; i++ ){
10.     out.println( ss[i] );
11.   }
12. }
```

Which of the following should replace **XXXX** in line 2 to obtain working code?

- O a. The **FileNameFilter** class.
- O b. The **FileNameFilter** interface.
- O c. The **FileFilter** class.
- O d. The **FileFilter** interface.
- O e. None of the above will work.

Answer b is correct. The inner class must implement the **FileNameFilter** interface. There is no **FileNameFilter** or **FileFilter** class. Therefore, answers a and c are incorrect. Answer d is incorrect because the **accept** method in the **FileFilter** interface takes only a **File** reference. Answer e is incorrect because the **FileNameFilter** interface will work.

Question 9

You have created a **File** object that corresponds to a file on your hard disk. What is returned when you call the **lastModified** method of this **File** object?

○ a. A **long** primitive value that represents the date the file was last modified as the number of seconds since the start of January 1, 1970

○ b. A **long** primitive value that represents the date the file was last modified as the number of milliseconds since the start of January 1, 1970

○ c. A **java.util.Date** object that represents the date the file was last modified

○ d. A **String** formatted with the last modified date in the default style for your operating system

Answer b is correct. The value returned is a long primitive in milliseconds, even if the underlying operating system does not measure time to that precision. You could create a **Date** object with the value returned, but the actual value is a **long** primitive. Therefore, the other answers are incorrect.

Question 10

Which of the following Java entities are not **abstract** classes or interfaces? [Check all correct answers]

❑ a. **InputStream**

❑ b. **PrintStream**

❑ c. **Socket**

❑ d. **Reader**

❑ e. **DataInput**

Answers b and c are the only entities that are concrete classes. **InputStream** and **Reader** are **abstract** classes, and **DataInput** is an interface. Therefore, answers a, d, and e are incorrect.

Need to Know More?

 Harold, Elliotte Rusty. *Java I/O*. O'Reilly & Associates, Inc., Sebastopol, CA, 1999. ISBN 1-56592-485-1. This book has excellent general coverage of IO topics.

 Harold, Elliotte Rusty. *Java Network Programming, Second Edition.* O'Reilly & Associates, Inc., Sebastopol, CA, 2000. ISBN 1-56592-870-9. This book covers all forms of network communication.

 http://java.sun.com/docs/books/tutorial/essential/io/index.html is the starting point for the online tutorial on the IO classes.

 http://java.sun.com/docs/books/tutorial/networking/index.html is where the tutorial that relates the IO classes to programming network communication starts.

 http://www.unicode.org is the home page of the nonprofit consortium that maintains the UNICODE standard. This is the place to start if you have character encoding problems.

Sample Test

Question 1

Given the following definition of the Demo class and the DerivedDemo class

```
1. public class Demo extends Object {
2.    String Title;
3.    public Demo( String t ){
4.       Title = t;
5.    }
6.    public void showTitle() {
7.    System.out.println("Title is " + Title);
8.    }
9. }
10. class DerivedDemo extends Demo {
11.    public void setTitle( String  tt )
          { Title = tt ; }
12. }
```

what happens if you try to compile this code, create a DerivedDemo object, and immediately call the showTitle method of that object?

○ a. The message "Title is null" is written to standard output.

○ b. The compiler complains about the DerivedDemo class.

○ c. A NullPointerException is thrown in line 7.

Question 2

Which of the following class declarations are not correct Java declarations? [Check all correct answers]

☐ a. public synchronized class FastClass extends Thread

☐ b. private protected class FastClass

☐ c. public abstract class FastClass

☐ d. class FastClass extends Thread

Question 3

You are writing a toolkit of classes in the "wesayso" package to be used by other programmers in your company. Because of security considerations, you don't want other programmers to subclass your VitalDataAccess class, but you will have to provide for access by classes in other packages. How should this class be declared?

○ a. protected static class VitalDataAccess extends Object

○ b. public final class VitalDataAccess extends Object

○ c. public abstract class VitalDataAccess extends Object

○ d. public static class VitalDataAccess extends Object

Question 4

Given the following partial listing of the Widget class

```
1. class Widget extends Thingee{
2.    static private int widgetCount = 0;
3.    static synchronized int addWidget(){
          widgetCount++;
4.        return widgetCount;
5.    }
6.    String wName;
7.    public Widget( int mx, String T ){
8.    wName = "I am Widget #" + addWidget();
9.    }
10.   // more methods follow
```

what is the significance of the word "private" in line 2? [Check all correct answers]

❏ a. Because widgetCount is private, only methods in the Widget class can access it.

❏ b. Because widgetCount is private, only the addWidget method can access it.

❏ c. If another class tries to access widgetCount, a runtime exception will be thrown.

❏ d. Because widgetCount is private, only methods in the Widget class and any derived classes can access it.

Question 5

The following lists the complete contents of the file named Derived.java:

```
1.   public class Base extends Object {
2.       String objType ;
3.       public Base(){objType = "I am a Base
             type" ;
4.       }
5.  }
6.
7.  public class Derived extends Base {
8.      public Derived() { objType = "I am a
            Derived type";
9.      }
10.     public static void main(String args[]){
11.         Derived D = new Derived();
12.     }
13.  }
```

What will happen when this file is compiled?

○ a. Two class files, Base.class and Derived.class, will be created.

○ b. The compiler will object to line 1.

○ c. The compiler will object to line 7.

Question 6

Given the following listing of the Widget class

```
1. class Widget extends Thingee{
2.    static private int widgetCount = 0;
3.    public String wName;
4.    int wNumber;
5.
6.    private static synchronized int
         addWidget(){
7.       return ++widgetCount;
8.    }
9.    public Widget(){
10.      wNumber = addWidget();
11.   }
12. }
```

what happens when you try to compile the class and use multiple Widget objects in a program that uses multiple Threads to create Widget objects?

○ a. The class compiles, and each Widget gets a unique wNumber that reflects the order in which the Widgets were created.

○ b. The compiler objects to the addWidget call of a static method in line 10.

○ c. A runtime error occurs in the addWidget method.

○ d. The class compiles, and each Widget gets a wNumber, but you cannot guarantee that the number will be unique.

Question 7

In the following class definitions, which are in separate files, note that the Widget and BigWidget classes are in different packages:

```
1. package conglomo;
2. public class Widget extends Object{
3.     private int myWidth;
4.     XXXXXX void setWidth( int n ) {
5.         myWidth = n;
6.     }
7. }
    // the following is in a separate file
8. import conglomo.Widget ;
9. public class BigWidget extends Widget {
10.     BigWidget() {
11.         setWidth( 204 );
12.     }
13. }
```

Which of the following modifiers, used in line 4 instead of XXXXXX, would allow the BigWidget class to access the Widget.setWidth method (as in line 11)? [Check all correct answers]

❑ a. private

❑ b. protected

❑ c. blank—that is, the method declaration would read void setWidth (int n)

❑ d. public

Question 8

Given the following code fragment with a continue to a labeled statement, predict the printed output:

```
1. int i, j;
2. lab: for( i = 0; i < 6; i++ ){
3.        for( j = 5; j > 2; j-- ){
4.            if( i == j ) {
5.                System.out.print(" " + j );
6.                continue lab;
7.            }
8.        }
9.    }
```

○ a. The output will be 3 4 5.

○ b. The output will be 3 4.

○ c. The output will be 3.

○ d. The statement on line 5 is never reached, so there is no output.

Question 9

You are writing a set of classes related to cooking and have created your own exception hierarchy derived from java.lang.Exception as follows:

```
Exception
    +— BadTasteException
            +— BitterException
            +— SourException
```

BadTasteException is defined as an abstract class.

You have a method eatMe that may throw a BitterException or a SourException. Which of the following method declarations will be acceptable to the compiler? [Check all correct answers]

❑ a. public void eatMe(Ingredient[] list) throws BadTasteException

❑ b. public void eatMe(Ingredient[] list) throws BitterException, SourException

❑ c. public void eatMe(Ingredient[] list) may throw BadTasteException

❑ d. public void eatMe(Ingredient[] list)

Question 10

Given the following code fragment

```
switch( x ) {
  case 100 :
    System.out.println("One hundred");break;
  case 200 :
    System.out.println("Two hundred");break;
  case 300 :
    System.out.println( "Three hundred");
      break;
}
```

choose all of the declarations of x that will not cause a compiler error. [Check all correct answers]

❑ a.
```
byte x = 100 ;
```
❑ b.
```
short x = 200 ;
```
❑ c.
```
int x = 300 ;
```
❑ d.
```
long x = 400 ;
```

Question 11

Which of these statements about the value that appears in a switch statement are correct? [Check all correct answers]

❑ a. The value can be of type char.

❑ b. The value can be of type byte.

❑ c. The value can be of type long.

❑ d. The value can be of type boolean.

Question 12

Which of the following loop expressions will not compile (assume there are no other variable declarations inside the method that contains the expression)? [Check all correct answers]

❑ a.
```
int t = 10 ;
while( t ){
    System.out.print(" - " + t- );
}
```

❑ b.
```
while( x > 0 ){
    int x = 1 ; x-;
}
```

❑ c.
```
int i = 0;
do { System.out.print(" - " + i++ );
}while( i < 10 );
```

Question 13

Here is part of the hierarchy of exceptions that may be thrown during file IO operations:

```
Exception
    ┼─ IOException
            ┼─ FileNotFoundException
```

Suppose you had a method X that is supposed to open a file by name and read data from it. Given that X does not have any try-catch statements, which of the following options are true? [Check all correct answers]

❑ a. The method X must be declared as throwing IOException or Exception.

❑ b. The method X must be declared as throwing FileNotFoundException.

❑ c. Any method that calls X must use try-catch, specifically catching FileNotFoundException.

❑ d. No special precautions need to be taken.

Question 14

Which of the following statements about finalize methods are incorrect? [Check all correct answers]

☐ a. The purpose of a finalize method is to recover memory and other system resources.

☐ b. The purpose of a finalize method is to recover system resources other than memory.

☐ c. You should always write a finalize method for every class.

☐ d. The order in which objects are created controls the order in which their finalize methods are called.

Question 15

Here is a method that creates a number of String objects in the course of printing a countdown sequence:

```
1. public void countDown()
2.    for( int i = 10 ; i >= 0 ; i- ){
3.       String tmp = Integer.toString( i );
4.       System.out.println( tmp );
5.    }
6.    System.gc()
7.    System.out.println( "BOOM!" );
8. }
```

When the program reaches line 7, how many of the String objects created in line 3 *will have been* garbage collected (assume that the System.out object is not keeping a reference)?

○ a. None.

○ b. There is no way to tell.

○ c. 10.

○ d. 11.

Question 16

Which of the following statements about Java garbage collection are true? [Check all correct answers]

❑ a. The following code will start the garbage collection mechanism:

```
System.gc();
Thread.yield();
```

❑ b. Calling Runtime.getRuntime().gc() will probably start the garbage collection mechanism, but there is no guarantee.

❑ c. The garbage collection Thread has a low priority.

❑ d. The method by which Java determines that a chunk of memory is garbage is up to the implementer of the JVM.

Question 17

You are writing code for a class that will be in the default package and will use the graphic components in the AWT package. Select the correct code fragment to start the source code file.

```
Fragment A
    import java.awt.*;
Fragment B
    package default ;
    import java.awt.*;
Fragment C
    import java.awt.*;
    package default;
```

○ a. Code fragment A

○ b. Code fragment B

○ c. Code fragment C

Question 18

What is the range of values that can be stored in a short primitive variable?

○ a. 0 through 65535

○ b. -32768 through 32767

○ c. -32767 through 32768

Question 19

Given the following method definition in a class that otherwise compiles correctly

```
1. public boolean testAns(String ans,int n){
2.     boolean rslt;
3.     if( ans.equalsIgnoreCase("YES") &&
         n > 5  ) rslt = true;
4.     return rslt;
5. }
```

what will be the result of trying to compile the class and execute the testAns method with inputs of "no" and 5?

○ a. A runtime exception will be thrown in the testAns method.

○ b. A result of false will be returned.

○ c. A compiler error will prevent compilation.

○ d. A result of true will be returned.

Question 20

Given that a class, Test, declares a member variable named "Scores" as an array of int as follows

```
int Scores[];
```

which of the following code fragments would correctly initialize the member variable Scores as an array of 4 int with the value of zero if used in the Test constructor? [Check all correct answers]

❑ a. int Scores[] = {0,0,0,0} ;

❑ b. Scores = new int[4] ;

❑ c. Scores = new int[4] ;

 for(int i = 0 ; i < 4 ; i++){ Scores[i] = 0 ; }

❑ d. Scores = { 0,0,0,0 };

Question 21

Given the following code for the Demo class

```
public class Demo {
  private String[] userNames;
  public Demo(){ userNames = new String[10];
  }
  public void setName( String s, int n ){
       userNames[n] = s;
  }
  public void showName( int n ){
    System.out.println( "Name is " +
      userNames[n]);
  }
 public String getName( int n ){return
   userNames[n];}
}
```

what would be the result of calling the showName method with a parameter of 2 immediately after creating an instance of Demo?

○ a. Standard output would show "Name is null".

○ b. A NullPointerException would be thrown, halting the program.

○ c. An ArrayIndexOutOfBoundsException would be thrown, halting the program.

○ d. Standard output would show "Name is ".

Question 22

Given the following code fragment from a class definition, which of the following statements are true? [Check all correct answers]

```
1.  int Aval  = 0x65;
2.  byte Bval = 065;
```

❑ a. The variable Aval has been initialized with a hexadecimal format literal, and Bval has been initialized with an octal format literal.

❑ b. Both Aval and Bval contain 65.

❑ c. The logical test Aval > Bval would evaluate true.

❑ d. The compiler would report a NumberFormatException on line 1.

Question 23

The following program is compiled and then run with this command line:

```
>java Demo alpha beta gamma

 public class Demo {
   public static void main(String args[] ){
     int n = 1;
     System.out.println( "The word is " +
       args[ n ] );
   }
 }
```

What happens?

○ a. "The word is alpha" is written to standard output.

○ b. "The word is beta" is written to standard output.

○ c. "The word is gamma" is written to standard output.

○ d. The runtime system reports an error in the main method.

Question 24

What happens when you attempt to compile and run the following code?

```
1. public class Logic {
2.    static long sixteen = 0x0010;
3.    static public void main(String args[]){
4.        long N = sixteen >> 4;
5.        System.out.println( "N = " + N );
6.    }
7. }
```

○ a. The compiler will object to line 4 combining a long with an int.

○ b. The program will compile and run, producing the output "N = 0".

○ c. The program will compile and run, producing the output "N = 1".

○ d. A runtime exception will be thrown.

Question 25

Given the following object hierarchy and code for the upgrade method

```
java.lang.Object
    |
    +—— mypkg.BaseWidget
                |
                +—— TypeAWidget
```

```
// the following is a method in BaseWidget
1. public TypeAWidget upgrade( ){
2.     TypeAWidget  A = (TypeAWidget)  this;
3.     return A;
4. }
```

what will be the result of trying to compile and run a program containing the
following statements?

```
5.   BaseWidget B = new BaseWidget();
6.   TypeAWidget A =  B.upgrade();
```

○ a. The compiler will object to line 2.

○ b. A runtime ClassCastException will be generated in line 2.

○ c. After line 6 executes, the object referred to as A will in fact be a
       TypeAWidget.

Question 26

Given the following code fragment, what will happen when you try to compile and run the showSmall method?

```
1. public void printArray( long[] x ){
2.    for(int i = 0 ; i < x.length ; i++ ){
3.       System.out.println("# " + i + " = "
          + x[i] );
4.    }
5. }
6. int[] small = { 1,2,3,4,5,6,7,8,9,0 };
7. public void showSmall() {
8.    printArray( small );
9. }
```

○ a. The code compiles and the JVM automatically promotes the int array to a long array.

○ b. The compiler complains that there is no method matching the use in line 8.

○ c. The code compiles but a runtime ClassCastException is thrown in line 8.

Question 27

In the following code fragment from an applet, we know that the getParameter call may return a null if there is no parameter named size:

```
1. int sz ;
2. public void init(){
3.    sz = 10;
4.    String tmp = getParameter( "size" );
5.    if( tmp != null X tmp.equals( "BIG" ))
          sz = 20;
6. }
```

Which logical operator should replace X in line 5 to ensure that a NullPointerException is not generated if tmp is null?

○ a. Replace X with &.

○ b. Replace X with &&.

○ c. Replace X with |.

○ d. Replace X with ||.

Question 28

What happens when you try to compile and run the following code?

```
1. public class EqualsTest{
2.    public static void main(String args[]){
3.       float A = 1.0F / 3.0F ;
4.       if( ( A * 3.0 ) == 1.0F )
             System.out.println( "Equal" );
5.       else System.out.println("Not Equal");
6.    }
7. }
```

○ a. The program compiles and prints "Not Equal".

○ b. The program compiles and prints "Equal".

○ c. The compiler objects to line 3.

○ d. The compiler objects to using == with primitives in line 4.

Question 29

Given that you have a method scale defined as follows, where scalex and scaley are int constants

```
public Point scale( int x, int y ){
    return new Point(
        ( int )( x / scalex ),
          ( int )( y / scaley ) );
}
```

what will happen when you call this method with double primitives instead of int, as in the following fragment?

```
1. double px = 10.02;
2. double py = 20.34;
3. Point thePoint = scale( px, py );
```

○ a. A compiler error is caused in line 3.

○ b. The program compiles but a runtime cast exception is thrown.

○ c. The program compiles and runs.

○ d. The compiler objects to line 1.

Question 30

What happens when you try to compile and run the following code?

```
1. public class EqualsTest{
2.    public static void main(String args[]){
3.       Long L = new Long( 7 );
4.       Integer J = new Integer( 7 );
5.       if( L.equals( J ) )
          System.out.println( "Equal" );
6.       else System.out.println("Not Equal");
7.    }
8. }
```

○ a. The program compiles and prints "Equal".

○ b. The program compiles and prints "Not Equal".

○ c. The compiler objects to line 5.

○ d. A runtime cast error occurs at line 5.

Question 31

The GenericFruit class declares the following method to return a float calculated from a serving size:

```
public float calories( float serving )
```

A junior programmer has written the Apple class, which extends GenericFruit, and he proposes to declare the following overriding method:

```
public double calories( double amount )
```

What result do you predict?

○ a. It won't compile because of the different return type.

○ b. It won't compile because of the different input type in the parameter list.

○ c. It will compile but will not override the GenericFruit method because of the different parameter list.

Question 32

You are designing an application to recommend dog breeds to potential pet owners. To maximize the advantage of working in an object-oriented language, you have created a Dog class, which will be extended by classes that represent different kinds of dogs.

The following code fragment shows the class declaration and all of the instance variables in the Dog class:

```
1. public class Dog extends Object {
2.    float avgWeight;
3.    float avgLifespan;
4.    String breedName;
```

Which of the following would be reasonable variable declarations for the SportingDog class, which extends Dog? [Check all correct answers]

- ❑ a. private float avgWeight ;
- ❑ b. private Dog theDog ;
- ❑ c. String[] hunts ;
- ❑ d. String breedName ;

Question 33

In the following code for a class in which methodA has an inner class

```
1.  public class Base {
2.    private static final int ID = 3;
3.    public String name;
4.    public void methodA( int nn ){
5.      final int serialN = 11;
6.      class inner {
7.        void showResult(){
8.        System.out.println("Rslt= " + XX);
9.        }
10.     } // end class inner
11.     new inner().showResult();
12.   } // end methodA
13. )
```

which variables would the statement in line 8 be able to use in place of XX?
[Check all correct answers]

❏ a. The int ID in line 2

❏ b. The String name in line 3

❏ c. The int nn in line 4

❏ d. The int serialN in line 5

Question 34

The GenericFruit class declares the following method to return a float calculated from a serving size:

```
public float calories( float serving )
```

A junior programmer has written the Apple class, which extends GenericFruit, and he proposes to declare the following overriding method:

```
public double calories( float amount )
```

What result do you predict?

- ○ a. It won't compile because of the different return type.
- ○ b. It won't compile because of the different name in the parameter list.
- ○ c. It will compile but will be incompatible with other uses of the method because you can't cast the double return type to float.
- ○ d. It will compile and be compatible with other uses of the calories method.

Question 35

Given a base class and a derived class defined as follows

```
public abstract class BaseTest
        extends Object implements Runnable
public class AdvancedTest extends BaseTest
```

what happens when you try to compile another class that includes the following method?

```
1. public boolean checkTest( Object obj ){
2.   if(obj instanceof BaseTest) return true;
3.     System.out.println( "Not a BaseTest" );
4.     if(obj instanceof Runnable) return true;
5.     System.out.println( "Not Runnable" );
6.     return false;
7. }
```

○ a. The compiler objects to the use of an abstract class in line 2.

○ b. The compiler objects to the use of an interface in line 4.

○ c. The code compiles just fine.

Question 36

You have written a class that extends Thread, which does time-consuming computations.

In the first use of this class in an application, the system locked up for extended periods of time. Obviously, you need to provide a chance for other Threads to run. Here is the run method that needs to be modified:

```
1. public void run(){
2.    boolean runFlg = true;
3.    while( runFlg ){
4.       runFlg = doStuff();
5.
6.    }
7. }
```

What statements could be inserted at line 5 to allow other **Thread**s a chance to run? [Check all correct answers]

❏ a.
```
5.    yield();
```

❏ b.
```
5.    try{ sleep( 100 );
   }catch( InterruptedException e ){}
```

❏ c.
```
5.    suspend( 100 );
```

❏ d.
```
5.    wait( 100 );
```

Question 37

You need to create a class that implements the Runnable interface to do background image processing. Out of the following list of method declarations, select all of the methods that must appear in the class to satisfy the Runnable interface requirements. [Check all correct answers]

❏ a. public void start()

❏ b. public void run()

❏ c. public void stop()

❏ d. public void suspend()

Question 38

You have an application that executes the following line:

```
Thread myT = new Thread();
```

Which statements are correct? [Check all correct answers]

❑ a. The Thread myT is now in a runnable state.

❑ b. The Thread myT has the priority of the Thread that executed the construction statement.

❑ c. If myT.start() is called, the run method in the class where the construction statement appears will be executed.

❑ d. If myT.stop() is called, the Thread can later be started with myT.start() and will execute the run method in the Thread class.

Question 39

Here is a partial listing of a class to represent a game board in a networked game:

```
1. class Board extends Object{
2.    Image[] pics = new Image[64];
3.    int active = 0;
4.    public boolean addPic( Image mg,
                    int pos ){
5.      synchronized(XXX)
6.      { if( pics[pos] == null ){
7.          active++ ; pics[pos] = mg;
8.           return true;
9.        }
10.         else return false;
11.     } // end synchronized block
12.   } // end addPic method
13.   // remainder of class
```

Which alternatives for line 5 would allow you to prevent collisions due to more than one Thread using the addPic method to modify the array of Image references? [Check all correct answers]

❑ a. 5. synchronized(this)

❑ b. 5. synchronized(pics)

❑ c. 5. synchronized(mg)

❑ d. 5. synchronized(active)

Question 40

You are working on an applet that does animation. A single object, animC, derived from java.awt.Canvas, holds all the animation data and a memory image. A single Thread, animT, uses this data to create a new image for the next animation frame and then calls the following method:

```
1. synchronized void waitForPaint(){
2.    painted = false; repaint();
3.    while( !painted ){
4.      try{ wait();
5.      }catch(InterruptedException x){}
6.    }
7. }
```

The paint method in animC executes the following code after the new animation frame has been shown:

```
synchronized(this){painted = true; notify();}
```

After animT has entered waitForPaint and before the paint method has been executed, which of the following statements are true? [Check all correct answers]

❏ a. Other Threads cannot modify data in the animC object.

❏ b. Other Threads can modify data in the animC object using synchronized methods only.

❏ c. Other Threads can modify data in the animC object using synchronized or unsynchronized methods.

❏ d. If the animT Thread is interrupted, it will exit the waitForPaint method.

Question 41

Which methods are not instance methods of the Thread class, or are instance methods deprecated in Java 2? [Check all correct answers]

❑ a. start()

❑ b. stop()

❑ c. run()

❑ d. suspend()

❑ e. sleep(long msec)

❑ f. toString()

❑ g. join()

Question 42

You are using a Panel to contain a set of five buttons. Which layout manager should you use to ensure that at least a portion of each button is displayed even when the Panel has been resized to an area too small to show the full area of all buttons?

○ a. new GridLayout(1,5)

○ b. new FlowLayout(FlowLayout.LEFT)

○ c. new GridBagLayout(5)

○ d. new CardLayout()

Question 43

You are writing a simple utility application based on Frame. This application will have a menu bar, a label, and a text field. You have decided to do without a layout manager.

Which of the following statements will be required in the constructor to place the label at the top left corner of the Frame, with 5 pixels of clearance below the menu bar and 5 pixels in from the left border (assume that label1 has already been constructed and added to the Frame)? [Check all correct statements]

❏ a. setLayout(null);

❏ b. setLayoutManager(null);

❏ c. label1.setLocation(5, 5);

❏ d. label1.setLocation(getInsets().left + 5,
                          getInsets().top + 5);

Question 44

When you are building a menu system, the highest level of organization is the MenuBar. Which class handles the next level of organization?

○ a. java.awt.MenuComponent

○ b. java.awt.MenuItem

○ c. java.awt.Menu

○ d. java.awt.PopupMenu

Question 45

Which of the following layout managers does not alter the height of a component? [Check all correct answers]

❏ a. BorderLayout

❏ b. GridBagLayout

❏ c. CardLayout

❏ d. FlowLayout

Question 46

Which constant names are valid positioning options in the GridBagConstraints class? [Check all correct answers]

- ❑ a BOTH
- ❑ b. EAST
- ❑ c. NORTHEAST
- ❑ d. NONE

Question 47

Once created, some Java objects are immutable, meaning that they cannot have their contents changed. Which of the following classes produce immutable objects? [Check all correct answers]

- ❑ a. java.lang.Double
- ❑ b. java.lang.StringBuffer
- ❑ c. java.lang.Boolean
- ❑ d. java.lang.Math

Question 48

Given an object created by the following class

```
1.  class Example extends Object{
2.    public void  Increment( Integer N ){
3.      N = new Integer(  N.intValue() + 1 );
4.    }
5.    public void Result( int  x ) {
6.      Integer X = new Integer( x );
7.      Increment( X );
8.      System.out.println( "New value is "
9.             + X );
10.   }
11. }
```

what happens when a program calls the Result method with a value of 30?

○ a. The message "New value is 31" goes to the standard output.

○ b. The message "New value is 30" goes to the standard output.

○ c. None of the above.

Question 49

What happens when you compile and run code containing the following lines?

```
1.  Integer A, B, C;
2.  A = new Integer( 3 );
3.  B = new Integer( 4 );
4.  C = A + B;
5.  System.out.println( "Final value " + C );
```

○ a. The code compiles and prints "Final value is 7" when run.

○ b. The code compiles but generates a runtime exception in line 5.

○ c. The compiler balks at line 4.

○ d. The code compiles and prints "Final value is null".

Question 50

Given the following method in an application

```
1. public String setFileType( String fname ){
2.   int p = fname.indexOf( '.' );
3.   if( p > 0 )fname = fname.substring(0,p);
4.   fname += ".TXT";
5.   return fname;
6. }
```

and given that another part of the class has the following code

```
7.   String TheFile = "Program.java";
8.   File F = new File(setFileType(TheFile));
9.   System.out.println("Created " + TheFile);
```

what will be printed by the statement in line 9?

○ a.
```
     Created Program.java
```
○ b.
```
     Created Program.txt
```
○ c.
```
     Created Program.java.txt
```

Question 51

What will happen when the following method is called with an input of "Java rules"?

```
1. public String addOK(String S){
2.    S += " OK!";
3.    return S;
4. }
```

○ a. The method will return " OK!"

○ b. A runtime exception will be thrown.

○ c. The method will return "Java rules OK!"

○ d. The method will return "Java rules".

Question 52

Which of the following code fragments are legal Java code? [Check all correct answers]

❏ a.
```
String A = "abcdefg";
A -= "cde";
```
❏ b.
```
String A = "abcdefg";
A += "cde";
```
❏ c.
```
Integer J = new Integer( 27 );
J -= 7;
```
❏ d.
```
Integer J = new Integer( 27 );
J-;
```

Question 53

What happens when you try to compile and run code containing the following lines:

```
1. Float A = new Float( 1.0F );
2. String S = "value is " + A;
3. System.out.println( S );
```

○ a. The compiler objects to line 2.

○ b. The program compiles and prints "value is 1.0".

○ c. A runtime exception occurs in line 2.

Question 54

Which AWT component can generate an ActionEvent?

○ a. java.awt.List

○ b. java.awt.Scrollbar

○ c. java.awt.Canvas

○ d. java.awt.Panel

Question 55

Which of the following Collections classes can return object references in the order of addition? [Check all correct answers]

❑ a. java.util.ArrayList

❑ b. java.util.Hashtable

❑ c. java.util.Map

❑ d. java.util.Collection

Question 56

Which of the following interfaces in the java.util package does java.util. Hashtable implement?

○ a. java.util.HashMap

○ b. java.util.Map

○ c. java.util.SortedSet

○ d. java.util.Iterator

Question 57

The Math.random() method returns what kind of primitive value?

○ a. An int with values randomly distributed between Integer.MIN_VALUE and Integer.MAX_VALUE

○ b. A float with values randomly distributed between 0.0 and 1.0

○ c. A double with values randomly distributed between 0.0 and 1.0

○ d. A long with values randomly distributed between Long.MIN_VALUE and Long.MAX_VALUE

Question 58

What kind of stream is the System.out object?

○ a. java.io.BufferedWriter

○ b. java.io.PrintStream

○ c. java.io.FileWriter

○ d. java.io.OutputStreamWriter

Question 59

Which of the following events has a matching adapter class that implements the appropriate listener interface? [Check all correct answers]

❑ a. java.awt.event.MouseEvent

❑ b. java.awt.event.KeyEvent

❑ c. java.awt.event.ActionEvent

❑ d. java.awt.event.FocusEvent

❑ e. java.awt.event.ItemEvent

Answer Key

1. b	21. a	41. b, d, e
2. a, b	22. a, c	42. a
3. b	23. b	43. a, d
4. a	24. c	44. c
5. b	25. b	45. d
6. a	26. b	46. b, c
7. b, d	27. b	47. a, c
8. a	28. a	48. b
9. a, b	29. a	49. c
10. b, c	30. b	50. a
11. a, b	31. c	51. c
12. a, b	32. c	52. b
13. a	33. a, b, d	53. b
14. a, c, d	34. a	54. a
15. b	35. c	55. a
16. b, c, d	36. a, b	56. b
17. a	37. b	57. c
18. b	38. b	58. b
19. c	39. a, b	59. a, b, d
20. b, c	40. c	

Question 1

Answer b is correct because the **DerivedDemo** class does not define a constructor; the compiler expects to find a default constructor in the **Demo** class. The expected form of a default constructor is one with no arguments (which you don't have in the **Demo** class), causing a compiler error. Answer a could occur if other problems were fixed because the member variable "Title" is initialized to **null**. Answer c would never occur because the **String** concatenation process adds "null" if the object reference is **null**.

This question demonstrates how important it is when taking a test not to jump to conclusions about the question. On reading the code, you might think the question is going to be about access to variables, but it turns out to be about the absence of a constructor.

Question 2

Answers a and b are correct. Answer a is correct because **synchronized** cannot be used as a class modifier. Answer b is correct because neither of these keywords can be used as a class modifier. Answer c is incorrect because this is a valid declaration; **abstract** is used for a class that has one or more **abstract** methods. Answer d is incorrect because this is a legal class declaration. In general, you can expect test questions that ask you to identify incorrect code, so read each question carefully.

Question 3

Answer b is correct because the **final** modifier is used with class declarations to ensure that the class cannot be extended. Answers a and d are incorrect because the **static** modifier cannot be used with class declarations, only with methods and variables. Answer c is incorrect because the modifier **abstract** implies that the class *must* be extended.

Question 4

Answer a is correct; the **private** keyword restricts access to within the class. Answer b is incorrect because there may be other methods in the class. Answer c is incorrect because it is the compiler that recognizes the **private** keyword and controls access. All access considerations are taken care of by the compiler, not the runtime system. Answer d is incorrect because derived classes cannot see **private** variables in the parent. You are just about guaranteed to run into access modifier questions and questions that say to check all correct answers but have only one correct answer on the test.

Question 5

Answer b is correct; the compiler error message is Public class Base must be defined in a file called "Base.java". Although it is common for a single Java source file to generate more than one class file on compilation, two **public** classes cannot occupy the same Java source file. Answer a does not occur; the compiler will object because the **public** class name does not match the file name. If the source file had been named Base.java, answer c would be correct.

Question 6

Answer a is correct. The use of **synchronized** in line 6 ensures that number assignment will not be interrupted, no matter how many **Thread**s are trying to create **Widget** objects. Answer b is incorrect because line 10 is in the correct form, although **Widget.addWidget** could also be used. Answer c is incorrect because the **addWidget** method has no code that can generate a runtime error. Answer d is incorrect because the use of **synchronized** in line 6 ensures that number assignment will not be interrupted, no matter how many **Thread**s are trying to create **Widget** objects.

Question 7

Answers b and d are correct. Answer b is correct because the **protected** modifier allows access by derived classes as well as classes in the same package. Answer d is correct because the **public** modifier allows access by all. Answer a is incorrect because **private** prevents any access from another class. Answer c is incorrect because the default access allows only access within the same package.

Question 8

Answer a is correct. Every time the statements on line 5 and 6 execute, the **continue** resumes the loop started on line 2. A complicated loop logic question such as this is likely on the test. Don't panic—use the scratch paper to work through the loop logic if necessary.

Question 9

Answers a and b are correct. Answer a is acceptable because **BadTasteException** is more general than **BitterException** or **SourException**. Answer b, which lists each exception separated by commas, is also acceptable. Answer c is incorrect; "may throw" is not a legal expression. Answer d is incorrect because these exceptions don't descend from **RuntimeException**; they must be declared in the method declaration.

Question 10

Answers b and c are correct. The type used in the **switch** statement must accommodate all of the values in the **case** statements. For this reason, both b and c are acceptable. The compiler checks two considerations: The variable in the **switch** statement must be capable of assuming all of the values in the **case** statements, and it must be convertible to an **int**. Answer a is incorrect; **x** cannot be a **byte** type because the **case** constants 200 and 300 are not compatible. Answer d is incorrect because **switch** statements cannot use **long** values. You would have to have a specific cast—**switch((int)x)**—before the compiler would accept it.

This question is probably the most frequently missed question in my online tests, and the reason people miss it illustrates a very important point. On first reading the question, people jump to the conclusion that it is going to be about the allowable types in a **switch** statement in general. The lesson to be learned here is that you should take the time to understand exactly what each question is asking.

Question 11

Answers a and b are correct; a **char** or **byte** can be used, but only if all the **case** statement constants are in the correct range. Answer c is incorrect because a **long** cannot be used in a **switch** statement. This restriction is related to the fact that the compiler constructs a table with 32-bit entries that point to the code for each case to handle a **switch** statement. This also explains why case values must be evaluated as constants at compile time. Answer d is obviously incorrect; only integer types can appear in a **switch** statement.

Question 12

Answers a and b are correct. The code in answer a fails to compile because **t** is not a **boolean**. Only an expression resulting in a **boolean** value can be used in a **while** test. Answer b fails to compile because **x** is defined only inside the code block and is not available to the **while** test. If **x** had been defined elsewhere, the compiler would have objected to the second definition inside the loop. Answer c is incorrect because the code in answer c does compile.

Question 13

Answer a is correct because **IOException** is a "checked" exception. Answer b is incorrect because of inheritance; declaring **IOException** is sufficient. Answer c is incorrect due to a bit of a trick in the statement; there are alternatives to using **try-catch**. For example, the calling method *could* be declared as throwing

IOException, thus passing responsibility for catching the exception back up the calling chain. Answer d is incorrect because **IOException** exceptions are "checked"—they must be declared and caught.

Question 14

Answers a, c, and d are correct. Answer a is correct because the statement is incorrect. Memory is recovered by garbage collection, and finalizers are for other resources. Answer c is correct because the statement is incorrect; objects that do not use system resources other than memory do not need finalizers. Answer d is correct because the statement is incorrect; there is no guarantee about the order of object finalization. Answer b is incorrect because the statement is correct.

Question 15

Answer b is correct because there is no way to tell when the garbage collector **Thread** will run. The programmer cannot count on garbage collection starting at once. The language specs say that the Java Virtual Machine (JVM) will make a "best effort," but this does not guarantee anything. The important point here is the wording "will have been garbage collected," which implies that you can be sure that it happens. Answers a, c, and d are incorrect because they imply that you can be sure.

Question 16

Answers b, c, and d are correct. Answer b is correct because, as discussed in the explanation of Question 15, the code may start the garbage collector, but there is no guarantee. Answer c is correct because the Java Virtual Machine (JVM) assigns a low priority to the garbage collection thread. Answer d is correct because picking the best garbage collection method is left up to the individual JVM implementer. Answer a is incorrect because it implies that you can be sure that the garbage collector will start.

Question 17

Answer a is correct. The default package is what you get when there is no package statement. Answer b is incorrect because it tries to put the class in a package named "default," which will cause a compiler error because **default** is a Java keyword (used in **switch** statements). Answer c not only uses the wrong **package** statement but also puts it in the wrong position. Any **package** statement must be the first noncomment statement in a Java source code file.

Question 18

Answer b is correct. To remember whether the negative or positive range is larger, think of the byte range -128 through 127 and recall that the high bit is used as a sign bit. Answer a is incorrect because **short** variables are signed; 0 through 65535 would be unsigned. Answer c is incorrect because as discussed for answer b, the negative range is always 1 greater with signed integers.

Question 19

Answer c is correct; the compiler recognizes that the local variable **rslt** will not always be initialized. Answers a, b, and d are incorrect because the class will not compile as written.

Question 20

Answers b and c are correct. Answer b works because primitive number arrays that are member variables are automatically initialized to zero when constructed. Note that this is not true of variables declared inside methods. Answer c works, but the loop would be necessary only if an initial value other than zero were required. Answer a is incorrect because it creates an initialized array but is a local variable, not a member variable. Note that the question says "in the Test constructor." Problems related to duplicate variable declarations are difficult to catch. Answer d is incorrect because initialization by means of a bracketed list can be used only in the statement that declares the variable.

Question 21

Answer a is correct. The constructor creates a new array of type **String[ ]** in which every item has a **null** value. Answer b is incorrect because a **NullPointerException** would be thrown only if the constructor had not created the array. Answer c is incorrect because the array index 2 is legal (because the array has been constructed with a size of 10). Answer d does not occur because the **String** conversion process substitutes the word "null" when it finds a **null** reference, not a blank.

Question 22

Answers a and c are correct. The hexadecimal literal evaluates to 101 decimal, and the octal literal evaluates to 53 decimal. Answer b is incorrect because line 1 uses a hexadecimal literal and line 2 an octal literal. Answer d is spurious because the Java runtime, not the compiler, reports exceptions.

Question 23

Answer b is correct because the index of "alpha" is zero. This also explains why answers a and c are incorrect. The **args** String array, like all Java arrays, is addressed starting with zero. Answer d is incorrect because the runtime system finds the **main** method without problem. At least one question involving the correct signature of the **main** method and the interpretation of the command line is likely to appear on the test.

Question 24

Answer c is correct. The shift operation is legal. Answer a does not occur because the 4 represents the number of bits to be shifted. Because shifts greater than the number of bits in a **long** do not make sense, shifts are always **int** values. Answers b and d are incorrect because the shift operation is legal. The bit pattern for the hex constant, when right-shifted four positions, leaves a single bit in the one position. If you are not used to working in binary, be sure to get in some practice before the test.

Question 25

Answer b is correct; the Java runtime checks all class casts for compatibility. A base class cannot be cast to a derived class type. Answer a does not occur because of the explicit cast in line 2. If this cast were removed, the compiler would object. Answer c is incorrect and is there to see if you are paying attention—objects never change their type, no matter what the type of the reference.

Question 26

Answer b is correct. The compiler knows that the signature of the **printArray** method requires an array of **long** primitives. Answer a is incorrect; primitive array types do not have a hierarchy and cannot be cast to another primitive array type. You may be thinking of the automatic promotion of an **int** primitive to **long**. Answer c is incorrect because the compiler can detect the error. When dealing with arrays, be sure to remember that an array is an object whose type includes the type of the primitive or reference variable it can contain.

Question 27

Answer b is correct; this is the "short-circuited" AND operator that does not evaluate the second term if the first one results in **false**. Answer a is incorrect; this operator would attempt to run the **equals** method on the **tmp** variable even if it were **null**, causing a **NullPointerException**. Answers c and d are incorrect because these two OR operators would attempt to run the **equals** method on the **tmp** variable even if it were **null**, causing a **NullPointerException**.

Question 28

Answer a is correct because a floating-point number cannot exactly represent the fraction 1/3—multiplying by 3 does not recover the original number. This also explains why answer b is incorrect. You should be extremely careful when testing for equality between two floating-point numbers. Answer c does not occur because the compiler has no problem with this initialization of variable **A**. Answer d does not occur because == can be used with primitives and reference variables.

Question 29

Answer a is correct; the compiler will not convert a **double** to an **int** without a specific **cast**. Answer b is incorrect because the program does not compile and because cast exceptions are thrown only by reference variable casts. Answer c is incorrect because the code does not compile. Answer d does not occur because line 1 is the correct way to initialize a **double** primitive value. A numeric constant with a decimal point is automatically assumed to be a **double**.

Question 30

Answer b is correct; the test results in a **false** value because J is not a **Long** Object. This also explains why answer a is incorrect. All of the reference variable **equals** tests compare content only after they have determined that the input **Object** is of the correct class. Answers c and d do not occur because the signature of the **equals** method takes any **Object** reference.

Question 31

Answer c is correct; this declaration will not override the one in **GenericFruit** because of the different parameter list. Answers a and b are incorrect because the compiler will consider this an overloaded method name, so it will compile.

Question 32

Answer c is correct; this array of **String** objects could be used to store the names of game animals the **SportingDog** is used to hunt. Answers a and d are incorrect; shadowing the base class **avgWeight** and **breedName** variables would only cause trouble without gaining anything. Answer b is incorrect because there is no need for **SportingDog** to "have a" **Dog** because it "is a" **Dog** by inheritance. The Sun test objectives document mentions the distinction between "is a" and "has a," so you may see these terms on the test.

Question 33

Answers a, b, and d are correct. Answers a and b are correct because inner classes can access any static or member variable in the enclosing class. Answer d is correct because, although it is a local variable, it is declared **final**. Answer c is incorrect because the local variable **nn** is not declared **final**. This special usage of the keyword **final** causes the compiler to provide storage for this variable in a permanent location. This is necessary because an inner class object created in a method may outlive the method.

Question 34

Answer a is correct; the compiler sees an attempt to override the **calories** method in the parent class because the method name and input parameter type are the same. However, overriding methods cannot have a different return type, so a compiler error results. Answer b is incorrect because the name used in the parameter list is not part of the method signature; it is the variable type that is significant. Answers c and d are incorrect because the code will not compile. Note how the slight differences in wording between this question and Question 31 make a large difference in outcome. Be sure you can spot the difference between overloading and overriding a method.

Question 35

Answer c is correct. The compiler has no trouble with this method code. Answer a is incorrect because an **abstract** class can be used in **instanceof** tests. Answer b is incorrect because an interface can be used in **instanceof** tests. Knowing how the **instanceof** operator is used is essential to programming in Java, so if you missed this one, go back and review.

Question 36

Answers a and b are correct. Answer a is correct because **yield** lets the thread scheduling mechanism run another **Thread**. Answer b is correct because **sleep** allows time for other threads to run. Answer c is incorrect; there is no **suspend** method with a time input. The **suspend()** method (with no input parameter) would permanently suspend your **Thread**, and, of course, **suspend** is a deprecated method anyway. Answer d is incorrect: It would not compile as written because calls to **wait** must provide for catching **InterruptedException**. Furthermore, the call to **wait** would have to be in a **synchronized** code block.

*Note: It is an essential part of this question that the **run** method is in a class that extends **Thread** because both **yield** and **sleep** are **static** methods in the **Thread** class. If this **run** method were in a **Runnable** class, the syntax **Thread.yield()** and **Thread.sleep()** would be required.*

Question 37

Answer b is the only correct answer. The only method required by **Runnable** is **run**. The other answers, although they may sound reasonable, are not required by the **Runnable** interface.

Question 38

Answer b is the only correct answer. The priority of the new **Thread** will be that inherited from the **Thread** that called the constructor. Answer a is incorrect; the **Thread** is in the "new" state, so **start()** must be called to put it in the runnable state. Answer c is incorrect because **myT** is a **Thread** object created without a reference to a **Runnable** object; the **run** method in the **Thread** class will be executed. The **run** method in **Thread** is, of course, an empty method, so nothing would happen. Answer d is incorrect because once a **Thread** has been stopped, it cannot be restarted.

Question 39

Answers a and b are correct. Answer a would work because it would obtain a lock on the entire **Board** object, and answer b would work because it would obtain a lock on the **pics** array. Answer c would not work because having a lock on **mg Image** would not protect the array. Answer d would not even compile because **synchronized** statements must have an object reference and **active** is a primitive variable.

Question 40

Answer c is correct. When **animT** calls **wait**, the lock on the **animC** object is released. Answers a and b are incorrect. Other **Thread**s can modify data in **animC** using any method because **animT** does not hold a lock on the object while in the **wait** state. Answer d is incorrect because when a **Thread** is interrupted, an **InterruptedException** is thrown. Because this exception is caught inside the **while** loop, **animT** reenters the **wait** method.

Question 41

Answers b, d, and e are correct. Answer b is correct because **stop** is a deprecated method. Answer d is correct because **suspend** is a deprecated method. Answer e is correct because **sleep** is a **static** (class) method, not an **instance** method. Answer a is incorrect because **start** is an instance method of **Thread** that makes a new **Thread** runnable. Answer c is incorrect because the **run** method is an instance method of **Thread**. Answer f is incorrect because all Java objects have a **toString** instance method, so **Thread** does too. Answer g is incorrect because **join** is a **Thread** instance method. The convoluted way this question is stated should convince you of how important it is to read each question carefully.

Question 42

Answer a is correct; a **GridLayout** attempts to display an equal portion of each button when the **Panel** is resized. Answer b is incorrect because a **FlowLayout** leaves out buttons that don't fit. Answer c is incorrect because this is not a valid **GridBagLayout** constructor. Answer d is incorrect because a **CardLayout** shows only one component at a time.

Question 43

Answers a and d are correct. As far as answer a, **Frame** has a default **BorderLayout**, so you must set the layout manager to **null** or the **Label** will end up filling the Center position. Answer d shows the correct way to position the label with compensation for the **Frame** insets. Answer b is incorrect because it uses the **setLayoutManager** method, which does not exist. Questions that state bogus method names are possible on the test. Answer c is incorrect because it does not take the **Insets** into account. If you don't compensate for the **Insets**, the menu bar will partially or completely cover the label.

Question 44

Answer c is correct. **MenuItem** objects are attached to **Menu** objects that are attached to a **MenuBar**. Answer a is incorrect because **MenuComponent** is the **abstract** class from which the other menu-related classes inherit. Answer b is incorrect because a **MenuItem** is the object that you actually select. Answer d is incorrect because a **PopupMenu** is a **MenuItem** container that can be attached to any **Component**. Although you could attach a **PopupMenu** to a **MenuBar**, that is not the usual convention.

Question 45

Answer d is correct. A **FlowLayout** attempts to fit in components without changing their height. Answer a is incorrect because the East, West, and Center components of a **BorderLayout** have their height changed. Answer b is incorrect because a **GridBagLayout** typically alters both the height and width of components. Answer c is incorrect because components in a **CardLayout** are resized to fit the container.

Question 46

Answers b and c are correct because both are positioning options. **EAST** causes a component to be positioned on the right edge of the available area, centered vertically. **NORTHEAST** causes a component to be positioned at the upper-right corner of the available area. Answer a is incorrect because **BOTH** is a resizing option, not a positioning option; it allows a component to be stretched in both directions. Answer d is not a positioning option. **NONE** is a resizing option; it prevents a component from being resized.

Question 47

Answers a and c are correct. **Double** and **Boolean** are wrapper classes that produce an immutable object. Answer b is incorrect because the **StringBuffer** class is provided with many methods for manipulating its contents. It is the **String** class that creates immutable objects. Answer d is incorrect because the **Math** class cannot be used to create an object; it consists entirely of **static** methods. This is an important item to remember when you see a question involving a **Math** class method.

Question 48

Answer b is correct. Inside the **Increment** method, the reference to **N** is local. The **Integer** created with 31 has nothing to do with the reference to **X** in the **Result** method. This also explains why answer c is incorrect. Answer a is incorrect because although a new **Integer** object with an **int** value of 31 is created, it does not affect the object **X** in the **Result** method.

Question 49

Answer c is correct. The + operator is not defined for **Integer** objects, only for **String** objects. Answers a, b, and d are incorrect because line 4 causes a compiler error.

Question 50

Answer a is correct. **TheFile** still refers to the same immutable **String** object created in line 7. Answers b and c are incorrect because the manipulations inside the **setFileType** method cannot alter the original object.

Question 51

Answer c is correct; the += assignment creates a new **String** that concatenates the original **String** text with the literal. Answer a is incorrect because a new **String** is returned. Answer b is incorrect because the += assignment is perfectly legal. Furthermore, if it were illegal, the compiler would have caught the problem. Answer d is incorrect because although it is true that the original input **String** is unchanged, the statement in line 2 creates a new **String** object. You are practically guaranteed to get at least one question that involves knowing legal **String** operations.

Question 52

Only answer b is correct. **String** is the only class for which an assignment operator += is defined. This operation constructs a new **String** assigned to variable **A**. Answer a is incorrect because the -= operator is not defined for **String** objects. Answers c and d are incorrect because no arithmetic operators are defined for **Integer** objects. Remember that **Integer** objects cannot be changed, so answer d is illegal no matter how plausible it looks.

Question 53

Answer b is correct. The compiler recognizes that the + requires **String** concatenation. This also explain why answer a does not occur. Answer c does not occur because the compiled code uses the **Float.toString()** method to convert the value stored in **A** to a **String**.

Question 54

Answer a is correct. An **ActionEvent** is generated when an item in a **List** is double-clicked on. Answer b is incorrect; a **Scrollbar** generates an **AdjustmentEvent** when moved. Answers c and d are incorrect because **Canvas** and **Panel** can't generate an **ActionEvent**. **ActionEvent**s are considered "semantic" events because the raw mouse or keyboard events are interpreted in terms of the logic implemented by the **Component** that gets the event.

Question 55

Answer a is correct. **ArrayList** maintains an internal list in the order of addition. **ArrayList** is the new Collections API class closest to the original Java **Vector** class. Answer b is incorrect; the order of elements in a **Hashtable** depends on the treatment of key hashcodes. Answer c is incorrect because **Map** is an interface that does not require the order of addition to be retained. Answer d is incorrect because **Collection** is the root of the collection interface hierarchy. It does not require the order of addition to be retained.

Question 56

Answer b is correct; **Hashtable** implements the **Map** interface. Answer a is incorrect: **HashMap** is a concrete class, not an interface. Answer c is incorrect because **SortedSet** is an interface that requires the contents to be sorted, whereas **Hashtable** does not sort. Answer d is incorrect because the **Iterator** interface is used by classes that iterate over a collection.

Question 57

Answer c is correct. **Math.random** returns a **double** value. This value may equal 0.0 but will always be less than 1.0. This is also why answers a, b, and d are incorrect.

Question 58

Answer b is correct. **System.out** is a **PrintStream**. In general, the use of **PrintStream** is discouraged in Java 2 because it does not properly handle Unicode characters. However, **System.out** remains a **PrintStream** for compatibility with older programs. The classes in answers a, c, and d are incorrect because they are all designed to correctly handle Unicode characters.

Question 59

Answers a, b, and d are correct. Answer a is correct because there are, in fact, two adapters that take **MouseEvent** events: **MouseAdapter** and **MouseMotionAdapter**. Answer b is correct because there is a **KeyAdapter** class. Answer d is correct because there is a **FocusAdapter** class with two methods. Answer c is incorrect because the **ActionListener** interface specifies only one method, **actionPerformed**, so there is no need for an adapter. Answer e is incorrect because the **ItemListener** interface specifies only one method, **itemStateChanged**, so there is no need for an adapter. Note that in general, adapters are provided only where the listener interface specifies two or more methods.

Glossary

100% Pure Java

Classes and applications that meet Sun's criteria for total independence from underlying operating system support may display this label.

absolute positioning

If a **Container** has a **null** layout manager, the programmer may position and size **Component** objects in pixel coordinates. This is called absolute positioning.

abstract (Java keyword)

Classes or methods defined as **abstract** define a runtime behavior but do not provide a complete implementation. You cannot create an object from an **abstract** class, but an object created from a class that extends the **abstract** class can be referred to with the **abstract** class name. When applied to member methods, it declares that the implementation of the function must be provided by subclasses, unless they are also declared as **abstract** classes. Any class that contains **abstract** methods must be declared **abstract**. An **abstract** class can't be declared **final**.

abstract path name

The operating system-independent internal representation of a path inside a **File** object. It consists of an optional prefix string, which typically represents a disk drive, plus a list of zero or more names. The last name in the list may represent a directory or file.

accessibility

The **javax.accessibility** package specifies interfaces to connect user interface components with assistive technologies that make it easier for people with disabilities to interact with Java applications.

adapter

The **java.awt.event** package has a number of classes that conveniently allow programmers to create event listeners. These "adapter" classes provide empty methods that fulfill the requirements of various event listeners. For example, the **KeyAdapter** class implements the **KeyListener** interface, so if you need a class that implements **KeyListener**, you can extend **KeyAdapter**.

Adjustable (interface)

The **java.awt.Adjustable** interface defines methods for dealing with scrollbar-like controls.

American Standard Code for Information Interchange (ASCII)

A widely used encoding standard for text and control characters. Java uses Unicode internally but appears externally to be using ASCII because the printing characters of ASCII are a subset of Unicode.

anonymous class

A local class that is declared and instantiated in one statement. The term "anonymous" is appropriate because the class is not given a name.

applet

A Java program that runs almost independently of the operating system within a Java Virtual Machine (JVM) provided by a Web browser. An applet is normally distributed or downloaded as part of a Web page from a central Web server, and then the applet executes on the client machine. Browser security limits an applet's access to the client-machine file system and other resources.

application

A Java program that runs on a user's system with full access to system resources as opposed to an applet,

which is strictly limited by the security restrictions in a Web browser. By convention, the start-up class for an application must have a **main** method.

ArithmeticException

A runtime exception thrown by the Java Virtual Machine (JVM) when integer division by zero occurs. Note that floating-point division by zero does not cause an exception.

array

A collection of data items, all of the same type, in which each item is uniquely addressed by a 32-bit integer index. Java arrays behave like objects but have some special syntax. Java arrays begin with the index value 0.

Arrays class

This class in the **java.util** package contains many **static** methods for operations on arrays of primitives and object references.

ASCII (*See* American Standard Code for Information Interchange.)

assignable

An object reference is assignable to a reference variable if it is the same type as the variable or has the variable as an ancestor in the class hierarchy. A primitive type is assignable to a variable if it can be converted to that type without a specific **cast**.

assignment

Operators that place a value in a variable, such as the = and += operators.

atomic

A sequence of computer operations is said to be atomic if it cannot be interrupted by another **Thread**.

automatic variable

A variable that is declared inside a method. It is called automatic because the memory required is automatically provided when the method is called. "Local variable" is the preferred term.

bitwise

A bitwise operator performs an operation on Java integer primitive types on an individual-bit basis.

break

A Java keyword that is used in two contexts. The plain **break** statement simply causes execution to continue after the present code block. When used with a statement label, **break** causes execution to continue after the code block that is tagged by the label. Contrast this behavior with that of the **continue** keyword.

byte

The 8-bit integer-type primitive used in Java. Java treats a **byte** as a signed integer.

Byte class

The wrapper for 8-bit byte primitive values.

bytecode

Essentially an instruction for the Java Virtual Machine (JVM) in a platform-independent format. The Java compiler reads Java source code and outputs class files that contain bytecodes.

cast

A Java expression explicitly changes the type of the expression to a different type by using the **cast** syntax, which consists of the new type in parentheses. **Cast** is also a reserved word in Java but is not currently used.

catch

The Java keyword **catch** is used to create a block of code, or "clause," to be executed when a specific exception is thrown in a block of code set up by a **try** statement. Each **catch** must specify the type of exception caught.

CGI (*See* Common Gateway Interface.)

char

The integer primitive variable that Java uses to represent Unicode characters. A **char** variable is treated as a 16-bit unsigned integer, whereas all other integer primitives are treated as signed.

Character class

The wrapper for 16-bit **char** primitive values.

checked exception

Exceptions for which the compiler requires you to provide explicit handling code.

class

An object-oriented programming term that defines the implementation of objects that can inherit or share certain characteristics. In Java, all program behavior is defined by classes, and all classes descend from the **Object** class. Think of a class as a blueprint for creating objects; just as you can create more than one building from a blueprint, you can create more than one object from a class.

Class (class)

This class in the **java.lang** package allows you to find out the runtime type of any object. An instance of this class is created for every class and interface in a running Java program as the Java Virtual Machine (JVM) loads the program.

class file

The compilation of a Java class results in a class file. The name of the file matches the name of the class and the file type is ".class".

class method

A method that is declared **static** and thus is attached to the class as a whole. Some Java classes, such as **Math**, are used entirely through class methods.

class modifiers

Java keywords **public, abstract**, and **final** that define characteristics of a class.

class variable

A variable that is attached to a Java class rather than to an instance of the class. Variables that are declared **static** are class variables.

ClassCastException

This exception is generated when the Java Virtual Machine (JVM) detects that an attempt has been made to cast an object reference to an incompatible type.

clone method

A method in the **Object** class that can create a copy of an object.

Collection interface

This interface defines the basic behavior for objects in the Collections application programming interface (API).

Collections application programming interface (API)

The set of classes and interfaces, new for Java 2, that provide a wide array of methods for manipulating collections of objects.

Color (class)

The **java.awt.Color** class encapsulates the red, green, and blue intensities of a screen color. In addition, **Color** has an alpha component that represents opacity.

Common Gateway Interface (CGI)

The conventions that govern data communication between a Web server and auxiliary programs. For example, Web search requests to search engines such as Yahoo! use the CGI convention.

Comparator interface

By implementing this interface, your custom class can make use of the large number of sorting and searching methods in the **Arrays** class.

completeness

Whether a behavior is fully developed or needs to be further developed by subclasses. In an incomplete, or **abstract**, class, the implementation of some or all behavior is left to sub-classes. A **final** class is considered the end of a hierarchy and can't be subclassed.

Component (class)

The **java.awt.Component** class is the parent of all nonmenu screen components in the Abstract Windowing Toolkit (AWT). This is an **abstract** class, so **Component** objects are never created directly.

constraints

In layout managers that implement the **LayoutManager2** interface, a constraint is an object passed to the layout manager that directs the way a particular component is treated. For example, the **String** "North" in a **BorderLayout** is a constraint.

constructor

A special type of member function that is called when an instance of a class is created. The constructor performs many steps to initialize data storage.

constructor chaining

One constructor calling another constructor. Java enforces a set of rules on chaining constructors to ensure that superclasses get a chance to perform default processing.

Container (class)

The basic functionality of all Abstract Windowing Toolkit (AWT) containers stems from this class. In addition to the functions it inherits from **Component**, a **Container** object has a list of all components it contains and may have a layout manager that controls arranging these components.

contentPane

In the Swing primary container classes such as **JFrame**, interface components are added to the **contentPane** container rather than directly to the **JFrame**.

continue

This Java keyword is used in two contexts. When used inside a looping construct, the plain **continue** statement causes execution to continue with the next innermost loop execution. When used with a statement label, **continue** transfers control to the labeled loop. Contrast this behavior with that of the **break** keyword.

controller

In the Model-View-Controller design pattern, controller functions communicate user input to the model and view(s).

conversion

In a Java expression, changing the type of the expression by one of several methods. Conversion can occur when you are assigning the results of an expression to a variable, when you are invoking a method with a specific **cast**, or in a numeric expression. Java also provides for converting any type to a **String** in **String** expressions.

daemon Thread

Threads may be tagged as daemon threads by the **setDaemon** method to distinguish them from user threads. Daemon threads are generally Java Virtual Machine (JVM) utilities such as the garbage collection **Thread**. The name comes from typical Unix usage.

deadlock

A situation in which two or more **Thread** objects cannot proceed because each holds a resource the other needs.

decorator

A design pattern in which a core class has additional functions added by an attached object rather than by subclassing.

decrement

The decrement operator ( ) subtracts one from the primitive numeric variable to which it is attached. This operator can be used with all primitive numeric types.

deep copy

This term is used when you are describing the cloning of objects. A deep copy must be made by creating new copies of all objects referred to by the original object.

delegate

In the Swing convention, the object that handles the look and feel for a component. From the point of view of the Model-View-Controller design pattern, a delegate combines view and controller functions.

delegation

The Java 1.1 event model is sometimes referred to as a delegation model because event-generating components delegate event handling to specific event listeners. This is in contrast to the original event model, in which the component that generated the event had no connection to the eventual handler.

deprecated

Disapproved of; a number of methods in Java 2 that are left over from earlier versions are tagged in the Java Development Kit (JDK) 1.2 documentation as deprecated. Some are deprecated because an improved naming convention has been adopted and some because their use has been found to be harmful. Note that these methods are still in the library in JDK version 1.2 but are not guaranteed to be there in subsequent versions.

deserialize

To reconstitute a Java object that was stored by serialization; typically performed by an **ObjectInputStream**.

Dimension (class)

The width and height of a component are typically read and set with **java.awt.Dimension** objects. For instance, in the **setMinimumSize** method, a **Dimension** object is passed.

doclet

A Java program written with classes in the **sun.tools.javadoc** package that can customize javadoc output. (*See* javadoc.)

double

The 64-bit floating-point primitive type used in Java.

Double class

In addition to being the wrapper for 64-bit **double** primitive values, this class has special constants such as **NaN,** that are used to detect various problems with floating-point arithmetic.

drag-and-drop

The part of the Java Foundation Classes (JFC) that supports the transfer of data between Java applications and between Java and native applications using the dragging and dropping metaphor.

dynamic method lookup

The Java Virtual Machine (JVM) locates the correct method to call at runtime, based on an object's actual type, not the type of the reference that is used.

editable

You can control whether the user can edit the text displayed in a **TextArea** or **TextField** with the **setEditable** method.

enabling events

The **enableEvents** method in **java.awt.Component** is called to specifically enable events as determined by an event mask. Events are also enabled when specific listeners are added to a **Component**.

encapsulation

Encasing information and behavior within an object so that its structure and implementation are hidden to other objects that interact with it.

Enumeration interface

The interface in Java 1 that specifies how a collection will generate a series of the elements it contains using the **nextElement** and **hasMoreElements** methods. The **Iterator** interface in Java 2 is intended to replace **Enumeration**.

equals

The **equals** method compares one object reference with another and returns **true** if the objects are equal in content. The default **equals** method in the **Object** class returns **true** if both references refer to the same object. Classes such as **String** provide an **equals** method that checks for equality of content.

Error (java.lang.Error)

This class, which is a subclass of **Throwable**, is the parent of all Java error classes. Errors generally signal a condition from which the program cannot recover, as opposed to exceptions that may be recoverable.

event listener

Any object that has an interest in user interactions with a particular control can register with that control as an event listener for specific events. When the event occurs, each listener for that type of event is notified.

event mask

The event mask in a **Component** object determines the types of events it will generate. Constants that correspond to the various events are defined in the **java.awt.AWTEvent** class.

Exception (java.lang.Exception)

This class, which is a subclass of **Throwable**, is the parent of all Java exceptions. The compiler insists that all **Exception**s, except those that descend through the **Runtime Exception** branch of the hierarchy, be provided for in the code.

extends

The Java keyword used in the definition of a new class to indicate the class from which the new class inherits.

field

A variable that defines a particular characteristic of a class.

File (class)

The **java.io.File** class manages directory and file pathnames, not actual data files. **File** objects can be used as input to methods that do open files, but the main purpose of the class is to manipulate names independent of the operating system.

file separator

The character used to separate the components of a path and file name. Because Windows and Unix use different symbols, the only portable way to build a path and file name is with the system-specific constants provided in the **File** class.

final

The Java keyword that declares that a class can't be subclassed. When applied to a member method, it declares that the method can't be overridden by subclasses. When applied to a member variable, it declares that the variable is a constant; after its value has been set, it can't be changed. A **final** class can't be declared **abstract**.

finalize

The **finalize** method of an object is executed by the Java garbage collection mechanism when the memory occupied by the object is about to be reclaimed. The **Object** class has a do-nothing **finalize** method, so all Java objects inherit a **finalize** method.

finally

The **finally** keyword is used to attach a code block that must always be executed to a **try** block.

float

The 32-bit floating-point primitive type used in Java.

Float class

In addition to being the wrapper for 32-bit float primitive values, it defines several important constants.

Font (class)

A **Font** object represents a particular font face characterized by the family plus style information and point size.

font family

From a typographic point of view, fonts are characterized by a design style or font family such as Times Roman or Courier.

garbage collection

The process by which the Java Virtual Machine (JVM) locates and recovers memory occupied by objects that can no longer be used by the program.

Graphics (class)

The **java.awt.Graphics** class provides a context for drawing components and images on the screen. All drawing is done through a **Graphics** or **Graphics2D** object.

Graphics2D (class)

The **java.awt.Graphics2D** class extends **Graphics** and is used throughout Java 2.

hashcode

In general computing terms, a characteristic number generally derived from the contents of a data item. Operations on this number allow a program to locate a data item much faster than it could with any search method.

hashCode method

Every object in Java has a **hashCode** method that generates an **int** primitive value. The **Object** class provides a simple method that, in most implementations, returns just the reference value that points to the object. By overriding this base method, the designer can create an optimized hashcode.

Hashtable class

A **Hashtable** object stores **Object** references indexed by "key" objects using the hashcode of the key. It is typically used to store references with a **String** key, but any class that implements the **hashCode** method will work as a key.

heavyweight components

Interface components that make use of a corresponding operating system peer.

IDE (*See* Integrated Development Environment.)

IEEE (*See* Institute of Electrical and Electronics Engineers.)

implements

The keyword used in a class declaration to precede a list of one or more interfaces. When more than one interface is implemented, the names in the list are separated by commas.

import

An **import** statement in a Java source code file tells the Java compiler in which package to look for classes that are used in the code. The **java.lang** package is automatically imported; all others must be specified in **import** statements.

increment

The increment operator (++) adds one to the primitive variable to which it is attached. This operator can be used with all primitive numeric types.

IndexOutOfBoundsException

This exception is generated when an attempt is made to address an array element that does not exist. The **ArrayIndexOutOfBoundsException** and **StringIndexOutOfBounds Exception** are subclasses of this class.

init (applet method)

By convention, the initial class of a Java applet is expected to have an **init** method. The Java Virtual Machine (JVM) in the Web browser calls the **init** method after the applet object has been created but before it is displayed.

initializing, initialization

Setting a starting value for a variable.

inner class

A class or interface that is nested within another class. Inner classes have access to all member fields and methods of their enclosing class, including those declared as **private**.

InputStream (class)

The **abstract** base class in the **java.io** package for many classes that read data as a stream of bytes.

Insets (class)

The border widths on all four sides of a container are typically represented by a **java.awt.Insets** object.

instance

An object of a particular class is called an instance of that class.

instance fields

Member fields that are distinct for each instance of a class.

instance methods

Member methods that can be executed only through a reference to an instance of a class.

instance variable

A variable that is part of an instance of a class, as opposed to a class (or static) variable that is part of the class itself.

instanceof

This logical operator is used in expressions to determine whether a reference belongs to a particular type. The operator expects a reference on the left and a reference type on the right. If the reference can legally be cast to the reference type, the operator returns **true**.

Institute of Electrical and Electronics Engineers (IEEE)

A professional society that maintains various standards for computer hardware and software, among others.

int

The 32-bit integer primitive type used in Java. Note that **int** primitives are always treated as signed integers.

Integer class

The wrapper for 32-bit **int** primitive values.

Integrated Development Environment (IDE)

A programming system that integrates several programming tools in the same package. An IDE typically includes a source code editor, a compiler, a debugger, project tracking functions, and graphic screen-design functions.

interface

In Java, an interface is similar to a class definition, except that no detailed implementation of methods is provided. A class that implements an interface must provide the code to implement the methods. You can think of an interface as defining a contract between the calling method and the class that implements the interface.

interrupt

An instance method of the **Thread** class. The results of calling this method depend on the state of the **Thread**. If it is in a **sleep** or **wait** state, it is awakened and an **InterruptedException** is thrown; if not, the interrupted flag is set.

interrupted (Thread private variable)

This flag is set to **true** if a **Thread** is interrupted. It can be accessed only by the **interrupted** and **isInterrupted** methods.

interrupted (Thread static method)

A **static** method used by the currently running **Thread** to determine whether it has been interrupted.

InterruptedException

This exception can be generated when a **Thread** that is sleeping or waiting is interrupted. The **Thread** cannot continue with what it was doing but must handle the exception.

IOException

The parent class for all exceptions associated with input/output processes such as opening and reading a file.

isInterrupted

An instance method of the **Thread** class by which a **Thread** can be interrogated to see if it has been interrupted.

Iterator interface

This interface is intended to take the place of the **Enumeration** interface as the preferred way to examine elements in a collection. It provides methods similar to those in **Enumeration** but with shorter names, and it adds a **remove** method.

Java 2 Enterprise Edition (J2EE)

The collection of Java standard library classes plus extensions designed for supporting multi-tier Web applications. If you need to develop large-scale Web applications, this is the package for you.

Java 2 Micro Edition (J2ME)

Sun's package of Java classes designed to support applications that run in relatively small systems, such as telephones and Palm Pilots.

Java 2 Standard Edition (J2SE)

The package of Java classes and utilities for normal development. The programmer's exam assumes that this is the edition of Java you are familiar with.

Java 2D

Sun's term for a group of classes that provide many advanced graphic methods.

Java ARchive (JAR)

This format enables a single file to contain a number of resources such as class files or images. The basic format is that of the well-known zip utility, but it has some Java-specific additions.

Java Development Kit (JDK)

The package of utilities, a class library, and documentation that you can download from the **http://java.sun.com** Web site as the Java 2 Standard Edition (J2SE) package. You may see the JDK for the Java 2 platform referred to as the 1.2 or later version. Sun now seems to favor calling this the Software Development Kit (SDK).

Java Foundation Classes (JFC)

A group of five toolkits Swing, Java 2D, Accessibility, Drag & Drop, and Application Services for various aspects of advanced user interface building. Most of these classes were developed as add-ons for Java 1.1 but are now integrated into Java 2.

Java Virtual Machine (JVM)

The part of the Java runtime environment that interprets Java bytecodes and connects your program to system resources. The specifications for the JVM are public and have been used to create Java interpreters on a variety of systems.

javac

The program that starts the Java compiler.

javadoc

The Java utility for automatic documentation. Source code with comments in the correct format can be processed by the javadoc utility, which creates Hypertext Markup Language (HTML)-formatted reference pages. If this processing is done correctly, your application documentation is merged with the documentation for the rest of the language.

JComponent (class)

The **javax.swing.JComponent** class is the base class for the Swing visual components. The immediate ancestor of **JComponent** is **java.awt. Container**; thus, a **JComponent** object can contain other components.

JDK (See Java Development Kit.)

JFC (See Java Foundation Classes.)

join

This instance method in the **Thread** class coordinates **Threads**. The **Thread** that executes the method waits for the **Thread** whose method is called to die.

JVM (See Java Virtual Machine.)

label

A Java statement can be labeled with an identifier followed by a colon. Labels are used only by **break** and **continue** statements.

layout manager

The generic term for an object that can control the position and size of screen components within a **java.awt.Container** object. The **LayoutManager** and **Layout Manager2** interfaces in the **java.awt** package define the methods that one of these objects must provide.

lightweight components

Interface components that do not have an operating system peer. All screen drawing and event processing for lightweight components is carried out by the Java Virtual Machine (JVM).

List interface

This interface provides for an ordered collection of object references. This is not to be confused with the **java.awt.List** class, which creates a listbox.

listener

In the Java 1.1 event model, an object that receives a certain class of events because it has registered with the generating component. Listeners are defined as interfaces so that any class can implement the listener interface and receive events.

local class

An inner class that is defined within a member method. Not only does the local class have access to all class members, but it also has access to local variables that are declared **final**.

local variable

A variable declared inside a code block. (*See also* automatic variable.)

lock

A variable associated with each object that can be manipulated only by the Java Virtual Machine (JVM). For a **Thread** to execute a **synchronized** code block, it must have ownership of the lock that belongs to the **synchronized** object.

long

The 64-bit integer primitive type used in Java. Note that **long** primitives are always treated as signed integers.

Long class

The wrapper for 64-bit **long** primitive values.

low-level event

This term is used for events close to the raw events provided by the operating system, such as mouse movements.

main (application method)

By convention, the initial class of a Java application must have a **static** method named **main**. The Java Virtual Machine (JVM) executes this method after loading the class, to start the application.

manifest

Every Java Archive (JAR) file has a contained manifest file that carries additional information about the other files in the JAR. This can include digital signatures, encryption information, and a variety of other data. The **java.util.jar.Manifest** class is used to give the programmer access to the data in a manifest.

Map interface

A class that implements this interface must associate key objects with value objects. Each key must be unique. The **Hashtable** class implements the **Map** interface.

maximumSize

Components descended from **JComponent** can have this parameter set with the **setMaximumSize** method.

MAX_PRIORITY

A constant in the **Thread** class.

member

A field, function, or inner class that is declared as part of a class. The class encapsulates the member and can control access to the member.

member class

An inner class that isn't declared as **static** and isn't declared within a member method.

MenuComponent (class)

All **java.awt** classes used to display screen menus descend from **java.awt.MenuComponent**.

method

Java code is organized into methods that are named and declared to have specific input parameters and return types. All methods are members of a class. (*See* member.)

method signature

The combination of a method's name and parameters that distinguishes it from other methods. The return type isn't included as part of the signature.

minimumSize

Components descended from **JComponent** can have this parameter set with the **setMinimumSize** method. Layout managers will not attempt to give the component less than this amount of space.

MIN_PRIORITY

A constant in the **Thread** class.

model

In the Model-View-Controller design pattern, the model object contains the data.

modulus, modulo

The modulus (also called modulo) operator (%) returns the result of the division of the left operand by the right operand. This operator can be used with integer and floating-point types.

monitor

The mechanism by which the Java Virtual Machine (JVM) uses object locks to control access by **Thread**s to objects.

multiple-inheritance

Subclassing more than one class, which isn't allowed in Java.

multitasking

When an operating system, such as Windows NT, appears to be running several programs simultaneously. Each program runs separately with its own memory and resources.

multithreading

When there are several independent paths of execution within a program. Each thread may have access to the main memory and resources of the entire program.

name space

The total set of names for classes, methods, and other program items that the Java compiler has to keep track of to uniquely identify an item.

NaN (Not a Number)

A special floating-point constant used to represent the results of arithmetic operations that don't have a correct numerical representation, such as division by zero. **NaN** constants are defined in the **Float** and **Double** classes. The only way to determine whether a numerical result is **NaN** is with the **isNaN** method. Trying to test for the **NaN** value with the == operator or **equals** method does not work.

narrowing conversion (primitives)

A conversion of primitive types that may lose information. For instance, converting an **int** to a **byte** simply discards the extra bits.

narrowing conversion (reference type)

A conversion of a reference type to a subclass; e.g., from **Object** to **String** is a narrowing conversion. The Java compiler insists on explicit casts and installs a runtime check on all narrowing conversions. At runtime, a **ClassCastException** is thrown if the conversion is not legal.

NEGATIVE_INFINITY

A constant defined in the **Float** and **Double** classes; it is the result of floating-point division of a negative floating-point primitive by zero.

nested top-level inner class or interface
An inner class that is declared **static** and treated the same as any other Java outer class. These inner classes don't have access to the **static** members of the enclosing class.

new
The Java keyword that is used to indicate construction of a new object or array.

NORM_PRIORITY
A constant in the **Thread** class.

notify
A method in the **Object** class that makes one of the **Thread**s on the object's wait list become runnable. Note that the **Thread** does not actually run until the Java Virtual Machine (JVM) scheduling mechanism gives it a chance.

notifyAll
Similar to **notify**, but it makes all **Thread**s on the object's wait list become runnable.

null
The special literal value used for the value of a reference variable that hasn't been initialized. Note that **null** has no interpretation as a primitive variable.

object
A specific instance of a class.

Observable
A class in the **java.util** package that provides basic methods for adding and notifying objects that implement the **Observer** interface. In the **Observer-Observable** design pattern, **Observable** is the object that contains data.

Observer
An interface in the **java.util** package that specifies the **update** method. **Observable** objects use this method to notify the **Observer**.

OutputStream (class)
The abstract base class in the **java.io** package for the classes that write data as a stream of bytes.

overloading
A class can have more than one method with a given name, provided the parameter lists are different. This is called overloading the method name.

overriding
If a method in a subclass has the same return type and signature as a method in the superclass, the subclass method is said to override the superclass method.

package
A group of affiliated Java classes and interfaces. Packages organize classes into distinct name spaces. Classes are placed in packages by using the **package** keyword in the class definition. A package limits the visibility of classes and minimizes name collision.

parent
Also known as the superclass, a class that is the immediate ancestor of another class by inheritance.

path separator
The character used to separate paths in a list, such as the Windows environment variable PATH. Because this varies among operating systems, the **File** class has a constant that you should use rather than hard-coding a particular character.

peer

The operating system object that corresponds to a Java Abstract Windowing Toolkit (AWT) interface object.

pointer

A mechanism used in C for indirect access to objects and variables. Java does not allow pointer manipulations, so give up your clever C programming tricks!

polymorphic

In object-oriented programming, the ability of an object to have many identities, based on its inheritance, interfaces, and overloaded methods.

POSITIVE_INFINITY

A constant defined in the **Float** and **Double** classes; it is the result of floating-point division of a positive floating-point primitive by zero.

preferredSize

Components descended from **JComponent** have this parameter, which may be set with the **setPreferredSize** method. Layout managers that respect **preferredSize** attempt to allow the **Component** to occupy this space.

primary container

One of the Swing objects that has an operating system peer and can serve as the basis for an independent window.

primitive

The following Java types: **boolean, char, byte, short, int, long, float,** and **double.** These are not objects, and variables of these types are not object references. Primitive values are accessed and stored directly in binary form rather than through the object reference system.

priority

All **Thread**s have a priority, a numeric value from 1 through 10, which is used by the Java Virtual Machine (JVM) to decide which **Thread** runs next. Not all operating systems provide the full range of priorities that the language prescribes.

private

Variables and methods that are tagged with the **private** keyword can be accessed only by methods that are declared within the same class.

promotion

The compiler's use of widening conversion of a number to the type required by a particular operation. For example, a **byte** primitive being used as an index to an array is promoted to **int** for the purposes of the operation.

protected

Variables and methods that are tagged with the keyword **protected** can be accessed only by methods of classes in the same package or by methods within classes derived from that class (in other words, classes for which that class is the superclass).

protocol

A set of rules that govern a transaction.

public

A Java keyword that modifies the visibility of classes and members, so that they may be accessed by all objects, regardless of the package to which they belong.

random access
Having random access to a file means that the programmer can move a file pointer to any spot in the file and begin reading or writing. This is in contrast with streams, which can be read only from beginning to end.

Reader (class)
The **abstract** base class in the **java.io** package for classes that read data as a stream of 16-bit Unicode characters.

reference
In Java, the programmer never works directly with the physical memory address of an object but instead works with an object reference. The Java Virtual Machine (JVM) is responsible for fetching and storing object data indirectly through the reference.

reference variable
Except for primitives, all variables in Java are referred to indirectly and thus are called reference variables. Objects, classes, interfaces, and arrays are reference variables.

Reflection application programming interface (API)
Classes that make up this API allow a program to discover the constructors, methods, and variables available in any class and the interface the class implements.

Remote Method Invocation (RMI)
The technology that enables one Java program to execute a method on an object resident on another system.

resume
The **Thread** instance method used to allow a suspended **Thread** to continue. This method is deprecated.

Runnable
An interface in the **java.lang** package that defines the **run** method used by **Thread**s.

RuntimeException (java.lang.RuntimeException)
This class is the parent of all of the exceptions that do not have to be declared in a method **throws** clause.

scope
The attribute of an identifier that determines its accessibility to other parts of the program.

SDK (*See* Software Development Kit.)

semantic event
This term is used in contrast with a low-level event. A semantic event incorporates some additional logic. (*See* Low-level event.)

serialize
To turn a Java object into a stream of bytes, typically using an **ObjectOutputStream**.

Set interface
An extension of the **Collection** interface that holds object references with the restriction that the **Set** prevents duplication of references so every reference is unique.

shallow copy
A copy produced by the **clone** method in the **Object** class is shallow because it simply copies reference variables' values.

short
The 16-bit integer primitive variable type. Remember that **short** variables are always treated as signed integers.

Short class

The wrapper for 16-bit **short** primitive values.

sign bit

The most significant bit in the Java **byte**, **short**, **int**, and **long** primitives. If this bit is turned on, the number is interpreted as a negative number.

signature

A method's name and the type and order of parameters in its argument list

singleton

A design pattern in which only one instance of a class can be created and access to this instance is controlled by a **static** class method.

sleep

The **Thread** that calls this **static** method of the **Thread** class sleeps for the number of milliseconds specified.

socket

Connections over a network between computers are represented on each end as sockets. A socket has a computer address and a port number, so a given computer can support many sockets.

Socket (class)

An object of the **java.net.Socket** class represents a single socket connection and can provide an **InputStream** and **OutputStream** for communication through the socket.

Software Development Kit (SDK)

The package of utilities, a class library, and documentation that you can download from the **http:// java.sun.com** Web site as the Java 2 Standard Edition (J2SE) package. Sun used to call this the Java Development Kit (JDK).

SortedSet interface

An extension of **Set** that keeps references in a sorting order as determined by the **compareTo** method, which each object in the set must implement.

stack trace

The formatted text output that can show the history of how a particular **Thread** came to be executing a method that created an exception or error.

start (applet method)

By convention, the Java Virtual Machine (JVM) in a Web browser calls an applet's **start** method after the initial display of the applet and whenever the Web page that contains the applet is re-exposed.

static

Tags a method or variable as belonging to the class rather than to an instance of the class.

static fields

Member fields of a class for which one, and only one, copy exists, regardless of the number of instances of that class.

static methods

Member methods of a class that can be executed without the need to reference a particular instance of that class.

stop

This **Thread** instance method causes a **ThreadDeath** error to be thrown, thus bringing a **Thread** to an abrupt end. The method is deprecated due to unpredictable results in certain circumstances.

stream

One of the ways Java looks at inputs and outputs such as files is as a sequence or stream of bytes. In contrast with random access, streams can be read only from beginning to end with a limited or nonexistent ability to back up.

StringIndexOutOfBoundsException

Methods in the **String** class throw this exception if an out-of-range character position is specified.

subclass

A class that extends another class directly or indirectly. In Java, all classes (except **Object** itself) are subclasses of the class **Object**.

super

The Java keyword used to refer to parent class constructors, methods, or variables.

superclass

In the Java class hierarchy, an ancestor of a class; the immediate ancestor is the direct superclass. (*See also* **extends** and **parent**.)

suspend

A **Thread** instance method that halts a **Thread** until the **resume** method is called. This method is deprecated because the suspended **Thread** can keep a lock on an object, thus creating a deadlock condition.

Swing

The set of advanced interface components developed as improvements over the original Abstract Windowing Toolkit (AWT) components. Swing components were optional add-ons for Java 1.1 but are part of the standard extensions for Java 2.

synchronized

The Java keyword that activates the monitor mechanism for a method or a block of code.

System class

The **System** class is composed of **static** methods and variables initialized by the Java Virtual Machine (JVM) when a program starts in order to provide a variety of utility functions.

Thread

The **java.lang.Thread** class encapsulates and defines the behavior of a single thread of control within the Java Virtual Machine (JVM).

ThreadDeath

A special error used to bring a **Thread** to a halt.

ThreadGroup

The Java Virtual Machine (JVM) uses these objects to define a set of **Thread** objects and conduct operations on the set as a whole.

throw

The Java statement that throws an exception; it must have an associated **Throwable** object.

Throwable (java.lang.Throwable)

The class that is the parent of all Java error and exception classes.

throws

This Java keyword is used in method declarations to introduce a list of exceptions that the method may throw.

time stamp

Mouse and keyboard events, which are descendents of **InputEvent**, carry a **long** primitive variable that gives the system time when the event was created. This is generally called a time stamp.

toString

All reference types have a **toString** method, which the Java compiler uses when evaluating statements in which **String** objects and the + operator appear.

try

A **try** statement creates a block of code in which an exception may occur. One or more associated **catch** clauses must follow the **try**.

type

The interface to an object. In object-oriented programming, an object's interface is sometimes separated from its implementation, leading to a distinction between class and type.

UDP (*See* User Datagram Protocol.)

unary

Operators that affect a single operand. An example is the ++ increment operator.

unchecked exception

Exceptions that descend from **RuntimeException** are called unchecked because the compiler does not require you to provide explicit handling code for them.

Unicode

The international standard for representing alphabets. Java uses Unicode to simplify writing programs that are compatible with any locale. Java uses the 2 version of this standard (**www.unicode.org**), in which the American Standard Code for Information Interchange (ASCII) standard codes are represented with the usual values.

URL (class)

The **java.net.URL** class represents a Uniform Resource Locator (URL). With a valid **URL**, you can open an **InputStream** and read a resource from a Web server.

User Datagram Protocol (UDP)

A packet communication protocol that provides simple communication between programs. UDP is unreliable in the sense that a packet may be totally lost, but if the packet is successfully received, the data inside is reliable.

user Thread

Any **Thread** not tagged as a daemon **Thread**.

variable shadowing

Variables in the same scope can block direct access to other variables with the same identifier.

Vector class

A **Vector** object holds an extensible array of **Object** references.

view

In the Model-View-Controller design pattern, a view creates a particular presentation of the model data. A single model may have many views.

viewport

The logical window through which part of the view object in a **JViewPort** is seen.

visibility

The level of access granted to other classes.

wait

A method in the **Object** class. A **Thread** that calls this method releases its lock on the object, becomes inactive, and is placed on the object's wait list. Calls to an object's **wait** method must be in a block of code synchronized on the object.

wait list

A list of **Thread**s attached to a particular object waiting for notification.

wait set

Another term for a wait list.

widening conversion

Conversions of primitive types are called widening conversions when the conversion does not lose magnitude information. For example, converting a **short** to a **long** loses no information. A conversion of reference types from a subclass to a class higher up the class hierarchy is a widening conversion. For example, any reference can be converted to an **Object** reference, because **Object** is the root of the entire Java hierarchy.

widget

Programmer slang for a user interface component such as a button.

wrapper classes

A generic term for classes that correspond to each of the primitive types and provide various utility functions related to those types; e.g., the **Float** class that corresponds to **float** primitives.

Writer (class)

The **abstract** base class for classes that write data as a stream of 16-bit characters.

Index